Sounds Like Home

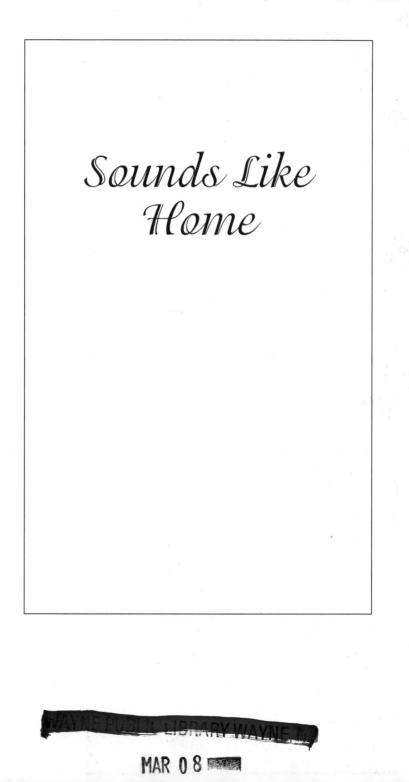

Sounds Like Home

Growing Up
Black and Deaf
in the South

Mary Herring Wright

Gallaudet University Press
Washington, D.C.

Gallaudet University Press
Washington, DC 20002

Library of Congress Cataloging-in-Publication Data

Wright, Mary Herring, 1924
Sounds like home: growing up Black and deaf in the South/Mary
Herring Wright.
p. cm.
ISBN 1-56368-080-7 (paperback : alk.paper)
1. Wright, Mary Herring, 1924– . 2. Deaf women–North Carolina–
Biography 3. Afro–American women–North Carolina–Biography.
I. Title
HV2534.W75A3 1999
362.4'2'092-dc21
[B] 99-12907
CIP

∞The paper used in this publication meets the minimum requirements
of American National Standard for information Sciences Permanence
of Paper for Printed Library Materials, ANSI.Z39.48-1984.

I dedicate this book to

my mom, Helena Herring,

and my four girls, Linda, Mary, Carolyn, and Judy.

They were my inspiration to keep on talking.

Many thanks to my daughter, the second Mary,

for all the help she's given me in getting

my book published.

Contents

Foreword

How transient is joy and grief
A moment stamped in bold relief
Then lost on memory's yellowed page
We trace them dim with dust and age

—author unknown

MEMORIES of my yesteryears are not dusty, and don't seem at all aged. I don't dwell in the past, but memories of my childhood are like beautiful jewels to be taken out every so often, played with, enjoyed, and packed away again. Those were years when sound had meaning, when I could hear. Now it's just vibrations, loud noises, constantly watching lips and every gesture, trying to get some meaning out of what is being said.

I began losing my hearing when I was about eight years old. By the age of ten, I was completely deaf. Although I have been examined by several specialists, none of them were ever able to determine exactly what caused my hearing loss. They are certain, however, that it is nerve deafness.

I decided to write my story because I wanted my children to have a lasting document that chronicled my experiences growing up as a deaf person. I also decided to write my story for my many deaf friends because my story, in many ways, is also their story. Many stereotypes about deaf people persist. Even today, some people continue to use the phrase "deaf and dumb" when referring to persons who are deaf. The use of the words *dumb* and *mute* are very inaccurate because many deaf people can speak. Therefore, none of them are really dumb or mute, even if they choose not to speak. The general public should understand that deaf persons are first and foremost human beings with the same fears, desires, anxieties, hopes and most importantly, intellectual abilities, that hearing persons have.

In the book, which roughly covers from the mid-1920s to the early 1940s, I talk about my experience of the transition from a hearing world to one of total silence. The book chronicles my ongoing adjustment as I travel back and forth each year between my deaf world at the North Carolina School for the Blind and Deaf and my hearing world at home. My adjustment to hearing loss occurred at a time when I was also experiencing the physical and emotional growing pains that come with adolescence. In addition, the story occurs over a period that covers two major events in American history—the Great Depression and World War II.

Finally, my story adds an important dimension to the growing body of literature on deaf people as I am an African American woman who is deaf. My book is unique and historically significant in that it provides valuable descriptive information about the faculty and staff of the North Carolina school for Black deaf and blind students from the perspective of a student as well as a student teacher. It also describes the physical facilities as well as the changes in those facilities over the years.

My story is one of enduring faith, perseverance, and optimism. I share it in the hopes that it will serve as a source of inspiration for others who are challenged in their own ways by life's obstacles.

Part One

A Bouquet of Roses

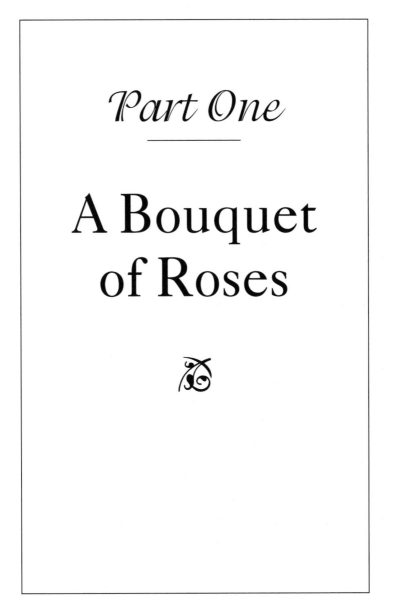

1

The Beginning:
Home and Family

MY LIFE began in a farmhouse on the back roads of a community called Iron Mine, located eight miles west of Wallace, a small rural town in southeastern North Carolina. Ours was a farming community with mostly tobacco and strawberries. Wallace had no industry and the business district consisted of Front Street (Main Street) and Back Street. The White-owned businesses were located on Front Street and consisted primarily of the clothing stores, the drug store, the grocery store, and the doctors' offices. There was also a post office, and just off Front Street was a hotel.

The Black-owned businesses were located on Back Street, which ran parallel to Front Street. The Bass Family Cafe was known for its good home cooking. Across the street was another cafe. The two shoe repair businesses were owned by the Pearsall family and by Mr. Powers. One of the grocery stores was owned by our cousin, Eugene Bennett, and the other was owned by Mr. Robinson. Back Street officially became Boney Street sometime during the 1960s, but is still known to most locals as Back Street. The Whites who lived in town worked in the stores, the bank, and maybe a few other businesses. The Blacks who lived near town either worked on Back Street or did house or yard work for the Whites. Very few, if any, worked in other towns because not very many people had cars or other means of transportation.

Iron Mine was a mixed neighborhood of Black and White families. Although most families were related to each other, the kinship of the Blacks and Whites wasn't discussed in public. Most everyone farmed or worked for someone who did. Several Black families owned large farms and nice homes. Everyone seemed to get along as far as race relations were concerned.

Outside of the city limits, neither Blacks nor Whites had electricity. We also used outdoor toilets. Usually, they were well-built little outhouses with two covered seats. A broom was kept in a corner to sweep and keep them neat. The only phone in Iron Mine was at the Smith farm. This belonged to Mr. Tom Smith; his wife was Martha, and their three boys were Colwell, Ted, and William. They had a country store in the yard. Papa farmed with them at times and all of Iron Mine received and sent messages at the Smith farm.

Now for my family: Papa; Mama; my beloved, one-and-only sister, Eunice; and four brothers, Bennie, Frank, Willie, and James Lloyd (we always called him Sam). Bennie was the first born, then Frank and Eunice. Another boy, named Clarence (also known as Bud), was next but he died at four years of age, before I was born—due to pneumonia I believe. Mama was watching someone playing cards and sent one of the children to the bedroom to see how he was. The child came back saying Bud was lying there "great long" (stretched out). Mama went to see. He was dead. She never liked cards after that. Willie came after Clarence and I was the next to arrive.

There's supposed to be a certain age when people begin to record memories. One of the first things I can recall is crawling across a plank on our porch. It led from the doorstep to the door while floorboards were being put down. I definitely remember crawling along it, hearing Mama screech and pick me up. However, I've never been able to convince any of my family of this. They insist I was far too young, I hadn't even started walking. As a child, the things I said were mostly ignored, hooted down, or taken with a grain of salt at best. This didn't faze me in the least. I always knew what I felt, heard, and saw.

I guess my brain really began registering things on a warm August morning in 1926 when I was going on three years old. Upon awakening and failing to hear pots and pans rattling in the kitchen, smell coffee perking, or hear the sound of Mama's voice, I went in search of her. The kitchen was empty. I had looked in all the rooms except the front bedroom in which my parents slept. This door was closed and I didn't see any of the other children or Papa. Sounds came from this room so I planted myself by the door. Each time someone opened it, I tried to sneak in but was pushed back and told to stay out of the way.

Finally Papa rushed into the bedroom, then back out, taking me with him as he left. Somehow we were in the truck. I say "truck," but I think it was once a car. Half of the body was cut away, then a box fitted on back and the whole thing painted blue. As I remember, we called it Bluebird. I sat there expectantly while Papa grabbed the crank, jabbed it in place, and cranked furiously. It caught, roared to life, then shook and rattled, ready to take off—and take off it did, over ruts and bumps, dust billowing from behind.

"Where we going, Papa?" I asked when I could hold still long enough.

"To get Miss Minnie."

I wondered who Miss Minnie was and why he was going to get her, but said no more. One didn't keep asking Papa questions. Besides, I was too busy grasping at something to hold onto as

Bluebird roared and rattled onward. Then we were in front of a little house somewhere, and Papa had rushed in to get Miss Minnie, who turned out to be a small, light-complexioned woman with big round eyes that looked like our calf's. I think I stared at her all the way back home. She paid me no mind and disappeared into the room Mama seemed to be in, taking her little black bag with her.

I was told to go play. How could I play, not knowing where my Mama was? I stayed right by that door, trying to see inside every time it was opened. I could smell the sharp smell of Lysol and hear queer noises. Finally someone took me by the hand and led me in, only I couldn't see a thing. Dark green shades covered the windows—only a slit of light here and there. Blankets covered the head and foot of the bed, and the sharp smell was stronger. By then I was terrified. Was Mama in this dark, queer-smelling room? If so, what for?

Then I heard Mama's voice. "Don't you want to see your new little brother, Hon?"

I peered toward the bed and saw my mother's face—a light blur. A bundle of something was beside her, but all I was interested in was finding Mama again. I had not the slightest interest in a brother, new or otherwise. However, someone unwrapped the top part of the bundle and I was told to look. It was a tiny face with tightly closed eyes. I peered at it, speechless, and left the room, still speechless.

That was my introduction to my baby brother, Sam. Where had he come from? This question was put to each member of my family or anyone else I could lay hold of. I was answered with a grunt or silence until I got to my brother Frank.

"Miss Minnie brought him," he told me.

"I didn't see him in the truck."

"That's because she put him in her little black bag," he assured me.

"She did?"

"Yeah, that's what the little black bag is for."

So that was it! What a smart brother I had, to know all of that, and he took the time to tell me. Well, I felt I should know something too.

"Dat's right, dat's right," I volunteered. "I went with Papa to get Miss Minnie and she hid him in her bag."

Having gotten started, I couldn't leave well enough alone. I had to make it even fancier.

"I went in the house with Papa. There were a lot of babies on shelves, and Papa let me pick him out."

"Sure enough?"

"Uh-huh."

I almost believed I was fully responsible for the arrival of Sam and have always had a special feeling for him, that in some way he was also mine.

Much later, I learned that Miss Minnie was a midwife. Back then most babies were born in their mothers' beds with either a doctor from town or a midwife to attend the birth. Our nearest hospital was James Walker Hospital in Wilmington, thirty to forty miles away. Some years after Sam was born, a White doctor in Wallace had rooms built over his office for White women to deliver but not for the Black women.

Sometime during the 1950s another White doctor, named Dr. Hawes, built a clinic in the next town, Rose Hill, and delivered babies of both races. Of course, the rooms for White women were on one end, and the rooms for Black women were on the other end, but he gave good care to all his patients. His fee was fifty dollars for nine months of prenatal care and delivery. If you preferred, he'd bring his nurse and a portable hospital bed and deliver at your home. It's said that he delivered three thousand babies before he died. Now Duplin County, where Iron Mine is, and the surrounding counties all have nice, up-to-date hospitals and ambulance service and provide all kinds of care.

Our home was a weathered six-room farmhouse with a long wraparound porch and a swing on one end. My mama's family had a large farm with lots of acreage. Her parents had nine children, and each time one married, a piece of land was sectioned off and given to that child. When Mama married Papa, she was given fourteen acres on the south end. That's where she and Papa built their house and raised their six children, plus about that many more children belonging to other people.

Our water source was a deep well near the kitchen door. It was fed by a spring of cold crystal clear water. The front yard of our home, like that of most farm homes of that time, was hard-packed dirt, shaded by large oak trees from which gray moss hung like old men's dirty beards. Peach, apple, and pear trees grew in backyards or fields. Our flower yards were on each side and toward the back, a profusion of different colors. They held mainly zinnias, marigolds, cock's combs, bachelor's buttons, four-o'clocks, and others whose names I don't remember. But I will never forget the tall, lavender and purple hollyhocks that grew in back of and beside our house. It was under those that I took my little brother to play.

For the next few years, most of my recollections revolve around Sam: Papa buying him a crib with rockers that he refused to sleep in, Bennie and Frank going to his bed each morning to bend over and nuzzle him or just bending over him with their eyes closed. I sometimes wondered if they were praying over him or catching a few more minutes of sleep after Papa routed them out of bed. Watching Mama nurse Sam fascinated me—it seemed a funny way to eat. This was also when I discovered the difference between the sexes. I always watched Mama change Sam's diapers and noticed he didn't look like I did. I asked her why.

"Because he's a boy and you're a girl."

This made me fret. I wanted him to look like I did—in fact, I wanted him to be a girl. I already had three big brothers and only one sister. All of them were older and none of them had time for me. I pondered on ways to make Sam a baby sister instead of a baby brother. I decided the most logical thing was to dress him like a girl. So one sunny summer morning while playing among the hollyhocks, I told him I was going to put one of my dresses on him.

"Huh," said Sam.

Running in the house, I got down my green Sunday dress (my best) that was hanging behind the door, my yellow hat with a narrow black ribbon that went around it and hung from the back, and last but not least, my best pair of pink silk bloomers. They had rubber around the legs. Step-ins (panties) were kept for girls in their teens. Soon all this finery adorned Brother Sam.

I beamed happily, "Now you are a little girl like me."

"Huh," said Sam.

His answer to everything, whether in answer to a question or a statement, was "Huh." A man of few words was Sam.

Now I needed a name for my new sister. I pondered on this for some time, but pondered alone. Sam was too interested in himself as a girl and his finery to worry about a name. I recalled Mama reading the story of Mary and Martha in the Bible, and since I was already Mary, what better name for a sister than Martha?

"I know, I know. Martha, that's a good name. It goes with Mary."

"Huh."

"Come on, Martha," I said, taking "Martha" by the hand to go play under the pear tree in back, but around the house came Mama.

At sight of Sam, she stopped and stared in wonder at her baby son—then came the blast. When it was over, "Martha" was once again Sam and my Sunday-go-to-meeting clothes were back behind the door. Mama also made sure my ears were full of words.

I think it was about this time that Bennie became ill with some kind of fever, malaria or typhoid. He was very sick and I remember Mama's worry and how she tended to him. I'd go look at him lying there in the bed with the tall wooden headboard. He was so thin and quiet. What I remember most about his illness is that Mama had to teach him to walk all over again once he was able to get out of bed. Sam was also learning to walk at this time. She gave each of them a stick for support, then got between them, and up and down the porch they went. Mama's eyes were shining with happiness. Her first- and last-born sons, learning to walk together. God had spared Bennie and now she was helping both boys learn to walk.

Aside from my family, other people have a special place in my heart and childhood days—Mary Elizabeth (or Mary Lizzie as we called her); her mom, Mrs. Helen Smith; and her stepfather, Willie Smith. The Smiths lived in town, but my parents raised Mary Lizzie on our farm. I don't know why they raised her, but I think it was because her mother worked and had no place to leave her. We all loved her dearly. She was a tall, pretty girl.

Mrs. Helen and Mr. Smith once took me to a circus, the only one I've ever been to. There I saw my first elephant, tiger, and lion. I was thrilled speechless, afterward, I traveled back to the car perched high on Mr. Smith's shoulder. When I was at home again with my family, the circus was all I could talk about. Someone asked me if I'd been afraid of the lions and other animals. I was indignant.

"What do you think I am—a fool?" (This was a favorite expression of my idol, Mr. Smith.)

"Mary!"

This from Mama, followed by a good dressing-down. *Fool* was classified with all the swear words we were forbidden to use or we'd end up in eternal fire along with the devil.

When she was grown enough to be on her own, Mary Lizzie moved to town to live with her parents. She learned to drive and used her dad's car to come out to see us often. I'd also go stay with them—more happy memories. Being in town was exciting. Theirs was a neat white house on the eastern side of town, with electric lights, an oil stove (instead of wood) for cooking, and a large gramophone or "talking machine" with legs (better known now as a record player). You could put on a record, wind it up with a crank, then close the top, making the music low and muted. And how exciting the house smelled—a mixture of cigarette smoke, oil stove, perfume, and whiskey. At home the chief smell was food cooking, coffee perking, and wood smoke from the heater and the kitchen stove. I loved that smell too. It meant "home."

I loved going uptown on summer afternoons with Mary Lizzie or Mrs. Helen. They'd use a little Vaseline to twist my hair in long sausage curls, and I got to wear a pretty dress, and *shoes and socks* in summer, on *weekdays*! How grand I felt, wishing Sam could see me stroll along Front Street. Mr. Smith owned the barbershop on Back Street. The lotions, talc powder, and hair tonics smelled so good. We'd wait for him to close up, then get in the car to ride back to the house, where he'd carry me in on his shoulder.

When I visited, Mrs. Helen took me fishing at the millpond not far from their house. The covered bridge over the water is still there. All I ever caught was trash and once a small turtle. While in town, I played with Ernestine "Teen" Stevens and Rick (I think her last name was McMillan). We caught tadpoles, played games, and, along with some girls who were considered "fast," played in an unfinished house across the street that we'd been forbidden to play in. Rick was older and sort of quiet, slim and very light complexioned with long brown hair. Teen was more my type: brown, short, plump, and ready to try new things—like going to the house that was off-limits. Rick wouldn't go and told Mrs. Helen on us. I got a scolding and so did Teen. We tore up Rick's Sunday hat to repay her. This earned me a spanking; I don't know what Teen got.

During one such visit, Papa showed up one afternoon in the old truck with Sam. I was happy to see them until I learned they had come for me. I couldn't explain it, because I was always glad to be going home from any place. This time I cried as though my heart would break. Mrs. Helen begged Papa to let me stay until the end of the week and they would bring me home.

"No suh, she's got to go home to keep Eunice company at the house and play with Sam. It's work time now."

My clothes were packed, and I was promised a new dress when I came back for another visit; then I was in the truck, still crying. Mrs. Helen gave me a final hug and kiss and a pretty quart jar of peaches. More kisses from Mary Lizzie and I was on my way, waving from the back window and trying to see them standing in the dusk also crying and waving. I never saw either of them again. I had only been home a short time when word came that they'd left town and moved to New York. Mrs. Helen had been caught with a jar of bootleg whiskey. They left the state to avoid prosecution. Only Mr. Smith returned for a visit; later, he was killed in a wreck.

Our family boarded teachers. One teacher, Miss Johnson,

stayed with us for a while, but I don't remember when she came. Miss Johnson had several boyfriends to come a-courting at our house. We had a heater in only one room, so they had to sit with the rest of the family or freeze in the unheated living room (or parlor, as it was called then). One suitor was Oliver Tate. I don't know what he used, but he had shiny black hair and a shiny face. They put their chairs side by side as far from the rest of us as possible and twittered at each other like two birds until bedtime, whereupon he bid us all goodnight and took his leave. Try as we might, no one ever understood a word they said. We wondered.

I think another boyfriend was my cousin, Oscar. He was long, lean, and lanky and seemed like his knees should go "clank, clank" when he walked. His style of courting was to recite a poem. I can remember one line he kept repeating: "If I was a cat, I wouldn't do that." Everybody laughed and laughed.

The third boyfriend was another cousin and one of my favorites, Willie E., known as Cap Jack. I loved to hear him sing and whistle "My Blue Heaven." His voice was so clear and tender. I can hear him yet as he would come through the path in the woods between his family's house and ours, whistling or singing. I'd stand still to listen until I saw him come out at the end of the field.

Maybe his singing ability helped him, for eventually he and Miss Johnson were married and she became Cousin Beulah. One summer after they married, she took me home with her. It was my first train ride. I kept rubbing my hands over the stiff plush covering the seats. It was fascinating to see houses, trees, and telephone poles rushing by the window. Her parents' home in Snow Hill was a pleasant white house on a hill at the corner of the street. It had a porch with a swing. Besides her mother and father, she had one sister and two brothers named Robert and Lotus.

While visiting Cousin Beulah's family, I made friends with a plump, older girl named Lucy. She took me with her to church to practice for a play, to someone's house to pick plums, and to other places. Most of my excursions with Lucy were made in a purple taffeta slip. Mama had made me a "best dress" from purple organdy, all fancy with ruffles, lace, and bows; the slip went with it. I knew better than to put on the dress for anything less than church services or some big event, so I wore what I considered the next best thing: the slip. I'd also wear my black patent leather Sunday shoes and white socks, and away I'd go with Lucy.

The visit was pleasant and I hated for it to end, but soon I was once again on the train going back home. A wonderful and fearful thing to ride, it huffed, puffed, chooed, and hissed out steam. A bell clanged while black smoke puffed up as it moved along very slowly, then picked up speed. Soon it was rocking down the rails like mad. I saw people go up front and pull down a white paper cup to get a drink of water. I longed to do the same but didn't dare leave the safety of my seat beside Cousin Beulah. At that time, she lived out on the highway with Cap Jack, his parents, and his cousin Jessie Mae.

Cap's mother was my mama's sister, and next to Mama I loved her more than any other woman I've known. We called her Sis Ette, and she was so sweet and gentle. I especially remember her hair. It was very soft, and strands would come out from the knot she wore it in and curl around her glasses on her forehead. She always called me "Hon" and would give me a pinch of snuff for running to get it down from a shelf and carrying it to her. This was done secretly as Mama had a horror of both snuff and the box it came in. To her, both were nasty. Sis Ette showed me how to put it in my cheek and pack it down, then spit. Most of mine came out with the spit. All of it had to be out before I got home or I'd get a real switching. Mama finally broke me from snuff by filling my mouth and lips with it and making me sit out in the hot sun and swallow the whole mess. Boy, was I sick! I heaved and heaved, and cried and heaved some more. I was cured.

Then there was Cap's father, Cousin Archie—short and partly bald with a thick black mustache. His morning ritual was to put on his clothes, then go to the end of the porch by the kitchen door and wash his face and hair (or head). This was done summer and winter. In the winter, when ice was in the water bucket, he'd crack the ice and wash in it anyway; he was real tough. His name for both me and Jessie Mae was "Little Gal." I didn't mind being a little gal, but Jessie Mae always protested.

"But Uncle Archie, I'm not a gal. A gal lives in a mule or horse stable," she'd say.

She was about twelve and fat, with red hair and green eyes, and everything tickled her. She'd laugh and laugh until her face was red and shiny with tears. She spent a lot of time playing house with me. I loved her too.

Another love of my life was, and still is, music. All kinds, but my favorites have always been the classics. No words, just music— loud, wild, and wonderful. If it was gay and lifting, I'd close my eyes and imagine sunshine, blue skies, flowers, and birds singing, and I'd feel happy. As a child, I just had to dance. I made up my own dance of hops, leaps, and skips. I had a really wild record going one day and was dancing my heart out when Eunice came in unexpectedly and caught me doing one of my originals. She laughed and laughed and said I looked for all the world like a one-legged chicken hopping up and down. I screeched and cried and begged her not to tell anybody, but my chicken-hop dance be-came a big joke among the family and friends, all except Mama. She just smiled a little and told me to dance if I wanted to and I did, but I made sure I was alone.

I couldn't stand sad music though. It made me depressed and

fearful. Mama's oldest brother, Julius Vatson (also known as Buddy Vat), gave me records of concerts and classical music. No one else liked them except maybe Bennie. He also loved music, often sitting in the corner by the gramophone at night, keeping it wound up and playing record after record. I can still hear the lovely sound of "Shine On Harvest Moon," sung by a group of Black men called the Jubilee Quartet. I can see the big, round October moon rising over the woods in front of our house, shining on the porch chairs turned against the wall for the night. I can see the shadows of the oak trees in the yard and the well at the corner of the house and smell the smoke from the oak and sweet gum logs burning in the heater. All the family would be gathered in from their day's work, full and content. Mama would be doing some needlework, patching some of the menfolks' overalls or shirts, or piecing a quilt together with Eunice helping her or studying. The rest of us would be sitting quiet, listening to the voice asking the moon to "shine on, for me and my gal." I was always lost in beautiful music.

Another song I especially loved to listen to was "Carolina Moon" by Kate Smith. It went:

Carolina moon keep shining, shining on the one who cares for me.
Carolina moon I'm pining, pining for the place I long to be.
How I'm hoping tonight, you'll go to the right window,
Scatter your light, tell her I'm alright, please do.

The room, lit by an oil lamp, filled with worn furniture and the glowing-hot cast iron heater, may not have looked like much to some people, but for me, it was the nicest room anywhere. Surrounded by all those I loved, I felt safe, warm, and contented—like I was the richest girl in the world.

I was happy to just stay at home, play with Sam, and follow Mama around the house as she attended the various chores. One such morning as Sam was napping, I had my first experience of seeing something I couldn't explain. I had a kitten I loved dearly—my first one. Its favorite place was napping on a sunny spot on top of our kitchen stove after it cooled off. However, my kitty died and I grieved for awhile, then things went on as usual. This particular morning, Mama had washed dishes and cleaned the kitchen, then moved on to make beds, with me right at her heels, running my mouth. I got hungry and Mama told me to go in the kitchen and look for a biscuit or something in the pie safe (where baked goods were stored). As I entered the kitchen, I stopped. There was my kitty sleeping in his usual spot of sun.

Delighted to see him, I shrieked to Mama, "Here's my kitty come back to me!"

As I did so, he raised his head, looked at me, then jumped to the floor, running behind the wood box with me in pursuit. Though I searched the kitchen, he was nowhere to be found. Mama told me it was just my imagination, that my kitty was dead and couldn't come back. Nonetheless, I knew he had. For me, seeing was believing, but I kept that to myself.

2

Iron Mine School Days

IRON MINE had a two-room wooden schoolhouse out on the highway beside our church. First and second grades were taught in one room, third to seventh in the other. After that, the children were either through school or had to find someone in town to live with in order to be able go to school in town and graduate from the eleventh grade. Only one school bus traveled to town and that was for Whites.

Children started to school when their parents felt they were old enough. I think I was about five and went because my brothers and sister were going and I wanted to go too. On my first day, we met two teachers along the road who proceeded to get acquainted with their future pupils. After hearing the names of the rest of the children, one patted my head and asked my name.

"Big Bud," I answered proudly.

My hair was very short and curly and I was a sturdy, plump little girl. My papa must have wanted another boy because he bought me bib overalls and shirts right along with my brothers, so I was known as "Big Bud" or "Skeeter." I wasn't officially enrolled my first year of school and did not attend regularly.

After Cousin Beulah, the next two teachers to live with us were Misses Staten and Beaty. One night, Mama, Sam, and I were at the old house (Mama's childhood home). Papa came by in the truck and stopped. I ran to get in and ride home. Two strange women were looking me in the eye. I jumped back down, not knowing anything better to do. When we got home, the teachers were shown to their room, or rather my and Eunice's room. Mama proceeded to get supper for them and I sat myself where I had a good view of the door to the bedroom to catch a glimpse of them each time it was opened. They came out when Mama called out in her best company voice that supper was ready.

Miss Staten was small with tiny feet (size three or four), very cute, and dimpled. She was from Brooklyn, New York, and it was a pleasure to listen to her talk; her voice was sweet and musical. I'd never heard anyone talk like that before. She'd often wear a pale yellow dress with black polka dots. Miss Beaty came from the opposite direction: South Carolina. She was "our kind of people," from a farm, and I felt at home with her. They settled into our family life like they had known us forever, even calling Papa and Mama, "Dad" and "Mama." The teachers' room and board was fifteen dollars per month. I guess for each one. I don't know, and I didn't worry about money in those days as long as I could get a penny from Papa for a pencil and ten cents for a tablet with "slick" paper; the five-cent paper was rough.

I started school in earnest. Naturally, I was overjoyed when it turned out Miss Staten was my teacher. She had first and second grades—there was no Head Start or kindergarten in those days. We had to jump right in and sink or swim. Miss Beaty had grades three through seven and the larger of the two rooms.

The little schoolhouse needed lots of things done to it. All Miss Staten had to do was smile, dimple up prettily, and ask any man or boy, and they'd fall over themselves getting it done. The

Miss Staten, one of my teachers at Iron Mine School. She boarded
with us for several years.

schoolhouse was repaired, new heaters were put in, and wood was
cut and stacked up. The big girls in Miss Beaty's room washed
windows and made curtains from white flour sacks brought from
home and trimmed them in bright prints. A table to hold the water
buckets and dipper was set up in a front corner. Miss Staten gave
a lecture on hygiene and each child had to bring a glass from
home and put his or her name on it. No drinking from each other's
glasses. We also had to leave our lunch bags, buckets, or boxes
up there after the teacher caught several students sampling their
lunches when they should have been studying.

IS THERE anything quite like waking up on a cold, frosty morning, all warm in your bed, and looking out the window at a bright sun just coming up, clear blue sky, and white ground? The fire would be roaring in the heater. Mama would be rattling and clinking pans and dishes in the kitchen where she was cooking breakfast: coffee bubbling in the pot, a pan of plump brown biscuits keeping hot on the apron of the stove, side meat and eggs frying, one of the boys coming in with a pail of rich milk right from the cow, and a pitcher of homemade ribbon-cane syrup, freshly filled from the barrel in the corncrib (or feed barn), set on the table.

After breakfast was eaten and lunches packed, and I'd had my usual morning screaming session—over knotted shoestrings, a lost book or pencil, and most often, Eunice combing and plaiting my hair so tight that the plaits stuck out like two horns behind my ears—we'd set out for school, walking of course. I was right at Miss Staten's heels, watching every step she took. She had a large assortment of tiny high-heeled shoes and they tapped along as she and Miss Beaty chattered and called out "Hey lady!" or "Good morning!" to all they passed. Sometimes other groups of children overtook us along the way and the boys vied with each other for the privilege of carrying the teachers' briefcases or whatever else they had that day.

Arriving at school, we could play outside until it was time to go in. When the bell rang, we lined up at the front door, boys in one line and girls in another, the shortest at the head of each line. At the second bell, we marched into Miss Beaty's room for devotion, which began with a song to get us in the mood (usually "My Country, 'Tis of Thee"). Then came the Lord's Prayer, Bible verses, and another song. Miss Staten's children then filed out into the smaller room and classes started for the day. We had

10:00 recess, dinner recess at noon, and another short recess about 2:30. School was dismissed at 3:30.

For me, going to school was a happy time under Miss Staten, for she made everything fun. She could sing beautifully and taught us pretty songs. We also had a large sand table in a corner of her room. She helped us make little houses, stores, a church, and a schoolhouse out of colored construction paper. These were arranged along streets on the sand table to make a town; tiny trees and flowers were added. It was quite pretty.

Each Friday, the last hour of school was spent in Miss Beaty's room where we had songs and spelling bees or storytelling. Sometimes, we had contests to see which boy could eat the most soda crackers, cold sweet potato pie, or other food the fastest without choking. Sometimes we took long hikes over the creek called Katy Ford or down to Doctor's Creek. Back at school, a large pot of vegetable soup and/or cocoa waited for us on the heater. After this was served around, we'd sing until time for school to get out. I can still hear Lydia Newkirk singing:

> It's collard greens, it's collard greens.
> First thing you do, better put 'em in the pot;
> Next thing to do, you'd better eat 'em while it's hot;
> It's collard greens.
> It's gasoline, it's gasoline.
> First thing you do, better put it in the tank;
> Next thing you do is put your foot on the crank;
> It's gasoline.

There were more verses, and she went through them all. The old schoolhouse fairly rocked with the clapping and stomping of feet keeping time with the lusty song. Miss Staten had never heard such songs and was delighted. Every time Lydia ended a song, Miss Staten had her start another one.

We started having a Christmas program and a tree for the community. In my first program, I was picked to lead a line of little girls on our makeshift stage. Each of us was wearing a long white nightgown and carrying a lighted candle. Mama made my gown special. She crocheted a lace yoke for it and lace bands for the long, full sleeves. My hair was fixed in sausage curls with a big white bow. I don't remember much of what I sang. By the time my group was called, I was too sleepy to care what I did. I wanted to go find Mama and lay my head in her lap and go to sleep. I did love my gown, and I wore it for years, until it came to above my knees and was hanging in shreds.

The county supervisor from Kenansville came down every so often to visit and inspect the school. This was Mrs. Turner, known as a warhorse because of her stern demeanor. She was plump, wore glasses, and looked as though she'd like to bite somebody. Everybody seemed scared of her. Once she had to spend the night at our house since that's where the teachers lived. It was my custom to go around and kiss everyone in my family good night after I was ready for bed and had said my prayers. Well, this night was no exception. After kissing my family and Miss Staten and Miss Beaty, Mrs. Turner was the only one left unkissed. We'd been taught never to slight anyone, but kiss Mrs. Turner? I looked at her sitting up there, glasses glinting and mouth tight, staring straight at me. I stood rooted with all eyes on me and everyone waiting. I looked at Mama, but she said nothing. Finally getting my courage together, I inched up closer and kissed her cheek and fled crying, but not before I saw her actually smile!

I believe it was during this winter that I had my first experience with death. I knew something was wrong with Sis Ette. She was always sitting in front of the fireplace doing nothing when I'd run in to see her. I'd hug her and smell medicine and know something wasn't right. I felt uneasy. Then one evening, instead of going straight home from school, Eunice and I went around the road and stopped to see Sis Ette. Mama had stayed there the night before. I ran in and stopped short. She wasn't in her usual place with her arms out to welcome me; she was in bed. The shades were down and a musty medicine smell was everywhere. I peered at her from behind Eunice. She looked so strange. Her eyes were sort of rolled up in her head and I wondered if she could see.

She could, for she saw me, held out a thin, weak hand, and said, "Come here, Hon."

I couldn't move and started crying, so Eunice took me home. Sis Ette died that night, and I still feel a great sorrow that I didn't go to the bed and hug her one last time.

Mama stayed with Sis Ette and left Eunice to get me and Sam dressed for the funeral. I don't remember what Sam wore, but I sure do remember my outfit—the shoes and stockings, that is. We couldn't bare our legs to the winter air by wearing socks; that was summer wear. Eunice couldn't find any of my long cotton stockings and didn't dare put me in socks, so she solved the problem by putting a pair of grown-up stockings on my little legs. They just twisted and wrapped around my legs, and along with my high-top lace-up shoes, I know it was a sight. I also wore my Sunday coat; it had a small collar of some kind of fur. Nothing mattered, though. I just felt sick inside hearing the crying and screaming. It was like a nightmare. From then on, I dreaded funerals and couldn't sleep well at night for at least two weeks when anyone I knew died.

After Christmas, the teachers got the older children started making things to be put on exhibit during commencement, when school closed in April. The younger children were given parts in plays and speeches to learn by heart, and we were drilled in spelling and arithmetic for the contests. All the schools were segregated and the children from all the Black schools in the county would gather at one school on that great day. It was a joyous time when our school was picked. Everything was clean and shining, and the aprons, rugs, and other things the girls and boys made were displayed on tables and on the blackboards. Prizes of blue ribbons or red-and-white ribbons would be pinned to the work judged the best. Also, for each grade, one child from each school would be sent up to spell or solve arithmetic problems by calling out the answers. Whatever school had the most wins would be judged Best School.

It was a big day for our families also. The women dressed up in their finest. The men left their spring plowing and planting, dressed in their Sunday-go-to-meeting togs and headed for the schoolhouse. When a truckload of teachers and kids from some other school arrived, we greeted them with this song:

> Iron Mine forever, hurrah, boys, hurrah,
> Down with the traitors and up with the stars.
> We will rally round the school boys, rally once again
> Shouting the battle cry of "Iron Mine"

When the trucks unloaded, we were supposed to go forward and welcome the visitors. Instead, we'd form little bunches and look over the other girls distrustfully, then with arms across each other's shoulders, we'd swish past them with our noses in the air. Some of them would huddle about uncertainly while the bolder town girls scornfully looked us and our two-room school over. Finally, we would all be herded into our nearby church for the contests. The schoolhouse had no stage nor enough seats.

I had practiced arithmetic cards so much that I could see them with my eyes closed and knew the answer to every one. When my turn came, I marched up and took my seat. The girl from the other school was called and she came up, and there was my shock. We were both supposed to be second graders. I guess she was, but she sure didn't look it—big, husky, and real tough. I had thought my beloved Miss Staten would flash the cards, but I didn't even know the teacher who did, and she looked as tough as the girl.

While I still stared open-mouthed, the first card flashed my way and I missed it entirely. Little Miss Tough knew the answer. The next card came up. I opened my mouth to call the sum but the teacher flashed it at the other girl before I could say a word. She knew that one too. Each time I tried to call out the answer, the card was flashed at the other girl. I looked out at all those faces, and saw Miss Staten looking real grim.

It was over after a while, and I'd only gotten in a couple of answers. I stumbled to my seat and broke down in tears, and when Miss Staten told me she was disappointed in me I wanted to die. To my surprise, Mama and Bennie both said they weren't. They were proud of me, for the other girl was larger and older, and the teacher held the cards a little longer for her, giving her time to answer, so it wasn't a fair contest.

That was all I needed to bring me around again. I was able to enjoy listening to one of the Carr girls, Estelle or Hattie, recite "Somebody's Mother." That scored for our school. Then there were sack races, beanbag throwing, and other games. By that time, Papa and Cousin Ab Boney had fish frying in a wash-pot and had a barrel of lemonade ready. Some of the older kids from different schools had gotten bold enough to ask each other what their names were and where they came from. A few even walked around the grounds together. We younger ones needed no such formalities. We just raced around eating, yelling, and hitting each other in passing.

The next day would be our last school day for the year. Mama, Cousin Ab, and maybe one or two more parents would come out. After passing out report cards, we would have a simple devotion ending with Cousin Ab leading in the song, "'Til We Meet

Again." The water would be running down my face. I would shuffle home behind the rest, clutching my report card that said I was promoted to the next grade and sniffling, thinking of the schoolhouse standing lonely and empty through the summer.

The teachers would pack their trunks to go home. Miss Beaty usually left first as she was a farm girl and had to hurry home to help with the spring work. Sometimes Miss Staten would stay with us for the summer with a trip off now and then.

3

More Childhood Memories

I REMEMBER waking up to beautiful summer mornings, listening to the birds singing in the peach trees outside my window. I'd get up and sit in the window in my nightgown, looking out at the fields, the chicken yard, and the crib. Seems I can still feel the gentle morning breeze and smell the freshly plowed dirt, flowering trees, and other scents belonging just to summer, all mixed with the smell of coffee and breakfast cooking. Sometimes I'd go out to the crib and climb through the second-floor window onto the roof and just lay there looking at the woods, house, and yard, feeling so happy. Always when I felt happy I seemed to hear beautiful music like none I'd ever heard on earth, and I wanted to sing, dance, or play some instrument to express all those happy feelings inside of me.

Then I'd hear Mama on the end of the porch calling, "Mary, you Mary, come here this minute," then grumbling about where "that child" could be.

Poor Mama. She always worried about my wandering and warned that some varmint was going to get me. None did except a two-legged one while I was at school years later. So the summer days marched by peacefully—except for thunderstorms. These I dreaded. At the first big boom of thunder, I'd run for Mama, hiding my head under her apron until it was over.

One of my favorite pastimes was following Bennie up and down the rows as he plowed. He would tell me the name of every bird we heard in the woods. My favorite birds were the trilling lark and the whippoorwills that swooped around at dusk. He also told me about different animals he and Papa trapped and about snakes. Bennie knew everything. Wasn't I lucky to have such brothers as him and Frank?

Frank could fix anything broken from a small toy to a car motor to a gun. He taught me to fight—to flex my muscles, ball up my fist, stick it under somebody's nose and say, "Smell my calf head." As a result, I was always fighting some little boy; girls were too easy. Frank also rode Sam and me piggyback and told us the story of Bro Rabbit and Bro Fox in his own style. Some days he'd take me to the field with him and give me a ride on the plow. When I became hot and tired of that, he would get a watermelon from some field, bust it in a shady spot, and leave me to eat to my heart's content. At noon he'd unhitch old Rhodie, his mule, from the plow, set me on her back, jump up behind me and we'd head for home and dinner.

As for Willie, I followed him to his rabbit boxes (traps) and explored the woods. We looked for and gathered lightwood to use for kindling to start fires. He found wintergreen bushes and taught me to chew the leaves. The part of "Auld Lang Syne" that goes, "We twa hae run about the braes" always reminds me of Willie and our childhood days.

But Sam was my joy and my despair. We played awhile and fought awhile. I never could bear to see him get a whipping, no matter what he'd done. When it was over, I'd go get Vaseline or whatever ointment I could find and rub his legs where they'd been switched.

I came in for my share of whippings too. One day, Mama had gone off, and Sam and I were playing house at the edge of the woods with some other child. I was the mama. I told him I was going to town, for him to be a good boy and I'd bring him chocolate candy. I trotted off to the house, found a box of snuff, mixed it with some sugar and carried it back to Sam, telling him it was cocoa. He ate every bit.

By the time Mama got back home, he couldn't walk—too drunk on snuff. Mama snatched him up with one arm and dug a little hole in the ground, then stuck his nose in it for him to smell fresh dirt, then another hole, another smell. When he was finally sobered up, Mama attended to my legs in such a way that I would rather have been drunk and smelling dirt.

Our days started at the crack of dawn. Papa was up first and then out to see how the animals had fared through the night. The dogs always greeted him with leaps and licks and yelps of joy, following him to the crib where the other animals slept. We had two mules, Ruth and Rhodie; a brown horse; a milk cow and sometimes a calf; and lots of pigs and chickens. Back at the house, Mama would be up, with a fire in the kitchen stove, putting on breakfast. If everybody wasn't up, Papa made the rounds and roused them all, mumbling about lazy young'uns laying in the bed all day.

Our first crop of the spring was strawberries. Papa and our neighbor on the south, old Mr. Lem, usually got a group of strawberry hands from some town to come live on the farm and pick strawberries for both farms. The picking usually took about three or four weeks, maybe longer. That was an exciting time. The old house (used for farmhands) was cleaned and swept and scoured. Bunk

Papa with his bird dog, Doc, sitting on the woodpile.

beds were made and the kitchen was fixed up and stocked with food. The big day arrived, and Papa left with the truck before daylight to go get the hands. We waited anxiously for them to arrive.

Finally, we'd see the truck up at the old house and people carrying in boxes and bags. As soon as we thought they'd had time to get settled in, Mama and us children would be on our way to get acquainted. A few would usually be old hands from previous years. There were also children of all sizes and ages, small fry for Sam and me, and older ones of courting age for the others. As fast as the berries were picked, the pickers were paid for each quart basket. At that time I think it was two or three cents a quart. The berries were then carried to the shelter where Mama and other women picked them over and packed them in crates. Papa shuttled back and forth, to and from the market where they were sold.

Before Sam and I got large enough to go in the field and pick, we would watch until the truck was about loaded with crates of berries, then stow away to ride to the market with Papa and beg for an ice cream cone or sucker. We vied with each other over who could make the goodies last the longest, then we'd argue over it. More often than not, Papa ran us out of the truck before leaving the shelter, saying he didn't have time for these worrisome young-'uns. He declared we weren't going with him anymore. We did and got more ice cream and suckers.

During this time, the smell of strawberries, honeysuckle, and dust hung heavy in the air, along with the heady smell of wild magnolias. We'd sometimes gather at the house of the strawberry hands after supper. Sometimes there'd be sanctified ones and they'd have preaching, praying, and singing. Other times, the old folks sat on the doorsteps talking while the young people and children played such games as Here We Go 'Round the Mulberry Bush, Farmer in the Dell, Kitty Wants a Korner, London Bridge, and Buck. The night, bright with silver moonlight, would be alive with black shadows and the sound of young voices, laughing and singing the verses to the games we played, high and shrill, happy to be alive and young. No one would think any of them had done a lick of work that day. Sore backs and knees from picking straw-berries were forgotten.

My favorite of the games was Bluebird in a Ring. A girl was picked to be "Bluebird" while the rest joined hands and formed a ring around her, skipping and singing,

> Bluebird in a ring, tra-la-la-la-la-la
> Why'n't you shake that motion, tra-la-la-la-la-la
> Why'n't you shake that motion, tra-la-la-la-la-la
> Why'n't you shake that motion, tra-la-la-la-la-la
> For she loves sugar and cream.

As the others sang, the girl put her hands on her hips and shook her "motion."

Those were happy, innocent years. The only thing we connected the word *drug* with was the drugstore in town. Camel, Kool, Lucky Strike, and Chesterfield were the only kind of cigarettes we'd heard of. We had plenty of hard work, but no TV, stereos, cars, or fancy clothes. The only places to go were school, church, each other's houses, and in the summer, to Wallace on Saturday evenings.

Papa, Mr. Pat Murphy, Dude Hayes, and McKinley Boone had the only cars or trucks in Iron Mine at that time. Neighbors would dress up and stand beside the road waiting for a ride to town. They didn't even have to raise a hand to stop Papa. He knew what they were there for already. Usually the truck would be loaded by the time he reached town and found a parking place on Back Street. Some handed him a quarter. Some said, "Much obliged, Mr. Ben." Others, so anxious to mingle with the crowds, just walked off. Papa would also transport dead bodies from the asylum in Goldsboro (now Cherry Hospital) to Wallace and he would pick up bodies from the train station. He also hauled neighbors' produce to market, moved furniture, and even hauled their dead to church and then to the graveyard. Only well-to-do people could afford a hearse.

Summer was when Mama's brother, Buddy Vat, came for a visit. He was one of only a few Blacks hereabout who had a college education and taught school. He lived in a lovely white two-story house in the nearby town of Warsaw until his death in 1944. He was always dressed in a three-piece suit with sharply creased pants, a round gold watch with a heavy gold chain across the vest, shiny black shoes, and black socks with his longjohns neatly tucked in. In summer he wore the same thing with a boater—a cream-colored, hard straw hat, with a flat top and a wide black band.

I loved Buddy Vat, but stood in awe of him. Mama took extra pains to fix very nice meals for him, and we had to behave and use our best table manners when he visited. He never complained or asked for anything extra, but we couldn't sit on his lap for fear of messing up the creases in his pants. When we children were sure he was out of the way, we'd sneak in and peek in his suitcase or satchel to see what he had. It was always clean socks, white shirts and underwear, and sometimes a bottle of store whiskey. I think Willie drank some of it once while Mama was gone, got high, and chased Eunice with some yard brooms or something.

I can't remember much about Buddy Vat's wife, Sis Mag. Only that she dressed fancy in the latest styles and that she died on his birthday while I was still small. She was planning a birthday dinner for him. She got up that morning to start the dinner, then lay down to rest. Mrs. Albert, who kept house for them, started off someplace and came back to get an umbrella. She found Sis Mag already dead, or she died right afterward, right on his birthday. I wore my white organdy dress with ruffles and bows to her funeral and that's all I know of her. She was the first person I remember being buried in a fancy coffin and transported in a hearse.

When Buddy Vat returned to Warsaw, the strawberries would be gone, as well as the hands, and we'd be busy with the tobacco crop. We'd wake up before daylight, cooking dinner along with breakfast. The dinner, with plates, forks, and spoons, would be packed in large dishpans and loaded on the wagon. Mama, Sam, and I rode with the dinner while Eunice usually drove a tobacco drag* or rode a mule with the boys. The fields would be a long

*A drag was a large wooden container that was used to transport tobacco from the field to the barn. Its name was probably derived from the fact that it was pulled or dragged behind the horse in the fields.

way from the house, so carrying dinner saved a trip home and gave us more time to rest. While the croppers would be filling the first drag with leaves, the women and children, who worked under the barn, would be piling sticks, setting up "horses"† and getting things in readiness for the drag of tobacco. It would finally appear piled high with leaves.

Papa stayed at the barn to supervise our work, making sure the tobacco was tied and piled right, and to take off sticks. Two people handed leaves, three or four to a bunch, to another person who tied them to a stick fitted on a "horse." When the stick was full, she'd tie off and yell, "Stick!" It was removed to a pile to be hung in the barn later. Sam and I would be put in the bottom of the drag to hand leaves up to the two handers. We had a break if we finished our drag before another one came up. Sam and I used our break to tie strings to large tobacco worms and pretend they were different animals. We even tried to race them.

At 11:30, the croppers came up to hang the piles of tobacco in the barn while Mama dished up dinner in the wagon bed. Other help went home or to some store for dinner. After dinner the dishes were packed away, then everybody tried to find a cool place to lie down and take a nap. That is, the old ones did. We kids played more games, argued, played tricks on some of the nappers, or got into arguments with other kids who lived nearby or happened to be passing. In an hour or so, Papa was up, telling everybody else to get up. Time to start work again. There'd be groans, but soon we were all busy again until an hour or so before sunset when the croppers came to hang up tobacco.

The women and children left for home to feed the animals, milk the cow, and cook supper. This was eaten around a long table with an oil lamp in the center amid the various bowls and plates

---

†A "horse" was a wooden device used for holding sticks on which the tobacco was tied. The tobacco was then hung in the barns to cure or dry out.

and bread and biscuits. Poor little Sam more often than not couldn't make it through supper and went to sleep with his head in his plate. After eating supper and washing dishes, we would all sit on the end of the porch where cool breezes from the south could blow over us. We'd talk over the day and let our supper digest. Mama had a horror of going to bed on a full stomach—it would surely give you nightmares if it didn't kill you first.

When the nights were silvery with moonlight and dark shadows, Sam, Willie, and I played hide-and-seek or caught lightning bugs (also known as fireflies). Sometimes Papa or one of the boys would cut a cool, sweet watermelon. However, if the night was dark and moonless, I'd huddle under Mama's apron. When the shiver owls (known to some as screech owls) started screeching I'd break out in goose bumps and stick my fingers in my ears. It's one of the eeriest, most unearthly sounds I can remember, like a woman in unbearable torture. It starts off as a thin, shrill scream, rises, hangs in the air and trembles, then slowly dies down and sighs off. But before you can get your wits together, it starts all over again. It was said that if you threw salt in a fire, turned your shoe upside down, or twisted your shirtsleeve tight, it would stop. I ran around doing all these and anything else I thought might stop that dreadful sound, but nothing worked.

One summer day a thundershower stopped our work so we went inside to take a nap, talk, or sleep through it. It passed over and the sun came out. We went back on the porch to get ready to go back to work. A fat white cloud with only a small amount of gray in it was moving east when, all at once a sharp bolt of lightning shot from it, causing everybody to jump and look uneasy. Mama herded us back inside, wondering about such a strange event. Miss Mag, a widow raising two daughters, three nieces, and a grandson, was living in the old house at the time. Only a short time had passed when Corina, one of Miss Mag's girls, came hurrying down the road to tell us that Miss Bell Turner had just been struck dead by that bolt of lightning.

Corina said the family had been napping through the shower of rain when someone came in their yard hollering about Miss Bell, so she came on to tell us. Miss Bell had been washing for the Smith family, on whose farm she lived, and had gone inside during the storm. After the sun came out she'd gathered up washing powder and bucket and started across the yard to the wash shed when the lightning struck, setting her clothes afire. It was most unusual for lightning to strike out of a small white cloud with the sun shining so all the oldsters said it was just her time, that God was ready for her.

At her graveside funeral, Miss Bell's wooden casket rested on a trestle of two sawhorses. The family and neighbors, including a small boy about two years old, all stood in a circle for the final rites. In the middle of a prayer, the boy suddenly asked loudly, "Who dat in dat box?"

Someone said, "Shhhh, that's An't Bell."

"Dat An't Bell?" He moved closer and peered in the coffin to make sure. "Yeah, dat's An't Bell."

At that point he was jerked back while still calling "An't Bell."

MAMA tried to instill in all her children good manners, proper English, fair play, and honesty. When Sam and I were old enough to be sent on errands, she told us to speak to everyone we passed or met along the way—to say good morning, good afternoon, or good evening, as the case may be. I never could bring myself to say good afternoon. It sounded uppity and citified, as any time between noon and dark was evening to us, so I'd say good morning or good evening. Sam said nothing, merely grunted.

One sunny morning Mama sent me over to Mrs. Susie Powers' house for something. Sam couldn't go so I was alone. I had been warned about men along the road, and when I looked up and saw I was meeting two of them, I lost no time in crossing to the other side even though it put me on the wrong side of the road. As they got closer, my heart thumped harder and my feet took on speed, but I remembered my manners. While they were still a couple of yards ahead I yelled, "Good morning!" Then I shot past them, running as though the boogerman was after me. Upon returning home those same two men were there, laughing and telling my folks how I had shouted good morning while still well ahead of them and ran past like a deer. They turned out to be some of Bennie and Frank's friends. At least I remembered my manners.

Mad dogs running loose was another summer worry. Some years before, one had run down and bitten a small cousin, who later died from rabies. So Mama always kept on the lookout for them, warning us what to do should we see a dog acting strange. One summer day, she and Cousin Lucy Bland were out across the highway chopping a field of peanuts. Sam and I were at Cousin Bert's house playing.

Someone came by yelling, "Mad dog coming!" We got inside quick, but I worried about Mama being out in a field with a mad dog loose. I needn't have worried. She said as soon as they heard "mad dog," they both dropped their hoes and were up a small pine tree in seconds. Neither knew the other could climb so fast. Someone killed the dog right past Cousin Bert's house.

Thelma was my Cousin Bert's daughter and my best friend as well. I had another cousin I loved like a sister. Her name was Edna and she lived with her grandparents, Aunt Mary and Uncle Tom. Her grandmother and my mother were sisters. She wasn't allowed to be out with the other neighborhood children, so I only saw her when she came to our house with Aunt Mary.

Thelma's family lived right beside the main highway, which was Highway 41. They didn't farm. Her father worked at the asylum in Goldsboro and only came home for a weekend now and then. Her two older sisters, Annie Ruth and Mary Bert, wore pretty summer dresses and went with the two older West boys from the nearby community of Shanghai. Going with them was considered very daring and wild. The Wests were a large family with twelve children. They were nice-looking people, but the children had the reputation of being wild and reckless, getting drunk and cursing. They also had their own church and store on their farm. James and Buddy West would come racing up in their car—even on weekdays—all dressed up. This was unheard of for farm girls, especially Blacks. Annie Ruth and Mary Bert would come out twittering and giggling to greet them. I was all agog. If one so much as looked my way, I was struck dumb. Not Thelma. She just stuck her thumb in her mouth and never acknowledged she even knew them.

I must have had an eye for handsome men even at that tender age. Thelma's oldest brother, George Henry, was the best looking of all—very tall, light complexioned, with a thin mustache, wavy hair, and deep-set eyes. He worked in Goldsboro with his father and drove a snappy roadster with a rumble seat.

He'd drive up, spot his mother standing on the porch or in the door and greet her with a breezy, "Howdy, Mrs. Lane."

She'd come right back with "Howdy, Mr. Lane" and they'd just smile at each other.

Love and pride were clearly there. He also had the gift of drawing. He'd draw beautiful paper dolls for Thelma and me to cut out.

Mama and Cousin Bert were best friends as well as cousins. After they got married, it seems they matched child for child. After George Henry and Mary Bert, Cousin Bert had Clyde, and Mama had Bennie. Then she had Annie Ruth, and Mama had Frank. Next were Cecil and Eunice, then Leroy and Willie, Thelma and me, and then Sam. Cousin Bert had Christina, but she died while still a baby and I never knew her. So Sam grew up with Annie Ruth's daughter, Doris. We all paired off and became best friends.

Thelma and I tried to see each other every day from the time we were just toddlers. Sometimes my family would hear the whole pack of dogs barking and making a racket out by the crib. Someone would go to the end of the porch and look down the bay road. Thelma would be standing in one spot calmly sucking her thumb, surrounded by snarling, yapping dogs. They never bit her. I, or someone else, would go shoo the dogs away and she'd come on to the house where we'd play happily until we'd hear the dogs again. We knew it was Cousin Bert this time, looking for her runaway.

She'd call "Oh, Bo Peep, have you seen my little gal?"

I'd tell Mama to say no, but lying wasn't one of Mama's faults and she'd say, "Yes, she's here."

Then the two of them would have a gossip visit, giving me and Thelma a little longer to play. We'd walk with Cousin Bert and Thelma a piece to mind the dogs. Sometimes we'd end up going all the way, at which point Mama would protest, "Bert, I didn't mean to come this far. Mercy, let me get back to the house and put on dinner." Then they would walk back a piece with us.

At meals, Mama was always a stickler for manners. She taught us to say, "I will thank you" for this or that, and then wait for it to be passed to us. If it was chicken, I'd say, "I'll thank you for the thigh." In vain, Mama said to just say, "I'll thank you for some chicken." For me, it was the thigh or nothing. Bennie finally broke me from that. By then he was sparking the pretty little teacher, Miss Staten, and wanted us all to show our best training and good manners. So at the table, when I'd start to ask for chicken, he'd fix his eyes on me.

I'd shut my mouth, or he'd hiss at me, "No, don't say it."

At that, I'd start crying and have to leave the table. To this day, I don't like chicken drumsticks.

Frank often got Sam into trouble. Once, Mama got after Sam about something else and told him to go get her a switch. We had to get our own switches to be whipped with and they'd better not be little things or back we'd go until we brought one of suitable size and limberness. When Sam came back, big brother Frank had given him a small round gourd with a long handle in place of a switch. We watched for Mama's reaction. She took the gourd, glanced at us, and gave Sam a few taps on his little red head with it.

We all had assigned chores to do besides regular farmwork. Bennie and Frank's was to feed and water Ruth and Rhodie three times a day. Eunice milked the cow. Sometimes she'd tell me and Sam to open our mouths wide, and she'd squirt warm milk in them. Willie also helped milk and take the cow to pasture. He and I washed dishes, swept the yard clean every Saturday, and shucked and shelled corn, which we carried out to Cousin Mamie's store to be ground into meal. Cousin Mamie had a gristmill behind her store and would grind corn for a small portion of the meal. It poured out of the mill, smelling all warm and sweet, into the clean white sack we had brought with us. It made cornbread such as you've never tasted.

Mama's pet project was caring for her hens and baby chicks but she couldn't stand really small kittens. Sometimes when she'd be napping by the heater, the kittens would be playing and frisking about on the floor. Papa would pick one or two up and set them where they could climb up on her. Upon feeling the little furry balls and sharp claws she'd wake up and shriek, "Ben!" How he would laugh. He tended to his pigs, hogs, and yard full of dogs. I especially remember Joe, Dinah, and Bell. Joe was white with black and rust spots. Dinah was all black with rust ears. I think they were both coonhounds. Bell was pretty, white with light-rust spots, and a bird dog. She was fat and gentle. I loved them all.

On the first cold, crisp fall night, Papa and the two older boys went coon hunting. Mama let me, Sam, and Willie all snuggle down in bed with her and listen to the hounds baying across the woods. It sounded like music to me. We knew the sound of each dog and could tell when they'd gotten a coon treed. Toward day, the hunters would break out of the woods with their bounty—coons, possums, or squirrels—in their knapsacks. The possums often would still be alive and hanging there grinning. I used to look at them grinning and wonder if they didn't mind having their necks broken. Papa kept the furs to sell along with those of the mink, muskrat, fox, otter, beaver, polecat, and other animals he caught. The coon and squirrel meat was kept to barbecue and stew.

By this time my sister was in her teens and prettier than ever. Naturally the neighborhood boys took notice and started coming a-courting. One of these boys was named George. I don't know where George came from, only that he stayed with Mr. Pat Murphy across the woods north of us and worked on his farm. He came one Sunday and he and Eunice sat by the heater, mumbling now and then while Mama cooked dinner in the kitchen. Finally he finished his courting session and announced he would be going.

No one said anything, so he stood up, stretched and said, "Well, you better come go up with me." This was addressed to Eunice.

She only giggled, so Mama said she reckoned we couldn't go this time. To think of Mama and all of us walking home with George struck me as funny indeed, and I laughed out loud. They all turned to see what ailed me so I hushed.

I liked most of the guys who came to court Eunice or at least tolerated them. That is, all except Len. He wore a purple suit.

My sister Eunice.

The pants fitted tight across his hind end with a small belt in back. He walked with a sort of shimmy-shake. When he came to walk Eunice to the Baptist Young People's Union (BYPU) at church on Sunday evenings, I'd be right behind them watching him shake and shimmy. When I could stand it no longer, I'd pick up the first good stick I could find beside the road and whack him flat across the seat of his pants. I know it hurt because I was a husky child and Frank, bless him, had taught me to use my muscles well. However, Len pretended or preferred to think that I was playing and kept on smiling and courting until I came down—wham!— again. He'd jerk then and tell Eunice to make me stop. She would tell me to stop, but not as though she really cared. As long as he didn't touch her, I'd lay off, but if he tried to put his arm around her or hold hands, down my stick would come again.

The ones I liked to see with her were Jesse Eakins, Paul Boone, and Thaddeus West. Jesse, whom I considered nice look-ing, had heavy black eyebrows and a friendly smile. Paul, too, was handsome, thin, and dark. And Thaddeus? I never knew how to classify him. But I liked his looks though he seldom smiled and was a man of few words. The best thing I remember about him is on cold winter nights, he'd come to see Eunice and sit behind the heater, not saying anything. Just smoking and listening to the rest of the family talk. Then he'd turn toward Eunice and put two of his fingers over two on the other hand, forming a square, and tell her, "Let's play Feed the Crow" (a children's game).

Much as I liked them, Eunice didn't choose any of these to be my brother-in-law. That was to be someone I'd never heard of.

Back then the church and schools were the center of our social life. Any time there was a play, box party (or box social), or other event at the schoolhouse, the whole neighborhood laid down whatever they were doing and headed there. One big event at church was hosting the Association, a meeting of all the local Bap-tist churches. Preachers, delegates, and other officials from differ-ent churches gathered in our neighborhood and some had to have sleeping quarters, as traveling a distance wasn't easy then. The meeting started on Thursday and lasted until Saturday or Sunday. Programs, meetings, and preaching were held each day and night. It seemed to be a festival as well, for booths were set up all over the churchyard. Some people had booths where you could have your picture taken, others sold jewelry, ice cream cones, candy, lemonade, barbecue, and balloons. Women prepared and brought boxes of food and laid it out on long tables. Others had preachers and other guests to eat in their homes.

Once, Mama fixed dinner for some Association guests and had mutton. I'd never known us to have that. We younger children called it goat meat. Mama said it was mutton and for us to call it that at the table. She needn't have worried about me calling it anything because I didn't like the smell and wouldn't ask for it in any case.

I was at the Association with the family one year, and while the boys strutted about and the girls flirted and giggled outside, Mama kept her three youngest under her wing inside. We sat by an open window where she was listening to the preacher but also had an eye out for any of her own who might pass by. Someone came and stood right under the window and started telling the other that one of Mr. Ben's boys had just gotten cut down the road over some girl. Upon hearing, "Ben," Mama was already halfway up before the man added "Boykins." After learning that it wasn't *her* Ben, she was still so unnerved she gathered us up, found Papa and the rest and we headed for home.

Our church was invited to take part in a program at a church in town one night. I was picked to say a speech I had been reciting right well about "I am only a little Christian." Mama had me done up in my white ruffled dress, all starched and ironed, with curls and hair bow. We had to ride on the back of Mr. McKinley Boone's truck to get to town. When we alighted there, the little town girls stood giggling at us while we were jumping out like chickens. My curls were blown in every direction, and I wasn't feeling so proud anymore. Mama smoothed and patted me back in order as best she could, and then we were herded inside the church.

The church was huge compared to our little Iron Mine church and I was told to be sure to say my piece loudly so people in the back could hear me. There were no microphones back then. I looked toward the back and it seemed miles away. My ego sank even lower. Then the program started, and the town kids were doing their thing. I lay my head in Mama's lap and pretended to be asleep, heart pounding and hands sweating, waiting to hear my name called. Three cute little girls got up and sang a beautiful song about turtledoves. One had a heavy, husky voice that I thought was simply out of this world. The song ended and it was my turn. I shut my eyes tightly and tried to snore. Mama and the director shook, called, and pulled on me. I wouldn't budge. Just snorted and sniffled and moaned. I sure wasn't about to compete with those wonderful children. Finally they gave up and called the little husky-voiced girl to recite a poem. It was also about doves.

" 'Coo' said the gray dove, 'coo.' "

I snorted on.

When it was over, we piled back in Mr. McKinley's truck, except Mama said that Sam and I would have to ride in the cab with her. Mr. McKinley had been sampling the stump-hole juice (bootleg whiskey), and we could smell it. Somewhere along the way he picked up two drunken White men who were hitchhiking and added them to the churchgoers in back. When they found out we'd been to church they tried to "get happy," like they were in church, and started singing "Will There Be Any Stars in My Crown?" Mama told them no there wouldn't, the way they were going, not a one.

I loved to hear hymns and spirituals. That was the joyful part in going to church. I could sit forever and listen to our choir sing "Sweet Hour of Prayer." Mama tried to teach me hymns when we were alone. I can still see us. She'd be sitting in a kitchen chair by the woodstove, where dinner would be boiling and simmering while I knelt beside the chair with my hands on her lap trying to understand all those little black notes and follow her voice. She would sing "Oh What Glory When Our Lord Shall Come," and

> You'll bring the one next to you,
> And I'll bring the one next to me.
> And in all kinds of weather,
> We'll all work together
> And win them one by one.

I never could do it. I learned the words but couldn't get the notes right.

At church we had a girls' quartet, also one for the young men. I don't know which I loved best, but the girls had thought up a new way of singing. Three of them would go up and start singing halfheartedly, flounder around, and pause like they didn't know what to do next. Then the one who was the leader and the best singer would stand up from somewhere in back and start singing along with them as she walked up to where they were, and they'd sing the house down. Then the men's group would go up and start with

> I'm going to walk around the sun,
> I'm going to chant it to the stars,
> I'm going to tell it to my Lordy Lord.

Chills would run up and down my spine. I'm thankful I heard all of that and stored it up in my memory, for I can hear them still.

4

Scary Times

LIFE was a mixture of happy times, sad times, busy days, and some idle days, but not many of the latter. Life would be scary at times, then peaceful and tranquil. One of the scary times was one Sunday evening when we'd all been to BYPU at our church—our main social doing on Sunday evenings. Eunice had on a beautiful pink silk dress that Cousin Lula had sent her from Norfolk, Virginia. It was long, as that was the style for older girls and young women to wear to dress up for church and such. It was sleeveless with a small cape trimmed with flower petals and pearls. She was beautiful with her long black hair. All the boys wanted to walk with her but she stood on the running board of Papa's old truck to ride with her hair and cape flying.

This particular Sunday we walked from church and took the road by Cousin Bert's house where Mama was visiting. The other children dropped off at their own houses, leaving Eunice, Willie, Sam, and myself. We passed Clyde at his Aunt Mamie's house just before getting to his. We could see Mama, Cousin Bert, and her sister Mamie sitting on the porch. We were halfway between the two houses when George Henry came out and started walking toward us sort of stiff legged. Just as he passed us, he called Clyde to come meet him. Then to our horror, George Henry pulled a single-barrel shotgun out of his pants leg, aimed it at Clyde and fired. Clyde staggered and we screamed and fled through Cousin Bert's yard at high speed with Cousin Bert, Mama, and Cousin Mamie right behind us. A high chicken wire fence crossed the backyard. Cousin Bert and Cousin Mamie stopped there and decided to go back and see what had happened. Eunice went right over that fence—long dress and all—without a single tear. Willie was long gone.

I had my beloved baby brother by the hand so I found a way around. I thought Mama did too. I passed her and Eunice. When we got onto the bay road toward home, I heard Mama somewhere behind me praying and hollering for God to have mercy on Bert and her boys. My short, fat legs were pumping and my heart was thumping as I dragged Sam along with me, but I repeated whatever Mama said.

I heard her say, "Jesus Christ have mercy."

I gasped, "Jesus Christ."

Poor little Sam's legs couldn't take anymore, so I had to stop and give him a rest. Mama and Eunice had also stopped. Mama was torn between getting home with her children and going back to see if Clyde was dead or hurt. She said she couldn't leave Bert in trouble.

About this time Willie came trotting up. He and Leroy had hidden someplace where they could see and hear all. He said Clyde wasn't hurt. He had ducked the shot and went on toward George Henry cursing him out. Mama said in that case, she'd take her children on home.

Next day, I had to go to Cousin Mamie's store for Mama and passed through Cousin Bert's yard. Her boys and some others were sitting on the woodpile laughing about what had happened. Someone had carried tales from one brother to the other over the West girls I think, and that caused the ruckus.

Upon seeing me, it was "Hey, Skeeter, how did Eunice get over that fence so fast?"

I didn't know. It seemed Mama went over it too. I'd been too busy getting myself and Sam to safety. It really was a wonder how Eunice had climbed over a high chicken wire fence in a long silk dress and not torn it a bit.

Somewhere along this time (1932 or 1933) I had another scary encounter. It was in March, a month I always dreaded because of high winds. I'd hear the wind late at night, whistling around the north corner of our house. Sometimes it seemed to howl and the house would shudder and creak. I'd be under the cover shuddering right along with it.

This particular night was a Sunday. We'd let the fire go out early and gone to bed because the wind was high. Through the window at the foot of my and Eunice's bed, I lay watching the moon trying to shine through the blowing dust. The moonlight was a queer yellowish color and I wished daylight would hurry and come. Turning my gaze from the window to try to go to sleep, there poised over my feet and not quite touching the bed was the upright form of a man dressed in a gray suit, white shirt, black bow tie, hard straw hat, and socks but no shoes. I couldn't see his features, but knew it wasn't anyone I'd ever seen before. His arms were straight against his sides and his eyes seemed to be closed. I couldn't believe I actually saw what I was looking at.

When I could move, I went burrowing under the covers and against Eunice's back, trying to wake her up. All she did was gnash her teeth and mumble. I gave up and lay there sweating, too scared even to call Mama. I couldn't stay covered up too long. I felt I was smothering. After a long time I peeped out, but he was gone. I made a hole for my nose to get air and lay huddled against Eunice the rest of the night. At breakfast, I told Mama what I had seen. I got the usual laughs and hoots and "listen to that gal's tales." Mama didn't laugh but looked thoughtful and later she questioned me closely about how the man looked and what he had on.

In bright sunlight and amid the busy-ness of everyday chores, I almost forgot about my night visitor. Papa went off in the truck and the rest went about whatever they had to do. Toward evening he returned and told Mama he'd seen someone who told him Snooks was dead. That was the nickname for her dead sister's boy, Orion Highsmith, who had lived with her and Papa at some time or other, but had left home before or soon after I was born to live in Norfolk. I never knew him. Mama started crying hard and Papa told her to hush because she didn't know if it was true or not. No one had notified her yet. Mama insisted it was true. She just knew it was ever since I'd told her about the man over my bed.

"Oh, pshaw," Papa said.

He said I hadn't seen anything and that I was just dreaming. I wished very much that I hadn't seen anything and wondered why Snooks would want me to see him when I didn't know him from anything. However, I had to protect my honor so I kept saying I did see him, and it all came back to me. I shut my eyes and went under Mama's apron.

Later, Mama sent me and Eunice over to Aunt Mary's house to tell her, although Papa insisted it was foolish to carry news without knowing if it was true or not. We found Aunt Mary in her kitchen, cleaning and dressing a chicken. She received the news calmly and kept on cutting up the chicken for awhile.

Then, she carefully laid the knife down, wiped her hands, said, "Well Lord, I can't help it," and let out a bloodcurdling scream.

She headed for her bedroom and rocking chair still shrieking. I stopped up my ears and headed for the door.

Soon afterward, a call came on the Smiths' telephone that Snooks really was dead. This is how we learned when his body would be shipped home. Papa met the train and brought the body to our house. Snooks lay in state on our front porch, where the neighbors gathered, until time for the funeral. I would not look at him. I'd seen enough already.

At Snooks's funeral, Cousin Helen Blackmore cried so, saying she wanted to go with him and lifting a leg to step into the open grave. She had on pretty pink garters with ruffles over her stockings. Her husband, Cousin Edmond, had both arms around her waist holding on while someone was heard to say, "Turn her loose and let her get in." Cousin Ab Boney sang his standard funeral song, "Swing Low, Sweet Chariot." His hoarse, raspy voice fascinated me.

Our house was a good ways from the highway and was surrounded by woods, so any forest fire was a real threat to us. The first fire I remember seeing in the woods close by was when some men from Raleigh had come to hunt with Papa. One was Dr. Vass. The other was a small man with straight, shiny black hair. I remember him in particular because I was in the yard screaming in fright at so much smoke and commotion with people running along the edge of the woods, shouting and fighting the fire. He knelt beside me and held me in his arms telling me it would be alright and not to be scared. When I calmed down enough, he gave me a fried chicken drumstick and cookies from his lunch box. Needless to say, I loved him and loved chicken thighs even more. I called him Dr. Hambone, but his name was Dr. Hampton.

Bennie and Frank were inseparable. Frank would go along with Bennie when he went to see the girls but was too bashful to talk to them himself. Late one Sunday night, I woke up hearing Frank tell Mama that when he and Bennie got to the branch (a low, wet part of the road) walking home that night, they heard humming and singing. When they looked they saw an old lady in a patch of briars beside the road, picking berries or something. They said she looked like our grandmother who had been gone for years. Frank panicked and ran, but Bennie wouldn't run with him, so he ran back to Bennie who walked on and whistled, making like he didn't see anything. All this time the old lady hummed and sang and busily picked her berries or whatever she was doing, paying them no mind. I heard no more, as I was a tight ball under the covers, with both ears stopped up.

I'll never forget one cold Sunday night in late fall. Bennie and Clyde had gone to carry Eunice back to town where she boarded with our pastor, Mr. Tim, and his wife to go to high school. Mama, Miss Staten, and Miss Beaty sat by the heater talking while Sam, Willie, and I played. All at once one of the grown-ups said, "Wasn't that a scream someplace?"

My heart jumped right up in my throat while my short, fat legs turned to jelly, and I headed for Mama's lap and apron. Before I could get there, they were all up and out on the porch listening. It was a beautiful night—cold and clear with a full moon just coming over the treetops in front of the house—and that made it seem worse. Then we heard more screaming.

"That's Bert's voice," Mama said. "She's in trouble and I'm going to her."

The teachers said they'd go too. We got bundled up and started down the bay road. My knees and teeth were shaking so hard I don't see how I ever made it. Getting nearer, we could hear people talking and crying. Then Willie pointed ahead to the dark woods of the swamp over across the field. We saw a light like a ball of fire falling into the trees and disappearing. Everyone was quiet then. We were passing Corina Johnson's house, and Mama said for me and Sam to stay there while they went on to see what was wrong.

We went in. A lot of other people were there too. One girl in a long red silk evening dress with lots of makeup and frizzy red hair was in front of the fireplace, carrying on. She'd talk, laugh hysterically awhile, then cry and moan, trying to tell what had happened. This was Catherine West (of the Shanghai Wests). Her sister, Leona, went with George Henry.

It seemed Catherine and Leona were riding in a car with some other men and one of these was sweet on Leona. They met George Henry at a crossroads where the other man had blocked the road with his car. The man got out, went to George Henry's car, and shot him in the heart. At that point Catherine and Leona jumped out of the car, ran to the nearest house, and pounded on the door. Catherine said a fat White man opened the door, held out his arms, and said, "Come in, Honey." She stopped and giggled about that and got some sour looks.

Anyway, George Henry was left lying on the ground in the headlights of his car. A White boy driving by saw and recognized him and stopped. The boy put him in his truck and carried him home. He died before they could get him out of the truck.

Poor Cousin Bert was inconsolable—her oldest, handsomest, and most talented son shot down like that. George Henry's brother Cecil got a shotgun to shoot Leona, whom he blamed for his brother's death. It seemed she had sent for George Henry to go to her house that night, and they were waiting for him at the crossroads. Frank stopped Cecil, saying it would only be more trouble for his mama. They held a graveside service for George Henry. Miss Staten sang—or started to sing—a solo and fainted in the middle of it.

5

Make Me a Child Again

Backward, turn backward, O Time, in your flight,
Make me a child again just for tonight!

Elizabeth Akers Allen, "Rock Me to Sleep, Mother"

THOUGH Mama had taught—or tried to teach—all of us not to chew tobacco, use snuff, or drink, some people always have to do their own thing. So it was with Frank. The first time my brother Frank came home high (our word for "drunk" in those days) was a winter night when he was about seventeen. Mama sat by the fire with her younger ones and the teachers. The door opened suddenly and he came through the door and headed straight for his room, not looking at anyone. There was a strange odor floating around after he passed by—sharp and strong.

Everyone stopped talking and sat listening. Most farmhouses had an outside door in just about every room. The boys' room had a door opening onto the backyard. We heard the back door of the boys' room opening and then the sound of retching. Miss Staten said she believed Frank had had too much "tea." Mama jumped up, hurrying toward the boys' room with me right behind her. Frank was lying on the floor with his head out the open door, sick to his stomach. The smell of bootleg whiskey was very strong and sour. Mama held his head and wiped his face, then told him to get up from there and go to bed before he caught his death of cold. He said dying was no trouble, then started singing, "I'm sitting on top of the world."

This was my first experience with seeing someone drunk, but not my last. I never saw Bennie high but once. We were sitting on Aunt Mary's porch one Sunday evening when Bennie came up the path walking straight and stiff. I didn't know what was wrong with him. Mama and Aunt Mary had him to lie across a bed and drink salt water. We left him there asleep and he showed up at home the next morning with a big hangover and a sore stomach.

Eunice was by this time in high school, having graduated from the seventh grade at Iron Mine Elementary. The high school hadn't let out yet, but our school had closed for the summer, and Eunice asked if I could go spend a week with her in town and go to her school to visit. I was beside myself with joy when Mama said it was alright with her; I never thought Papa cared whether I came or went. All week I looked forward to my upcoming trip. Finally, Friday arrived and Eunice was home again until Sunday. I couldn't be still, picking out clothes and packing them in Eunice's suitcase with her clothes.

So the time of departure came. Bennie got the truck keys from Papa and put the suitcase in back. I ran to kiss Mama and Sam goodbye, but before I could get to Papa, he laid his eyes on me and wanted to know where I thought I was going. Mama spoke up and said I was going to spend the week with Eunice.

"For what?" he demanded.

"Well-l-l," Mama said, "Eunice asked if she could go and I thought it would be alright."

"She ain't going nowhere, got no business down there."

"Papa, let her go," Eunice pleaded.

By this time I was in tears, all my bubbles of happiness busted.

Bennie got out of the truck and silently set the suitcase back on the porch. Eunice opened it and started taking my clothes out. My tears turned to shrieks.

"Put 'em back, put 'em back!" I screamed, jumping up and down while Papa sat there as staid and unmoving as Chief Sitting Bull.

Eunice lifted out my prized red silk pajamas. I snatched them and put them right back. If I couldn't go, my clothes would.

"Well Ben, can she go?" Mama asked for the umpteenth time.

His Adam's apple bobbed up and down furiously before he jerked up and said he didn't care where in the devil I went. I guess it was my shrieks and screams he wanted gone. So we were soon in the old truck bumping down the road. My big brother and sister started giving me a lecture on how to behave and stand a chance of getting what I wanted. I was told not to scream and cut up like I had done, to keep calm and keep a stiff upper lip. I felt my lip. It didn't feel stiff, still damp from crying, but I didn't care. I was on my way.

"Besides," Eunice added, "What would I want with your clothes if you weren't going? You do the craziest things."

Words and more words. I let them pass; I got to go was all that mattered.

Being with my sister was wonderful, and to be able to walk to school with her again was even more so. It was quite a long walk to be sure. Mr. Tim's house was on the western edge of town and Wallace Colored High School* was far on the eastern edge.

---

*The schools were segregated and Wallace Colored High School was the school to which Black children were assigned. Its name was later changed to C. W. Dobbins High School in honor of the first principal.

Walking through town was exciting, with my feet hitting hard cement sidewalks instead of dirt and mudholes. A gang of us always walked together.

The school was a long white wooden building, the pride of the Black community. It was newly built and smelled of fresh paint and the usual chalk and erasure dust. Eunice had many friends and I went first with one, then the other. Of the girls, my favorite was Annie Ruth Bennett. She was sweet and friendly and became my play mother. Of the boys, my favorite was T. C. Bass, an older boy, very nice looking with nice ways too. He gave me a Baby Ruth candy bar and took me to his classroom. Someone asked why I didn't eat my candy and to let me know it was alright she took a bite herself. Another did likewise and my candy made the rounds. Finally a small piece came back to me. Just as I was about to open my mouth and put it in, someone said loudly, "Mary's eating."

Mr. Dobbins, the principal, looked at me over the top of his glasses and marched toward me, hand out for the candy. I sat frozen. He took the candy and gave a small lecture as to how nice little girls didn't eat in school down there.

Oh, the injustice of it. I broke into tears and there were titters and giggles. T. C. came to my rescue, wiping my eyes. After school he took me to his father's cafe on Back Street and gave me an ice cream cone. He also told me that I was a pretty little girl and that he was going to wait for me to grow up and marry me. I was about eight years old at the time. He did wait, but I didn't marry him.

When school was out, all of us were back on the farm for another summer's work. On summer mornings I'd wake up and hear Papa's voice coming from someplace, giving instructions about what was to be done that day. Then I'd hear Mama calling all to breakfast and saying she had to go get the children (Sam and me) up. I'd jump down, throw on my clothes, race out to wash my face in cold well-water and be at the breakfast table beaming.

It was and still is a common practice in Black communities for families to raise children other than their own. I've already mentioned Mary Lizzie. Then there was Blue. He'd help Mama with us younger children as well as work in the fields. He'd roll up his sleeves and scrub out a tub of clothes like Mama did, so we called him "Mother."

When Blue married Pridgen (her real name was Mae), we loved her too. They lived across the woods behind us in an old farmhouse that she kept scrubbed spotless. I loved nothing better than spending nights with her, sitting before the fireplace. The curtains were very white, starched and ironed. The kitchen walls were whitewashed with lime and water, and she was such a good cook. In the morning there'd be a pan of golden brown biscuits, fresh butter, and milk. She did housework for White families at times. When Mama got sick, Pridgen would come across the field and woods to do for us and wait on Mama. She was like a big sister to all of us and so sweet.

The last night I remember spending with her was when her young niece or sister, Margaret, and Blue's younger brother, Allen, were there. Margaret and I went for a walk along the woods and ditch bank while Pridgen cooked supper. It got cold and we turned back to the house. When we got to the front door, Allen wouldn't let us in but told us to stay the h—— out. Thinking he was trying to be cute and playful on Margaret's account, we giggled and pushed harder, knocked him back, and walked in. A roar came from in front of the fireplace. There sat Blue in a tub of water, scrubbing away and hollering for us to get out of there and cussing Allen for letting us in. We fell over each other getting out.

That spring Pridgen changed. She didn't come over often and

seemed quiet. In July I was told she was sick, and Mama sent Sam and me to carry food to her. One Sunday morning after Sunday school, a bunch of girls went with Eunice and me to see her, but they wouldn't let me in the room. They said for me to come back in the evening when she'd be feeling better and I could see her then. So we went home, ate dinner, and later went back to church for BYPU and then back to Blue's house.

Other people had come too. I left the rest behind and went running in the house through the back door, so happy that Pridgen would be feeling better and could hug me and call me Hon again. I ran to the door of her room and stopped. Women were silently sitting around the room and Pridgen was lying on the bed straight and still, a white sheet pulled all the way over her. A breeze from the window made it flutter a little.

I was horrified and shocked. Running back out to go home, I met Mama and Blue coming through the yard gate. Mama saw me coming and opened her arms and just hugged me until I stopped crying. I would not go to Pridgen's funeral because it hurt too bad. There's so much sadness; but life still goes on.

PAPA would raise a field of ribbon cane to make molasses, which we also called syrup. It was harvested and stripped in early fall, usually on a cold, frosty day in October. Buster Teachey would come spend a night or two to cook the molasses for us. He was young, and sweet on Eunice. I think Bennie went with one of his pretty sisters whom they called "Sweet." Buster would get up early and get things started. A mill was set up and a mule hitched to it to pull two stone rollers. Someone would feed the cane stalks into the mill to squeeze out the juice, which would run into buckets. These were emptied into a long vat with a fire under it. Buster had long paddles he stirred the syrup with as it cooked. It was the sweetest smell. We children would get a clean corn shuck and dip it in the cooking syrup until we got chased away. After it was cooked and done, it was poured off into large wooden barrels and stored in the crib. We'd take a pitcher to the crib and fill it to keep on the table in the kitchen. Mama made the best syrup muffins.

Poor Buster. He didn't win my pretty sister either. I used to hear a song that goes, "A pretty girl is like a melody that haunts you night and day." That's what I thought of when I looked at Eunice. My days of hearing music and melodies were coming to a close but I didn't know it then. I went on my happy bumpity way.

AS WITH all kids, Christmas was the big event in my life—a time of mystery, good smells from the kitchen, cleaning and scrubbing, and the night of nights when that beloved but unseen man, Santa Claus, came and left things in our sacks. We hung up *sacks*—large white cloth sacks—not stockings. Stockings would never hold enough. Bennie and Frank ordered boxes of fireworks and they got up well before daylight on Christmas morning to shoot them off.

Mama would make out a long list of what was needed for her cakes and pies. The fruitcake was baked a couple of weeks before Christmas, wrapped, and put away. Hogs were killed and the smokehouse filled with hams, shoulders, sausage, cracklings, and lard, and liver pudding was hung from the rafters. Mama made lots of cakes besides the fruitcake: chocolate, raisin, coconut, and pineapple. We also had sweet potato and cushaw (winter squash) pies.

Willie and I would go in the fields and woods to get all the lightwood we could for Santa to build a fire to warm himself while he sampled Mama's cakes. A piece would have been cut from every cake when we got up. We'd hang our sacks behind the heater so he'd be sure to see them. Each sack had a note pinned to it, telling him our name and what we wanted. I always wanted a doll that could cry and had hair, and lots of apples, oranges, candy, nuts, and raisins. I don't know what Sam and Willie asked for, but I believe one or the other of them also got a doll one year. I remember Willie getting an air rifle.

One Christmas in the early 1930s we'd done everything up, then been washed and put to bed. I tried to stay awake to catch sight of Santa, but my eyes weren't willing. I don't know how long I'd been asleep when I felt someone shaking me and calling, "Mary, wake up." I woke up and then wished I hadn't.

Mama was holding an oil lamp, and the round red and white face of Santa Claus was just behind her. One look and I was out of the bed trying to get to my place of refuge—under Mama's apron. Santa was reaching for me with brown hands that didn't match his white and red face. I wasted no breath on words, just ran round and round Mama trying to get under her apron. Willie went under the cover and refused to come up. I don't know where Sam was. Santa finally decided to leave me alone and left. Mama put me back to bed and under the covers I went.

We later found out that Santa had been around the neighborhood to see all the good little girls and boys. He visited two of my girlfriends, Lorraine and Louise. Louise was cleaning out the fireplace when Santa called on them. He slipped up behind her and tapped her on the shoulder. Turning around, she stared in shock and fear, screeched, "God a'mighty," and then tore into the kitchen to climb up in the rafters where the sausage and liver pudding hung. Finally, Lorraine called her and said he was gone, but Louise was consoling herself by eating liver pudding.

Santa Claus also went to see another friend, Gladys. She'd done her chores and was sitting and staring into the fireplace thinking of what she'd get for Christmas when he tapped her on the shoulder. When she looked around, she could say nothing at first, then she burst into tears and said, "I've been a good girl, Santa, I've been good." It was many years before I'd learn that this particular Santa was my beloved cousin, Cap Jack. Before his time of rest came, he even got to visit some of the children of the ones he'd visited that night.

Papa's old home was about a mile or so down the road from where we lived. His sister, Sue, and her son, Buddy, still lived there. One night he came in from visiting them and told Mama a neighbor down there—a Mr. Clabber I believe—had just died with nothing to be buried in. It was a very cold night, bright with moonlight, and the ground was white with frost. It worried me that Mr. Clabber wouldn't have any nice clothes to wear when he went where Jesus was. So I was relieved when Papa came in again later and told Mama he'd been to Wallace and got Mr. Clabber something to be buried in. He and Mama always tried to help anyone who needed it.

A boy in my first-grade class, John Henry, had just moved to Iron Mine. He was as tall as the teachers and looked to be grown, so I wondered how he got put back in first grade. Now I know he was probably mentally retarded, but back then I'd never heard of it. Anyway, he wasn't in our school long. He caught pneumonia and died. He was washed, dressed in a suit and laid out on his family's best bed in their front room for the first night while Dude made his coffin.

Dude was a carpenter who made coffins on the side. We had no funeral home, so when people died they were bathed, dressed in their best clothes, and laid out on a bed while the coffin was being made. The neighbors, family, and friends gathered to sing, pray, and watch over the dead person all night. The body would be buried the next day. Some people claimed that sitting up with the dead was also to keep the cats away from the body. No embalming was done, and in most cases, I never heard of a doctor having to certify a death. In looking back, I believe that some could have been buried while in a coma and still alive.

Papa was on his way to the "sitting up." When he got near the house he could hear the women gathered there already singing. Cousin Bert Williams was going louder than the rest when all at once the singing turned to screams and shrieks with people tearing out the door. The dead boy had moved—sat up or something. Maybe he'd just been in a coma and they thought he was dead when they washed him. Maybe the singing woke him up. Anyway, he died again and was buried on schedule. I guess he was dead. Doctors weren't always called to verify a death then.

Another school year was coming to an end and commencement would be held at a church in Rose Hill this year. Miss Staten got the idea of dressing all the Iron Mine girls alike. She bought a whole bolt of pretty blue-and-white plaid cloth, with a little green in it, and a pattern for all the dresses to be made alike. The big day came and we gathered in the schoolyard early for William or Ted Smith to haul all of us—parents, teachers, and kids—in their big truck that was used to haul farm things, including mules.

Oh, weren't we proud of all our dresses just alike. That is, until we got there and started unloading. People stared. A bunch of us Iron Mine girls went down the road to a store for candy and sodas and almost had a fight with some of the Rose Hill girls who were snickering and counting how many dresses they saw alike.

It didn't worry me. I loved my dress and thought it and the color were very pretty. What worried me most about that day was that I wasn't able to make friends with a pretty little girl I saw there. She had come from Norfolk to visit. Although I smiled and tried to look my friendliest, she only stared, shook her curls, and turned away.

I went into the church in search of Mama but a program was underway and I was told to sit down, so I sat. The only thing I recall about the program was a bunch of plump, middle-aged women who were up front singing, or moaning rather. The song went, "My Lord, what a morning" over and over, and then,

> When the stars begin to fall
> You can hear the sinners mourn
> To wake the nations underground.

It went on and on and on. Someone started clapping, hinting that it was time for them to end the song. It encouraged them instead and they moaned louder. Some man behind me said loudly, "Hush and sit down!" They paid him no mind. He got up and left. Others did likewise. I'd been taught not to get up and walk out while someone was speaking or performing. But I loved happy music and this was the saddest sound I'd ever heard. I felt like crying and crying. I couldn't stand it and fled.

Religion has always been an important part of my life. Papa always had all of us at the table for the blessing. Each Sunday morning the Lord's Prayer and the Twenty-third Psalm were recited. We were taught not to lie, steal, use bad words, or drink. As children we obeyed; as adults we strayed on some of them. In our house was a picture of the Good Shepherd holding a white lamb in his arms, and I was told he cared for us the same way, so I had a certain safe feeling when I would just sit and look at it.

I became interested in heaven at a very early age. Saying my prayers, I'd get to "If I should die before I wake" and wonder what my family's reaction would be if I did die that night. Would anybody cry or be sorry? I felt Mama would and perhaps Sam, for he wouldn't have anyone to play and fight with. The others would probably be relieved that I wasn't there to scream and worry them.

So I'd think about all that I'd heard about heaven and how I'd like it. I'd heard people say it was a shiny place with gold streets, where everybody wore white and drank milk and ate honey. Well,

I had my white ruffled dress and I loved milk but the only honey I'd had was what Willie and Leroy brought me from the woods. It had baby bees in it that I had to spit out. I'd wonder if there wasn't anything else to go with the milk. Then I'd drop the whole thing and go to sleep.

Our church always had revival in September. Our pastor, Mr. Tim, was a very dear family friend as well. He and his wife, Miss Emma, had six daughters and one son. We always had a happy time when any of them came home from church with us for dinner and then all went back to church for evening services. One Sunday when I was very small, they passed the bread and wine around for sacrament communion and I cried for some. Mr. Tim came and took me out of Mama's arms and gave it to me.

Our church was small then, with a single gas lamp hanging from the ceiling up front and the back in shadows. The young people loved to sit back there to whisper and giggle. Cousin Archie would rise up, march to the back, and shake his finger at whoever he saw or heard and hush them up. He kept law and order in that church for as long as he was able to get there.

One night during revival, after he had finished preaching, Mr. Tim came down out of the pulpit for people to come up and join the church. He had preached a good sermon about going to Jesus, how he'd take care of us, and the joys of heaven. My brother Willie and most of his friends and the older children went up and accepted Jesus. Several times I rose up to go, even though I was under the age that children usually joined the church. I'd lose my nerve and sit down again. Finally, it looked like all who planned to join that night had done so and he was about finished. I couldn't be left behind. If all my family belonged and I didn't, I'd be shut out of heaven. Sam was a baby so he'd be OK. I don't know what I thought I was.

Anyway, gathering all my courage, I jumped up and ran to

Mr. Tim. Seeing me coming, he took both my hands and talked to me. I don't know what he said except he asked if I accepted Jesus as my Savior and if I knew what it meant to join the church. I nodded, unable to talk. My heart was thumping so hard I couldn't see the people around me. Afterward at home, I was teased unmercifully about being so fast to go up and join before I was old enough. They called me "Sister Mary."

The Sunday they were to baptize us in the creek was cold and rainy. Mama said it was too cold for me to go in that water and that I'd have to wait for the next baptizing. It was nine years later, when I was sixteen, that I was baptized. My brothers told me I half belonged to the church and half didn't, and if I died they'd put my coffin half in the church and have the other half out. I only hoped they'd let me all the way into heaven.

One Sunday we had a visiting preacher. I didn't understand why they called him a preacher. All he did was scream out a word or two, pound, stomp, shake his fists, and make a gasping sound in his throat. He made me uneasy and I was glad when he sat down and wiped his face and neck. Mr. Tim then got up and talked about how the devil was like a spider spinning a web to catch us. At home I mentioned to someone the difference in the sermons. Mama said that just went to show who was the better preacher.

I LOVED all the games we played, but especially jumping rope. There was a verse we'd jump by:

> Last night, night before
> A no-mannered pecker came a' knocking at my door.
> I came down to let him in,
> He hit me side the head with a bottle of gin.
> And all he said was ladybug, ladybug, turn all around,
> Ladybug, ladybug touch the ground,

Ladybug, ladybug show your shoes,
Ladybug, ladybug be excused.

I shut my eyes and jumped blissfully, feeling the air of the rope going over me, and my bare feet on the smooth, hard ground.

The highlight of our week was after we got all our chores done by noon on Saturday. Then we could wash up, put on fresh clothes, and go to a friend's house, but we had to be home by dark. Sometimes, a friend would promise to spend the night and we'd have to go after her. Now that was a big pleasure. We'd have to wait sometimes until she finished scrubbing floors or ironing clothes. Then she had to primp up and put a nightgown, a Sunday dress, and other clothes in a paper bag. We didn't have a "company room," so our girlfriends had to share my and Eunice's bed. Eunice and her friends would snicker and giggle about boys. I'd be worn out from my day's activities and fall right to sleep. On Sunday a big bunch would gather at someone's house and play games such as Blind Man, London Bridge, Buck, Farmer in the Dell, Little Johnny Waters, Loop the Loop, and so many more.

Across the Katy Ford lived a family named Carr. Sometimes I'd spend a night with them. Mr. Carr took a liking to me because he said I favored his little boy who'd been killed in a wreck. He seldom smiled, but I liked him very much. He had some large dark brown turkeys in his yard. I loved to watch them. One day he hitched up his mule and cart and brought me a young turkey.

I was thrilled with my new pet. It wasn't long before he knew me. I cooked cornbread and chopped onions to feed to him. I'd go out and sit on the front steps, and he'd be waiting. I'd scatter the bread crumbled up with the onions. It smelled almost like Thanksgiving dressing. After eating until his craw was big and full, he'd come stand before me and flap his wings a time or two while eyeing my lap, then hop on. I'd stroke his feathers and talk to him awhile, then go put him in his pen for the night.

One day Mama noticed one of her hens acting sick. She said it was a disease called limber neck and would probably spread. Sure enough, we found others lying about the yard in the same fix. I started worrying about my turkey and kept him shut up, or tried to, but somehow he'd find a way out and come to the doorstep and whistle for his breakfast or supper. I'd hurry out, feed him, and shut him back up in his pen. One morning I got up and there was no whistling at the doorstep. I hurried out to his pen and he was slumped over with a long, crooked neck. He tried to raise his head and look and me, flapped a little, and lay still again. Terrified, I flew to the house to ask Mama what to do. She said a little honey and turpentine might help, but she didn't have any honey.

I ran out the door and down the road, still barefoot and in my long white nightgown, to look for honey. At the first house, they didn't have any but Lorena, who lived there, offered to go with me and together we set out for the next house, Cousin Lucy's. No luck. The next was Cousin Frank Boney. She had a little honey but wanted to talk and ask questions about the family. I had no time for talk; I was crying by then.

"It's for my turkey," I sobbed. "He's sick."

I grabbed the honey and ran, leaving Lorena along the way. Back home I found the turpentine and an old spoon. I pried his bill open and poured the medicine down, praying that it wasn't too late and that he'd get well. Next morning, still no whistling. My turkey was dead. I buried him with my usual sobs, screams, and sniffles and missed him very much.

One morning while washing breakfast dishes, after he'd been dead for a good while, I heard the familiar whistle at the doorstep. *My turkey's back*, I thought happily. I ran out on the porch with my soapy hands only to find an empty yard. Running down the steps, I looked under the house and everywhere—no turkey. I ran to tell Mama. She said it was only my imagination, because I thought about him so much, like with my kitty that died. I thought differently, but said no more, just watched every day for my pet to come back and whistle again. He never did.

Professor Rogers, the principal of the largest Black high school in Wilmington (Williston High), often came to hunt with Papa.

This was another exciting time to look forward to. He'd come about daybreak and start blowing his car horn while still driving through the woods. He was a big handsome man and always had a cigar stub in his mouth. After greetings and hugs, he'd bring in paper, tablets, pencils, crayons, and scissors for us children. Uncle Foy (Papa's brother) and Aunt Lillie Bell, and sometimes their boys, Buddy and James, came too.

The men went bird hunting while Mama and Aunt Lillie Bell got busy cooking up a dinner fit for a king. Sam and I were right underfoot, ready to scrape cake batter or icing and smell all the food cooking. We had chicken (fried or stewed), ham, collards or other greens, sweet potatoes baked until the juice came out sweet and syrupy, rice and gravy, cornbread, hot biscuits, pickles, strawberry preserves, fresh sweet milk or buttermilk, coffee, and plenty of just-churned homemade butter.

After the men came in and dinner was eaten and dishes cleaned, we all gathered around the heater to talk. Professor Rogers always lit up a cigar to puff on while they talked over the day's hunt. Sometimes Papa tried a cigar, but cigars didn't become him for he wasn't a smoker. I'd get tickled watching him take short puffs and blow the smoke right back out. Being as it was winter and the days short, it was soon time for all to go. Mama and Papa always loaded Professor Rogers up with good things to carry home—meat, vegetables, and potatoes. Long after he was gone, the joy of the day and the smell of his cigar lingered.

Part Two

A New Kind of Life

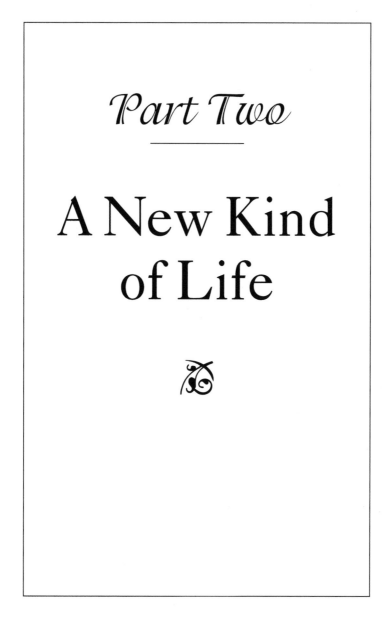

6

The Nightmare Begins

THE happy years of my childhood and many of the pleasant sounds I took for granted were about to change. School had started again, as usual, in late summer. The teachers had arrived, and I'd helped Miss Staten unpack her trunks and bags, sniffing the lovely perfume (I can still smell it) and folding piles of dainty handkerchiefs edged with lace and flowers. She gave me some of her handkerchiefs and other trinkets for helping her.

One evening when I was about nine years old, as I was walking home from school, I felt something in one eye. It was bothersome. Upon arriving home I went to the crib to get Mama to get it out. She could find nothing. I still felt it and my eye was red by morning but no one could find anything at all. This lasted for several days and I started seeing little rainbows around lights at night. This was related to my hearing loss, only we didn't know it then. At school, sometimes I'd look up from reading a book or writing to find Miss Beaty standing right by my desk staring at me.

"Mary, didn't you hear me speaking to you?" she'd ask.

"No ma'am," I'd say.

So she'd go over again whatever it was. Sometimes I'd miss

out on something anyway and she would tell me to stop being hardheaded and to pay attention.

One evening while sitting around the crib trying to learn to tie dry tobacco I fell asleep. Then Mama was shaking me to wake me up because it was time to go in the house. She said she'd been calling me loudly, and didn't I hear her?

"No Ma'am," I said. "No ma'am."

The others hooted and said that they knew I couldn't help hearing her, as loud as she called, and that I should stop putting on. Finally, one morning after Eunice had returned to school, I woke up and someone was saying how loud the car was that had brought Eunice home that night.

"What car?" I asked.

"Didn't you hear all that noise? It was loud enough to wake the dead," I was told.

I hadn't heard a thing. Mama got kind of quiet and thoughtful. Frank didn't tease or pick at me anymore. In fact, he became sort of gentle and kind. One day, he came up behind me and started talking but I didn't know it until he put his mouth close to my ear and called me loudly. I jumped. Mama was also standing by, looking at me so sadly. Frank told her he believed I couldn't hear.

I screamed, "I can too hear!" and ran off.

I was terrified at the thought of being deaf. Not hear the birds singing in the woods or the music on the records? Not hear Mama singing, pans rattling in the kitchen, the wind whistling around the house on a cold winter night, so many other things? A silent world? I'd just as soon be dead. Then I got mad. I decided I was not going to be deaf and started trying to always face whoever was talking to make sure I saw their lips move. I tried to keep up with whatever was being said. When I would see the rest of the family laughing and talking about something, if I couldn't understand and join in, I'd go out where the dogs were and talk to them. At least they were glad of my company. I felt they were my best friends.

School that I once loved so well was a nightmare. When the other children learned that I was losing my hearing, I was either shunned or pitied. When I didn't understand what was said, a few children would scream in my ear and ask why I didn't get a deer horn to hold to my ear and say "Eh? Eh?" They had seen pictures of old people with hearing problems holding a horn to their ear and thought I should use antlers from a mounted deer head.

I guess everyone also thought I was going blind. All I could see from my left eye was a white blur of light. I had to wear shades from morning until night, when I wasn't sitting by the heater, wringing towels out of a pan of hot water to hold to my eye. Our family doctor didn't know what the problem was, so he sent me to a specialist in Wilmington, so Papa carried me to Wilmington every two weeks. Dr. Smith was nice and I wasn't afraid of him. Sometimes our neighbor, Mr. Luther Powers, would take us to Wilmington for my appointment. I'd sit in back with Miss Susie. She'd tuck a soft woolen lap robe around both of us. Usually, I'd end up asleep with my head in her lap.

We went by train at other times and Professor Rogers would meet us at the station. One day Professor Rogers decided to go meet my doctor. He wasn't satisfied with him and made an appointment for me to see his own eye, ear, nose, and throat specialist, Dr. Sloan. He wasn't plump and jolly like Dr. Smith, and his office was on the tenth floor and much larger. He had so many nurses and shiny instruments that I was terrified. I cried and struggled so that Papa took me out in the hall to a broom closet until I quieted down. I continued to see Dr. Sloan every two weeks for several months.

I loved going to Professor Rogers's house, which we did whenever we took the train. It was a tall white house with a porch. He'd put me in his chair by the fireplace in the library. I'd never seen so many books—shelves all around, floor to ceiling. His youngest daughter, Harriet, would bring me apples and things to nibble on until dinnertime. Once, Professor Rogers took Mama and me on a tour of Williston High School. It was the finest school I'd ever seen.

At home I'd sit by the heater from the time I got up until bedtime keeping hot towels to my eye. I had to have drops put in it three times a day. If I went anyplace, I had to wear dark glasses (or shades). They were grown people's shades and they usually slid down my nose. I never went for long without cracking or breaking one side of them. As long as the bad eye was covered, I had to keep that pair. How I hated those shades; I won't wear them today if I can help it. Finally, my left eye cleared up and I could see well from it again, but the right eye had clouded, so I had to go through everything all over again. This lasted for a whole winter. Toward spring that eye also cleared up some, but not entirely, so I still wore shades.

When it was time for school to close, the teachers wanted me to have a part in something since I missed school so much. They gave me the part of Mother Hubbard with a few lines, but my hearing was nearly all gone by this time, so they had a girl lead me onstage and speak a few lines for me. It was humiliating to say the least. I'd always been so proud of learning my lines for a play or saying speeches. They thought I'd lost not only my hearing, but all my senses. I could still speak clearly and never understood why they wouldn't let me speak my lines for myself.

One Sunday afternoon while out on the highway with some of the kids, a boy named Hoover got into an argument with the girls and threw a bottle at one. It hit my eye, breaking the shades, so I stopped wearing them for awhile. I could see, but I was deaf, so no birdsong for me this spring. When we played the talking machine, I'd pick out a favorite record, then place my hand on top of the machine to feel the vibrations. I'd pretend I could still hear the music. At church, I'd keep my eyes glued to the choir members, trying to read someone's lips, pretending I could still hear the hymns I once loved to listen to. They would not give me any part in the Children's Day program that year. I stayed at Thelma's house while they had it. She had no part either, by choice. Thelma always flatly refused to be in any program and thought me foolish for caring enough to cry.

Mama prayed so hard for me to hear again. She taught me to read different parts of the Bible on having faith. When I'd kneel beside her chair to say my prayers at night, her hand would rest on my head and I knew she was praying too. We'd talk about what we'd do when my hearing came back, but it never did. God must have had other plans for me.

One of Mr. Luther's bird dogs had puppies and Papa got one for me. I had a house all ready for her right by my bedroom window. She was tiny and white with black spots and black around one eye. I named her Queen and she became my best friend and companion. The first night in her new home she yelped and cried all night. I was up early to feed and hold her. Soon she was at my heels from morning 'til night. She'd come in my room to wake me up if I wasn't outside when she thought I should be. None of the dogs were allowed in the dining room at mealtime, but Queen would sneak under the table, find my knee, and rest her chin on it. If I didn't slip her a bite, she'd nudge my knee and roll her eyes. Pretty soon, someone would notice she was under the table and tell her to get out of there or give her a kick. She'd go, but sneak right back. They'd ignore her or pretend they didn't know she was back, but there was always some grumbling about Mary and her old dog.

I wasn't suppose to read a lot as it strained my eyes, but not

being able to listen to family talk or go to school, I became quite
lonely and took to looking through all the old books Mama had
around the house. I read them all—some good, some bad. I found
one book of Greek stories about gods and goddesses, winged creatures, and horses. I'd carry the books into the living room, sit in
a rocker by the south window, and pull my shades down my nose.
With Queen at my feet, I'd read to my heart's content. I was right
there with all the people and places I read about.

Suddenly my book would be snatched from me and someone
of the family would be telling me about straining my eyes and
going blind and why didn't I go out and play or something. I'd go
out, wander about, play with the dogs, or walk across the fields
until Mama saw me and called me back to the house. She was still
afraid a varmint would catch me. That was her name for most
wood creatures, but I preferred them to most humans then.

After being outside for awhile, Queen and I would sneak back,
find my book, and settle down to read and sleep. I learned to keep
an eye on Queen. When she'd raise her head and listen, I knew
someone was coming. I would slip my book under the cushion of
the chair and be innocently looking out the window when they
got to the door.

One book very dear to me was *Heidi*. Miss Staten gave it to me
as a prize in third grade. I read it over and over, and always, I was
there in the mountains with Heidi and her grandfather. Like her,
I turned to the Bible and prayer. I enjoyed the Bible stories too.
My favorites of the Old Testament were Moses and Abraham. I
often discussed all I read with Mama and she was only too glad
to help me understand what it meant. I guess that's when I really
started to have a deeper faith and started searching for answers
in the Bible. My faith became more personal and Jesus seemed
closer.

Upon one of my other visits to Dr. Sloan, he decided that my tonsils and adenoids might be the cause of my deafness and that they should be removed. My parents arranged for Dr. Hawes to remove them in his office in nearby Rose Hill as it was closer to home, also probably less expensive. Very few people I knew ever went to a hospital.

The morning of my operation arrived. I asked if Thelma could go with me, so she, Eunice, and I got in the truck with Papa. In Dr. Hawes's office I was dressed in a white gown and placed on an examining table. Although I was frightened, I was calm until something was placed over my nose. I held my breath. They told me to breathe deeply. I couldn't; I screamed and kicked. Eunice and Papa had to help hold me. I was sure I was dying when I started getting weak and sleepy.

I woke up later in the day, lying on a cot someplace. My nose was stopped up and I had to keep my mouth open to breathe. Eunice asked how I was feeling but my throat was so sore and dry I couldn't say anything, so I just pointed to it and cried. The nurse or doctor told her to give me crushed ice. That helped, but it was so hot in the room that I was in misery. I'd sleep at times.

Sometime after dark, Papa came back with the truck. A cot was folded and laid in back, and I was covered with quilts and blankets. Eunice sat down beside me, and that's the way I rode home, looking up at the stars, so grateful for my sister to be there. Mama had the bed ready for me and made a fuss getting me tucked in. Sam made a big to-do and gathered apples from the tree for me, but I couldn't eat them, so Mama made apple dumplings with a rich spicy syrup to go over them. I cried because I couldn't eat them either, so she promised to make more when my throat healed.

Once again, we were all so sure that my hearing would return. Different ones would come up behind me and say something, then turn me around and ask, "What did I say?" I'd shrug because

I never knew unless I could see their mouths and read their lips. I pretended that it was okay and that I didn't care, but I just ached inside. Sometimes the hurt was too much and any little thing would set me off into a screaming, throwing tantrum. My brothers called me a spoiled brat and told Mama that she shouldn't take up time petting me. I wanted to be sure she was never far from me and had no desire to go off on long visits any more.

Mama had been very sick the winter before. No one told me but I knew that one night they weren't looking for her to live. I went out under the pear tree in the backyard and prayed to the God I had come to believe in to please not take my mama away. I thought of all I'd read about him helping people in the Bible. Sitting in my playhouse under the pear tree, I cried and prayed. The moon was just beginning to shine in the dusk when I saw something like a pan of water or ice thrown out a bedroom window. It sparkled and I went to see who was throwing something out, but the window was closed. It was winter so I went inside and asked Eunice who had dashed water out the window, but she said nobody had. I wondered about it, but not for long because the crisis with Mama seemed to have passed, and I went to the bed and hugged and kissed her. She was far from well though.

Papa got Miss Mary Keyes to come stay with us to look after Mama. On top of his hunting and farm work, he took a night job firing a boiler for the highway construction going through our neighborhood. He'd come home all black with coal dust, tired and red eyed. Queen had proven to be one of the best bird dogs around and Dr. Wysong offered to take her in payment for Mama's care, but because I loved her so much, Papa refused and worked instead.

For the first time in my life, Christmas was skimpy and my belief in Santa Claus wavered. After leaving my usual note of what to leave in my sack, I got up that Christmas morning and saw the small amount of candy and a piece or two of fruit in each of our bags and a toy apiece for Sam and me. I asked Eunice if there was really a Santa Claus. She said there was. So I asked how he got in, and she said down the chimney. Looking at our wood heater door, I suddenly knew no one had come down our chimney and crawled out through the heater, but I wouldn't ask any more questions. I was afraid I'd find out the truth, and the magic of Christmas would be lost.

So I accepted my small doll and tried to make clothes for her on Mama's sewing machine. I'd learned how to open and thread it and work the pedal. I'd done this one day while Mama was propped up on pillows in the bed watching me. I started working the pedal but had my hand in the wrong place. The needle went in my forefinger instead of the cloth and refused to back up. The pain was terrible and I screamed. Poor Mama lay there, helpless to do anything. Miss Mary Keyes came running from the kitchen and got me and the machine separated somehow and put oil and bandages on my bleeding finger. I was told to stay away from that machine from then on, but being me, I didn't. I was right back to sewing as soon as my finger healed.

Spring came slowly that year and Mama improved along with it. Eunice had gone back to Wallace to finish out the school year. Our dog, Bell, had a bunch of puppies out in the woods in an old hollow tree. On Easter Sunday, Papa cooked dinner; he even made a plain (pound) cake. Mama could come to the table and walk some, so Miss Mary Keyes returned to her own home. It was warm and sunny, and Papa told Mama to walk around some outside. He kept hold of her while Sam and I ran about, happy to see our Mama up and outside again. We visited Bell and her puppies. They were fat little balls of fur and so sweet and beautiful. We went through the back woods to the pond where the rowboat Bennie and Frank had made was tied under a tree. The water was still and peaceful with leaves floating here and there. We went by the chicken house, dog pens, cribs, and finally back to the house.

I shall always remember that Easter—the first one where I was really aware of its meaning. I had made Mama an Easter card of a cross with grass and spring flowers growing around it and "Easter Greetings" printed across the back. I didn't know then that people were supposed to buy fancy new clothes and parade for Easter.

By summer, life was back to normal. Mama was back in her garden and doing farm work, but I also think that was the summer we rented a room to a couple who had come to work on the highway. The teachers had gone for the summer. The woman's name was Minerva, but I've forgotten her husband's. Their little three-year-old, Janet, was a real brat. We had turned our living room into a bedroom for them. It soon became like a pigpen. Tension built up and it wasn't long before they moved on. We had a housecleaning and once again a living room, with Mama's pretty rug with the large red roses and green leaves around the border. The center table with the fringed cover and the rose bowl was once again sitting in the middle of the floor.

We still waited and hoped for my hearing to return. Each Thursday I had to go to Dr. Hawes's office for a shot in the arm. That I hated, and I screamed like he was killing me. I know he was as glad as I was when I'd finally had them all.

At that time Frank and Bennie had a yellow convertible with a rumble seat. Frank and one of his pals (I think it was Vander Murphy) were carrying me for a shot one evening. Sam was with us, and we were all in front since it was drizzling rain. We passed two pretty girls walking toward town and hollered out and asked if they wanted a ride. After a lot of giggling the girls decided they did. Frank opened the rumble seat and pushed Sam and me into it through the back window. The girls got in, smelling of perfume and powder and still giggling. One sat next to Frank, the other on Vander's lap. One looked back at Sam and me with the rain blowing in our faces and started to say something but turned back hastily when I gave her my meanest glare. I was so mad that I didn't even cry when Dr. Hawes stuck the needle high up in my arm. It was my last shot.

That wasn't the only adventurous ride with our brother Frank. Sometime the same summer Sam and I were at Miss Mag's house, playing while Mama and the rest worked. Near dark, Frank came by and told us to get in and he'd take us home. He didn't carry us home, but went to Wallace instead, to Back Street where a girl he liked, Mattie Tilly, worked as a waitress. We didn't know he was high until she came out to the car. Mattie knew Frank well enough to tell just by looking at him that he was high. She was older and knew more than we did. She looked at us, and told Frank to carry us home. She said he shouldn't have us out after dark like that and asked if Mama knew where we were.

I started sniffling then and Frank went and bought us ice cream cones. My tears dried up. But then he told Mattie to get in and go for a ride with us. She got in, apron and all, and what a ride! We went outside of town, across a creek bridge, and over a partially cleared field with stumps still in it. Two wheels went over one of the stumps and the car tilted dangerously. Sam and I screamed, and Mattie did too. I guess it scared Frank also, for he took Mattie back to the cafe, bought Sam and me lollipops, and took us home. Mama was walking the floor, worried to pieces. Sam had gone to sleep by then.

That summer I read about Hansel and Gretel. I lived that story for weeks. I could just hear the children singing when they could move again. I roamed the fields and woods with Queen, half hoping and half afraid I'd also come upon a witch's house and be turned to gingerbread. Meanwhile, summer was passing. The days had changed from the fresh, sweet green of spring to the lush green of July with its hot, dusty roads. Soon school would open again. I kept my mind closed against even the thought of school, knowing I couldn't go with my hearing gone.

I'd become reconciled to my silent world. The dogs, cats, and other animals were my friends. I read old schoolbooks, learning what I could. But sometimes I'd look at my family gathered at the table or sitting on the porch talking about something, and when they'd all laugh, I felt like I'd just as well be dead because I was so shut off from the rest of them. On the porch after dark when I couldn't see them talk, I'd lay my head in Mama's lap and feel her voice vibrate when she talked. I'd try so hard to understand a word or two. The tears would come but I made no sound, not wanting anyone to fuss and call me a "waterhead." Mama would stroke my hair and I'd calm down. At times though, I'd go into a temper, yell, and throw things. I knew they disliked me—all but Mama. So Queen and I roamed the dusty fields finding a watermelon here and there. I'd bust one and squat in the shade to eat what I could of it, and Queen would eat some too.

7

The Train Ride to a New World

IN 1935 my family decided to send me off to the state school for the deaf and blind in Raleigh. Mama broke the news to me, telling me that Norman Hayes, my cousin who was blind, went there. She talked about all the things he knew how to do and what a good time he had. I took the news in silence, not even imagining myself off in some strange place for school. To me school was the little wooden two-room building out beside the church, and to go meant walking the familiar road with my sister, brothers, and friends. I closed my eyes behind my cracked shades and could smell the blackboard dust, feel the warm morning sun on my back while having devotion in Miss Beaty's room, and hear all of us singing, "Lift Every Voice and Sing" or "My Country 'Tis of Thee."

Mama touched me. I opened my eyes to read her lips and gestures.

"They taught Norman to sing and play the piano," she said.

Music! I brightened up at that.

"Would they teach me?"

She nodded.

My beloved Mama.

"And I can come home for Christmas?"

Well, things weren't so bad. I could see myself coming back home, going to church, and surprising everyone by getting up and going to the piano. I'd sit down to play the most beautiful music and sing, "In the Garden" or "Every Day, Sing and Pray." I could just hear the applause and whispers of "I didn't know Mary could sing or play." I went in search of Sam to tell him about my future accomplishments. He didn't laugh or sneer at me, only nodded and grunted a little.

In fact, everyone started giving me special treatment. I wasn't fussed at and Queen was allowed under the table and any other place she wished to go. When the Iron Mine school opened, I went out there one day. Miss Beaty asked me if I was going to try to make it this year.

"No ma'am, I'm going to school in Raleigh," I said.

I still didn't really believe it though.

Papa and Eunice took me shopping at Collins Department Store. Two of our White neighbors, Estelle and Pauline Herring, worked there. They made a big to-do over helping me pick out dresses, underclothes, shoes, socks, and a nice sweater. Papa also bought a large brown suitcase with straps around it. All my new things were packed in it with the rest of my clothes. Eunice bought talcum powder, toothpaste, creams, headbands, and ribbons for me. Oh, I was a dressed-up girl and everybody was so nice to me. Even Willie and Leroy didn't tease or pick at me anymore.

The day for my departure drew nearer. I closed my mind and refused to even think. A letter arrived from the school with a ticket and a name tag to be pinned on me. I wouldn't look at it. Finally, the great and dreadful day arrived, but I tried to make it an ordinary day. I got up and put on a playsuit and ran outside to see Queen (Papa had shut her up). She licked me and wiggled as I hugged and talked to her.

It was like a holiday. Papa killed some chickens and Mama and Eunice fried them and baked cakes and other things so I'd have a meal for on the train. Sam and I went up to the grape arbor by the old house and picked a box of grapes for me to take. The sun was warm, the air sweet with the smell of grapes, and lots of little yellow butterflies fluttered about as white fluffy clouds drifted overhead. We played and ate as we picked, and I refused to even think I'd soon be leaving home and all those I loved so dearly. Back at the house we ate dinner, then I ran to hug and talk to Queen awhile. When I went back in the house, Mama got water and soap and laid out some of my new clothes for me. After I'd bathed and dressed, she put a towel around my shoulders and combed and brushed my hair into sausage curls. Then she ran a ribbon under my hair and tied a bow on the top of my head.

My suitcase was closed and the key hung on a string around my neck. I ran back to Queen. She seemed to know I was leaving and looked so sad. I couldn't see her then for the water standing in my eyes. She nuzzled me with her nose and the water overflowed.

They were all in the truck by then, waiting for me. Mama sat in front with Papa, my shoe box of food and my box of grapes in her lap. I got to the truck and looked back at Queen. Her nose was in a crack of the door. I ran back one more time, hugged her tight, and ran back to the truck. Someone helped me in. I was crying hard by then and couldn't bear to even look up. I was surrounded by my brothers, my beloved sister, Allen (who had moved in with us after Pridgen died), and Subud (Robert McMillan, one of my parents' foster children); Mama and Papa were in the cab. I wouldn't be coming back with them. When we got down the road where it turned and passed the grape arbor, I could see the house through a clearing. There it was—home, with the sun setting and tall twin oak trees at the end of the porch. They were the first things you saw when coming and the last when leaving—them and the big pine in the woods in front of the house. It sort of slanted.

I hurt and ached all over and couldn't stop crying. Eunice kept patting me and telling me to hush. Some of the neighborhood people who knew I was leaving were out to wave. Others stood by the road and Papa stopped for them. The truck was full when we reached the railway station. We all got out. Eunice took me to the five-and-ten and bought me a box of stationery for writing home and a couple of funny books (or comics). Back at the station others were also waiting. My cousin Norman was waiting with a girl named Catherine Bryant. She was pretty, with the clearest eyes. I found it hard to believe that she was blind. An older girl who was deaf kept making gestures for me not to cry, that there'd be lots of children for me to play with, and that I'd have a good time.

"And now wipe your eyes and hush," she gestured to me.

That was my friend, Margie Butler.

It seemed the train would never come. Mama went back in

the waiting room and sat down. I followed her and laid my head in her lap, trying to pretend we were all just down there to watch the train go by and I would soon be going back home to bed with Eunice, huddled up against her back. Comforted by such thoughts, I dozed off to sleep. Then someone was shaking me to get up. The train was coming! The ground was shaking as a jumble of white light came rumbling down the track. Papa pulled me away from Mama as I cried and hung on. Then somehow I was in the train. Papa put my shoe box of food, my funny books, and my grapes on my lap, patted my head, kissed me, and was gone. I tried to see out the window to get one more look at my beloved family, especially Mama, Sam, and Eunice, but the water in my eyes and the darkness kept them hidden. I saw just my own wet face reflected in the glass.

Then the train started chugging and moving slowly. This couldn't be me sitting here on this thing carrying me away from home, the fields and woods, Queen and the other dogs, the schoolhouse, and the church. I saw them all in my mind and cried harder. Then someone pulled my head up and hugged me, telling me not to cry and make myself ugly. It was Margie. Then another young girl came and sat across from me. She also made motions for me not to cry. That was Helen Johnson. When I had calmed down, Margie left to visit with others in the car. It turned out to be a special car carrying only deaf and blind students to school. A tall, very good-looking older boy came up, smiled at me, patted my head, and made some motions. I did not understand but was cheered just the same. This was to be my play father, David Mitchell from Wilmington.

The train was rocking on down the tracks now and my tears had slowed to just a drop now and then. Another girl who seemed to be Helen's friend had gotten on the train and was sitting with me and Helen, also making gestures for me not to cry and that I would have a good time, lots of good things to eat, and so on. Her name was Elizabeth. Another plump, pretty girl was named Sadie, and a smaller, frisky one was named Cora Armstrong. I started trying to gesture like them, not letting myself think of home. Every now and then I'd let out a long sigh and sniffles.

The other girls got out their boxes and bags of food, signed, swapped food, and ate, offering me some. I shook my head and opened my own shoe box. At the sight of the fried chicken and cake, the kitchen at home rose up before me with Mama and Eunice in it, busy fixing my food for the trip. My throat hurt and water spilled over from my eyes again. Forcing down a few bites, I closed the box. I wouldn't even open the grapes, knowing I'd see the blue sky, fluffy white clouds, yellow butterflies, dusty ragweed, goldenrod, and black-eyed Susies by the road. I'd see Sam and me climbing around on top of the arbor, eating grapes and throwing hulls at each other.

Once in a while Margie came up from the back of the car to check on me. Also David or Sadie would pass by, pat my head, and smile encouragingly. It grew late. Helen and Elizabeth started nodding. My own eyes grew heavy and I slept as the train rocked on through the night. I jerked awake and thought, *This couldn't be me, on this train going further and further from home and to where?* I didn't know and couldn't picture how the school would look or when we'd get there. I could hear—or feel the vibration from—a long wail of the train's whistle. I couldn't even cry anymore.

The conductor came by and started shaking the ones who were asleep. Margie came to tell me to get my things together; we'd be getting off. I gathered up my shoe box, grapes, and funny books, along with the little pocketbook Eunice had bought me with my change, autograph book, and hanky inside. It was quite a load. Helen opened the window and threw out scraps from her meal. So did Elizabeth. I thought about the good breakfast I'd have at my new school in the morning. Why worry with a big box of food I couldn't even eat? So out went my shoe box and the grapes followed. I felt relieved—nothing to remind me of home now.

The train came to a halt and I followed my newfound friends out and into a cold, empty, and gloomy waiting room. We sat and stood around for awhile until a man came in and signed something to the other children. I got up and followed them onto another train. This one was dim and kind of old and dirty. By now, I wasn't surprised at anything these people did or where we went. I was no longer home, just a lost soul out in the night. Finally, this train also ground to a halt. I looked out the window, and saw not a light anyplace, but the same man got up from someplace in the car and herded all of us off.

We seemed to be in the middle of nowhere—no buildings and no lights except from the train. We followed the tracks for awhile, then turned off on a graveled road. I could see a few lights up ahead now. Soon we were on a cement walk, passing dark buildings that some of the crowd turned off to go into. Then the girls I was with turned into a two-story brick building. The steps led up to a small, closed porch. Standing there was a plump, sweet-faced lady with short hair that was very white and soft-looking. She smiled and greeted each of the other girls. Margie pointed at me and signed something and went through the door leading upstairs.

The lady looked down at me and smiled, then bent and hugged and kissed me. I felt warm again. Taking my hand, she led me through another door along with Helen and Elizabeth. Going down a long hall, she opened another door. This was a long room, almost the length of the building, with a row of small white beds on either side. Everything was white like a hospital—walls, beds, spreads, chairs, and a few dressers. The other two girls already knew where their beds were and went to them. The lady was Mrs. Mallette, housemother for the deaf girls' dormitory.

She led me to a bed, turned back the covers, then took me to a heavy white door at the end of the room and showed me that it was the bathroom. It had rows of toilets in stalls, washbasins, and showers. Leading me back to the bed, she made motions for me to take off my dress and sweater and go to bed. My suitcase wasn't with me. After removing my shoes, socks, and dress, I wondered if these people prayed. Well, I was going to say my prayers regardless. Mrs. Mallette waited until I'd finished and gotten in bed, then turned out the lights and left me in the dark.

I went under the covers, couldn't stand it, and came up for air. A strange light swept across the sky and the row of windows on the opposite wall. Under the covers I went again. I soon felt like I was suffocating and had to have air. I didn't see the light—just a glow from the lights outside. Then again, it swept across the sky and windows. It was a broad band of light, wide at one end and narrow where it came up from behind the trees.

"Oh, Lord Jesus," I prayed. "Help me."

I wondered if it was Judgment coming. I was back under the covers. When I needed air again, I stuck only my nose out and mercifully slept.

When I opened my eyes again it was day. I was in a room full of about 25 girls. They were making their beds. I made mine, went to the bathroom, washed up, and tried to comb my hair like Mama did. Some of the big girls came from upstairs and combed and braided all of us younger girls' hair, but not Helen's, Elizabeth's, or another girl's. The other girl was larger than I was, and very pretty with a beautiful brown complexion, long wavy hair, and the prettiest eyes with long black lashes. She too could talk and seemed able to hear some. This was Mary Frances Hughes. The other girls stood around trying to sign to her and feel her hair.

I had put on my shades and stood waiting for whatever came next. Mrs. Mallette came and motioned for us all to go outside but first made Mary Frances braid her hair like the rest of us.

Outside we were lined up like soldiers and told to stand still until the breakfast bell rang. It was a large iron bell on a pole, and if we were outside, we could see someone pulling on the rope to ring it. When we were inside, the hearing teachers would tell us what to do. On this, my first morning, when the bell had rung, we marched single file across the grounds to another building. This one had three stories with a kitchen, storeroom, and dining room on the first floor. The chapel, office, library, and music rooms for the blind students were on the second floor. The third floor was classrooms. The dining room was filled with long wooden tables with rows of chairs on each side, and a metal plate, cup, and fork at each place. On each plate was a spoonful of thin grits, another of salmon and eggs, one thin hard biscuit, and a cup of water. I was assigned a seat but told to stand until time to sit down. The blind children sang the Lord's Prayer while the deaf students stood with folded hands and bowed heads. The blind girls had the first two tables—small girls at one and large girls at the other. Next came the deaf girls divided into two tables, then the deaf boys, and at the far end, the blind boys. We couldn't mix.

The housemothers stood watch over each group to make sure they did what they came there for—to eat and not to "talk"— especially not with the opposite sex. I sat down in front of that tin plate of watery grits, scrambled eggs, and salmon; thought of Mama's pretty brown biscuits, fried ham or bacon, the pitchers of syrup and sweet milk; and started to cry. Mrs. Mallette came to my chair and motioned for me to eat. I didn't want to displease her, so I took a bite of biscuit. It was hard, lumpy, and tasteless—no salt or baking powder. I stirred up the grits and salmon but just couldn't eat it. Mrs. Mallette let us know that the bell had rung, and we all stood up—finished or not—and marched back to the dorms to wait while the teachers, principal, and housemothers ate. Then another march to chapel for devotion and remarks from our principal, Reverend Williams. Then a march upstairs to the classrooms.

I was placed with the beginners. So were Mary Frances and another girl named Wilhelmina Hill. Mary Frances soon talked her way to a higher class. I had finished the fourth grade at home and tried to tell the teachers, but no one listened. I was shown a picture of an apple, the letter *A*, and how to say *apple* in sign language. Hill (as we called her) was dressed very nicely and primly, and she wore thick glasses. She protested about being where she was and said she was in the fifth grade. The teachers decided she was blind and sent her to the beginners' class for the blind students.

At the noon bell, we marched downstairs for dinner—another mess of something and a tin cup of water. I longed for the box of food and my grapes that I'd thrown out the train window. In the classroom after dinner it was more of the same. Different letters and pictures, but I was beginning to catch a sign or two. We didn't have school the next day. Instead we went to the nurse's room in each dorm, stripped to the waist, and were examined. They took blood to test for diseases and saw who needed their tonsils removed. The nurse recommended that my tonsils be taken out. When I protested that they had already been removed the previous summer, I wasn't believed. Mama had to convince them. She wrote them a letter and they must have contacted Dr. Hawes.

During the course of the day I got my first real look at the campus. The buildings were arranged in a square with two dorms on one side—one for the deaf boys and one for the blind boys—and two dorms on the opposite side—one for the deaf girls and one for the blind girls. The largest building, housing classrooms, the office, and the dining hall, was at the front facing the highway. All of these buildings were made of red brick. The back of the square consisted of three metal buildings—a shoe repair shop for the deaf boys, a mattress and broom-making shop for the blind boys, and a furniture or cabinetmaking shop for the deaf boys. The heating plant was also located there.

The North Carolina School for the Blind and Deaf was for Black children. When I was there, it could handle about 300 children altogether. At that time, however, I think we had more deaf students than blind students. The school for White blind children was in town and the school for White deaf children was in western North Carolina. Although we had our own principal, our school and the school in town were under the same superintendent, George Lineberry, who was White.

On Sunday morning I wondered what to do after our dab of grits, scrambled eggs, hard cold biscuit, and the usual cup of water was dealt with. Did we go to Sunday school or what? I saw an older girl standing at the back steps of our dorm gazing out toward the woods. Going up to her, I looked to see what she saw. There was a metal building and a brick one beside it with black smoke coming from a tall smokestack. A little farther, I saw a gravel road and a yellow wooden house with two stories. I touched the girl and, pointing at the yellow house, asked her if that was where we went to Sunday school. She nodded vigorously. I had no way of knowing she was totally deaf and unable to talk as well.

I had set out on my own to go to the "church" and had reached the tin building before someone noticed, ran after me, and hauled me back. I was told that it was against the rules to go that far from the dorm and that I would be whipped if I did it again. The tin building was where the boys learned shoe mending and we weren't to get anywhere near a boy—even me, who had spent all of my nine years in a house full of boys and felt more at home with them than with girls. However, after seeing several girls lashed across the back with a leather strap that Mrs. Mallette carried, I made sure I minded.

At 4:00 we marched to the chapel for vesper services. The blind students played the piano and sang, the deaf students signed hymns, and Reverend Williams did the scripture, prayers, and talk. This over, we marched from chapel to the dining hall for a Sunday evening supper of a peanut butter, molasses, and cheese sandwich, a cup of sweet milk, and an apple. Then back to the dorms where we could play, read, "talk," or whatever until 9:00. Then all lights were out.

Back in the classroom, I once again tried to tell Mrs. Whitaker, the beginners' teacher, that I had been promoted to fifth grade. After seeing some of my writing, she believed me. We went down to the office where Reverend Williams said I was to have a test and if I passed, then I'd be moved to the fifth grade. I passed! Then I was in Miss Hayes's room on the opposite side of the hall. Upon finding out I could still speak clearly, she made me talk to her, recite poems, and read stories to a class who couldn't even hear me. I felt much better. Only on warm sunny days, when I'd look out the window facing south and home and see fluffy white clouds, would I give a long, sniffling sigh, then try to read or do something to keep from crying.

Mrs. Whitaker was short, plump, middle-aged, and kindly, and given to wearing black skirts and white blouses with little black bows at the neck. Miss Hayes was equally plump, but younger, with a beautiful brown complexion and wavy black hair. I soon loved her dearly. I still remember "September," a poem by Helen Hunt Jackson, that Miss Hayes had me recite: "The golden-rod is yellow; / The corn is turning brown."

Life settled into a regular routine of meals, classes, play periods, study hours after supper (7:00 to 9:00), and lights-out. I learned to sign, made a few more friends, and talked with some of the teachers. Miss Stewart, our school nurse, was from Florida. Miss Kearney was the school secretary—tall, thin, and very stylish. They had a room together in our dorm. The highlight of my week was Friday or Saturday night when Mrs. Mallette sent for me to give me a letter from home. I'd look at Mama's familiar handwriting on the back and the postmark from Wallace, then find some spot where I could be alone to open it and read it over and over. Her letters were always full of news of family and friends. Papa would be gone hunting or doing some farm work, while Eunice, Willie, and Sam were in school. Even the dogs and farm animals were included in Mama's letters, especially Queen. I could see them all and would sit and dream of home awhile.

Mary Frances had adjusted to school like a pro and was into everything, even kitchen duty. For some reason she decided to take me under her wing. She would bring me bits of food she'd snitched from the teachers' tables when she was assigned to wash dishes. She even tried to teach me to do a shaky dance while rolling my eyes upward. I was hopeless but happy with my new-found friend. I didn't have her for long though. It turned out that Mary Frances's hearing was perfect, but her grades were so poor they had thought she was deaf and sent her to the school for deaf children. After saying good-bye, I never saw her again.

September turned into October, and the woods behind the school and the hills beyond were dazzling in russet, gold, red, and brown. I longed to go walk in them, but that was against the school rules.

The kids started getting excited about the state fair. I'd never even heard of it. I was told of all the wonders I would see: the rides, foot-long hot dogs, candied apples, and cotton candy. I, too, caught the excitement and started looking forward to the fair. All of us younger girls were measured for new dresses and shoes. The older girls made our dresses in sewing class, and the housemothers went to town, picked out several different styles of shoes, and ordered them in the different sizes. They also ordered sweaters, hats, and coats. I was told to write home for spending money though I already had a dollar. That was considered good money when apples, hot dogs, Cokes, and candy were only five or ten cents each.

So the big Saturday of the fair finally arrived. We had breakfast and were herded in front of the administration building, boys on one side, girls on the other. A couple of large farm trucks drove up. Girls loaded into one, boys into the other. Some housemothers and teachers had to ride with us. It was thrilling to ride through the streets of Raleigh and see other people and houses again, even if we *were* riding like cattle. People on the streets stared, but we cared not a bit. We were too happy to be out of our jail-like school for a change.

At the fairgrounds, everything was a wonder—the huge Ferris wheel and other rides, the midway and shows. Showgirls in heavy makeup and tight gowns or skimpy outfits were jiggling and shaking and inviting people to step up, buy a ticket, and come in to see their dances fresh from Broadway or some other far-off place. Our very prim and proper teachers, Miss King and Miss Harris, refused most of them and shoved us on, but finally said they'd let us see one that seemed more decent than the rest. The boys from school had already gone in, so in we went, hurrying to find seats up front where we could see better, eating popcorn or candied apples. Finally the curtain went up and the lights dimmed. Girls appeared onstage, very pretty and dressed in white cowgirl outfits. They danced and swayed until only one was left. She took off her scarf . . . her vest . . . her boots . . . her skirt . . . her blouse—by then Misses King and Harris were telling us to get up and get out at once, pushing and pulling while we ogled. I looked back at the door. The only thing she had left on was her hat, and she was astride a white pony.

We saw a boy turned to stone, a girl in a swimsuit in a snake pit, a fat lady, a bearded lady, and Mickey and Minnie Mouse (who turned out to be two little gray mice). We had free passes and rode on just about everything. I had my first ride on the Ferris wheel and the hopper horse (merry-go-round). At the end of a terrifying trip through the funhouse, we had to slide down a chute in the dark and were dumped out at the feet of bystanders. We had pictures made (four for twenty-five cents). Our teachers had tickets for our lunch, so we lined up at a diner and were given a hot dog or hamburger and a soda. Toward dark, we were again herded into the big trucks like so many cows and made the trip back to school, tired but happy. Some of us who'd had a dollar to spend carried back cotton candy, candied apples, pictures, and peppermint sticks to be nibbled after lights-out.

Memories of the fair were our source of pleasure until Thanksgiving, although Halloween was fun, too. There was a contest to see who could fix up the ugliest face. Boys and girls could be at the same party, but could not touch or get too close to each other. I slowly adjusted to campus life and learned which girls were friendly, which were mean and bossy. I avoided the mean ones with the exception of Hazel Gregory. No one could stay out of her way. She was a born troublemaker and into everybody's business.

After a couple of months Hill moved back to the deaf department. I'd see her staring at me solemnly; the glasses made her eyes look large and at first I felt uncomfortable. She didn't dress like the rest of us. I think she was twelve at that time, but all her clothes were straight: tailored dresses, plain skirts, sweaters and blouses, shoes with low heels, and cotton stockings such as Mama wore. She was usually alone. Somehow, we found out we both could still speak well and had a little hearing left. This formed a bond and we spent many hours telling each other of our families and home life. This helped to ease our homesickness. Her dad was a minister and also taught school. Her mother, brothers, and sisters were teachers. Unlike me, she lived in a large house in a city. Because she was quiet and prim, the other girls said she was too much like a teacher and left her alone.

Hill said she was in the fifth grade but had been placed in the fourth. She said she couldn't understand the other deaf kids' wild signs and the way they arranged their words. Another friend, Flossie, had also been put in the blind department and then found to be deaf. Like me, she had lost her hearing after being in school for awhile. She was older, a teenager, but outgoing and tried to be friends with everybody. When she found out that we were both from Wallace and that I used to hear, another bond was formed.

One Saturday a girl came racing to tell me my father was outside to see me. My heart leaped and pounded. Papa way up here? Unbelievable! Papa never went farther than Warsaw or Wilmington—close to home. Away I ran, only it turned out to be Professor Rogers, smiling and beaming, glasses shining, and a cigar stuck in the corner of his mouth. I was just as joyful and flew into his arms. He'd also brought his two daughters, Margarite and Harriet. They couldn't visit long, and after giving me a large bag of fruit and candy and some spending change, he told the principal and my housemother to be sure I was well taken care of and treated nicely. I was, and time passed.

Talk turned to Christmas and what we wanted. I said I'd wait to tell my Mama and Papa what I wanted when I got home. The other girls informed me that I wasn't going home until May when school was out. I said no, I was going for Christmas. It wouldn't be Christmas if I wasn't home because I had to hang my sack up by the heater along with Sam's and Willie's. They laughed and told me to wait and see.

Christmas came closer. Our teachers asked us to name three small things we wanted for Christmas. I asked Miss Hayes if I wasn't going home. She made no answer. I gave my list and waited for the day that classes would end for Christmas. It was a cold snowy day and I hurried to the dorm to pack some of my clothes. The teachers had theirs packed and were waiting in the front hall for cabs to pick them up.

I went first to one, then another with the same question, "Can't I go home for Christmas too?"

Some—Miss King and Miss Laws—looked at me with pity. Miss Hayes hugged me, got in her cab, and left me with my nose pressed against the window pane, crying my heart out. Finally, Mrs. Mallette found me there, scolded me for crying and ordered me to stop immediately. She gave me tissue to wipe my eyes and told me to go into the bedroom to wait for supper.

Left to right: Miss King, Miss Laws, and Miss Hayes on campus after a snowfall (1936).

The next day was Christmas Eve and looked like it—cold, gray skies and snow falling all day. The mailman came out from town and left a large pile of boxes in front of the office. They were for the children lucky enough to have parents who were able—and cared enough—to send them something from home. The secretary would sort them out and send them to the matron of each dorm to be opened and inspected before giving them to the children after supper.

We were told to go to chapel that night. There was a beautiful Christmas tree with lights that blinked on and off. After we were seated, Reverend Williams made a speech. I don't remember all he said, only that it was Christmas Eve and we should be happy and thankful for the goodies we were about to receive, and so on. Finally, as each name was called, a child went up to be given a brown paper bag. In each was a couple of apples, as many oranges, a handful of hard candy, and a few nuts. The small children also got a small toy or stuffed animal, and the older girls got talcum powder, combs, or handkerchiefs. After receiving my bag I sat down and looked inside, trying to decide whether to be thankful or to cry again. Before that could happen, chapel was dismissed and we were headed back for our dorms. I walked with Helen and Elizabeth, the three of us huddled arm-in-arm to keep warm. The campus was beautiful. Snow was still falling and that on the ground was deep and smooth and shiny under the lights. All of the dorm windows were lit up, which looked beautiful against the snow.

When we arrived at the dorm, I was told to report to Mrs. Mallette in her room. She took me across the hall to the sewing room and unlocked the door. There, on the long cutting table, were two large boxes she told me were mine from home. They had already been opened and inspected, so I had no problem getting inside. One box contained all the Christmas goodies my family enjoyed: some of each kind of cake that Mama and Eunice had baked—chocolate (my favorite), pineapple, coconut, raisin, and fruitcake. There were also lots of apples, oranges, candy, nuts, ham, chicken, and sausage. The second box was full of gifts from each member of my beloved family, new clothes, and spending money. Although I had nowhere to spend it, I was overjoyed. I had to let Mrs. Mallette keep both boxes as the older children would have soon cleaned them out. Each time I opened the food box for a piece of cake or anything to eat, wonderful images of the kitchen at home and of my mama and sister rose up before me, and for awhile I couldn't swallow for the hurting lump in my throat.

Other girls also had nice boxes and gifts and a lot of girls didn't. Some never received a piece of mail during all the nine months we were in school. I gave several girls a taste of my mama's cake and from then on until my box was empty, I was the most popular little girl on the first floor. On Christmas Day, the big girls even took me outside in the snow to make pictures with them. The snow had stopped during the night and the sun made the whole campus look like a fairyland. My homesick soul lifted greatly and I laughed and enjoyed it all. So passed my first Christmas in Raleigh.

Afterward, we settled back into the usual routine. I usually spent part of my after-school hours either in Miss Kearney and Miss Stewart's room reading magazines and funny papers or in Miss Hayes and Miss Hayward's doing the same thing. They all kept a large stack of books, magazines, and newspapers. I loved to read them and talk about my home and family. I guess I bored those poor teachers to tears, but they never seemed to mind and would let me talk. Bless them and my fourth-grade teacher from home, Miss Beaty. She even journeyed up to Raleigh to see me.

Toward the last of January I was sitting in the living room of the dorm trying to listen to Miss Kearney play a tune on the old upright piano, when she stopped long enough to tell me to see who was at the door. I checked the front door first and finding no one there, turned to the door on the south end. I opened it wide, saying, "Come in" without really looking up. It was bright outside, and looking at the people against the light I only saw silhouettes. Turning about, I started back down the long hall to lead them to Miss Kearney so she could find out who they wanted to see.

I noticed a young boy fell into step beside me at the same time that a strangely familiar hand touched my shoulder. I looked and saw, not only my dear mama and baby brother, Sam, but Eunice, Bennie, Frank, and Mr. McKinley Boone. It couldn't be! I think I screamed. I do know I was all hugged up with Mama, then Sam and Eunice, unable to say a word. Miss Kearney, hearing the commotion, came out to investigate.

All I could say was, "My mama."

She understood and introduced herself to them. We went to meet Mrs. Mallette and I raced upstairs to get Miss Stewart. The other teachers had gone home for the weekend. Then, of course, Margie and Flossie had to come see Mama. I went from one to the other of my family to feel them and pat them and make sure they were real. Bennie and Frank were embarrassed at this display of emotion but hadn't the heart to push me away as they would have done at home. Sam and Mama seemed as glad to touch and pat me as I did them. Even Eunice let me fuss over her when usually she'd tell me to stop slobbering and messing. All too soon it was time for them to go, as the sun was getting low and they had over a hundred miles to go to get home—no bypasses or four-lane highways back then.

Following them to the car, I hugged each one as they got in, even Mr. McKinley, saving Mama for the last. I hung on and cried as it seemed my heart would break right then. They'd only been with me a few hours and I had months and months until May, when I could go home and be a part of my family again. However, the goodies in the box they left me were a great consolation while they lasted.

The rest of the school year passed uneventfully until soon it was spring and Easter. Mama sent me a white organdy dress with green polka dots. We had a program in the chapel on Sunday evening. On Monday we had a picnic on the school grounds with dyed eggs, candy, cookies, and Kool-Aid.

8

HOME!!

IT WAS now April and we started counting the weeks and days until the middle of May when we would go home. I couldn't wait to show off all the things I had learned to do: sign language, handicrafts, and rug weaving. Finally our housemothers saw that all the small children on the first floor had their suitcases packed. We had fresh new underclothes laid out for us to wear home—an unbleached cotton slip, pink cotton panties, brown stockings, and brown or black oxfords. I saved out a pair of white socks to wear in place of the stockings and a pink headband that Eunice had sent me for Christmas. The last morning we had to strip our beds and turn the mattresses back. The dorm looked strange with all those beds in two long rows. It also looked lonely, and somehow I felt a little sad, for I had made friends and I'd miss them.

On the great morning, we were separated into groups according to which way we had to go. Some parents came in cars for their children. Others were loaded into the school truck and carried to the train or bus station, all wearing tags with our names and destinations printed on them. My group was the last to leave, and we'd be traveling as we came—by train. We got all the leftover teachers' food for supper and a brown paper bag of food for the overnight journey. About dark, we were loaded in cars and taken to the railway station, herded in, and parked on benches. Some

White blind children were also in our group. Our superintendent, Mr. Lineberry, strolled about inspecting us. I had noticed him before on our campus but never had talked with him. Now he stood gazing down at me, a tall, white-haired man with gold-rimmed glasses. He then asked in sign language what my name was. I started to sign it. He shook his head.

"No. Talk," he said, pointing to his mouth.

"Mary," I said.

"Mary what?"

"Herring."

"Glad to go home?"

"Oh, yes sir!"

He stood watching me for awhile longer, then said bye and moved on.

After awhile our tags were checked again and we then were herded out a door and down a dark and dirty-looking passageway and onto a cold railway car with hard seats. This particular car was for deaf and blind students only, so both Black and White students rode in the same car. We could sit where we pleased, but the Black students sat together and the White students sat together. We scrambled for seats and again I sat with Helen and Elizabeth. Although I had stayed friends with Helen, I'd found Elizabeth to be cranky and kind of sneaky. But the joy of being on my way home made everybody my friend or best buddy. After getting settled, I waited for the choo of the train to start and then the rattle and pull, but nothing happened. All the teachers had departed after seeing us settled except Mr. Slade, who taught the blind children. He had settled down in a seat up front and was reading a paper.

At some point I dozed off. I don't know how long I slept before I was jerked awake by the train grinding and jerking as though it was angry at being awakened at such an hour. It was very late by then. Finally the train started rocking along the tracks heading for Wallace. It didn't begin stopping to let off anyone until well after daybreak. Upon reaching Goldsboro, Helen and Elizabeth both got off. Helen lived in LaGrange, Elizabeth in New Bern. Then the stops became more frequent—Mt. Olive, Faison, Warsaw—I counted them all and then WALLACE!

Clutching my bag and comic books, I was helped down the steps by the conductor and there stood Papa, Eunice, and Sam. I hugged Eunice, Papa kissed me, and Sam didn't know what to do—he just stood there. Then Papa hustled us to the truck. It was strawberry time and he had to get back home to pick up another load to haul to market. The very air smelled like strawberries, wild magnolias, and dust. After turning off the highway and onto the dirt road leading to our house and farm, I started straining for my first sight of home in nine months. First I saw the top of the big pine rising up over the other trees, leaning slightly as though listening, then the tips of the twin oak trees at the end of the long porch. I hardly felt the truck hitting the bumps and mudholes. We rounded the first bridge and curve, trees on both sides of the road, then the second bridge and out into the open and there it was—*home!*

Getting out of the truck I found my foot had gone to sleep; I hobbled and skipped to meet Mama. How good to feel her hug me again, still wearing her apron that was my refuge in times of fright or trouble. Then I had to see the house—I ran from room to room. They seemed smaller than when I left and a little strange, but no less dear. Then Sam was pulling me to go out and see his new puppy, and there was Queen! I was down hugging and patting her while she licked my face and whined. Someone, Bennie I think, took a picture of Sam by the truck with his pup in his arms and me and Queen beside him. Then Willie came up from wherever he'd been and had me go with him to see the cow and her new calf, whose name was Sonny Boy. Soon I'd settled back into home life as though I'd never been away. Queen was at my heels as I made beds in the morning, washed dishes, swept the porch, and tended to dinner while the rest of the family picked and packed strawberries, set out tobacco, and chopped (hoed) the various crops.

Sam was my companion; we went back to our routine of playing for awhile and fighting for awhile. He, Mama, Eunice, and Willie quickly learned to fingerspell, so it was easier for me to communicate with my family. However, fingerspelling was something new and unheard of for the people around home. Eunice and Willie

Sam and his puppy and me and Queen in front of Papa's truck right after I came home from my first year in Raleigh.

seldom used theirs in public although Sam and Mama were proud of their ability and enjoyed having people gather around and gawk.

Some people wanted to learn to fingerspell too, and I was glad to teach them. A few would catch my eye in a crowd and wiggle their fingers and giggle at each other. Some boys I didn't know even made obscene gestures. That hurt. I'd tell Mama and lay my head in her lap and cry and say I wasn't going out among hearing people anymore. She said not to look at it that way. People didn't mean to be cruel, they only acted like that for the lack of sense and they were more to be pitied than anything else. Somehow, I couldn't feel pity—I only felt hurt and left out and sort of ashamed, as though I was somehow to blame for not being able to hear and chatter along with the other children as I once had. I even felt a little lonely for the school in Raleigh and the friends I'd made there, but not for long.

I was soon caught up in being home and it hardly seemed like I'd been away, more like a bad dream. I went back to my old routine of getting up early and making the beds while Mama and Eunice cooked breakfast and the boys fed the farm animals. We still had Ruth and Rhodie; our cow and calf; a pen full of chickens (shut up to keep them from eating the ripe strawberries and scratching up garden seeds); our pigs, big and little, noisily grunting and rooting about the pasture; Mama's flock of guineas; and the dozen or so assorted hunting dogs. After the early chores we'd eat breakfast—ham or side meat from the smokehouse, hot biscuits, fresh butter, syrup, milk, and coffee. I had to get used to being able to have second helpings and eat as much as I wanted to.

Then it was time for everybody to leave for the fields. At ten years old, I was old enough to tend to the dinner and set it on the table so Mama and Eunice wouldn't have to rush in and cook.

The vegetables were put on before they left and the meat was ready to cook. I was told how to cook the meat, the cornbread, the biscuits, and such, and to have it ready on time. Sam was left to be my company and to help with the breakfast dishes. I soon found out I'd get them done sooner and more peacefully alone. My next chore was to get our big straw broom and sweep every room and the porch. After that I could rest or play with Sam for awhile, as long as I ran into the kitchen now and then to put wood in the stove and stir the pots of vegetables. By 11:00, it was time for me to make biscuits, a large pan of cornbread, fry or boil whatever meat I was cooking, and make a large bucket of lemonade. And always my dear little Queen was close by, either behind the stove or under the kitchen table, keeping a watchful eye on me.

Fixing dinner wasn't always so easy or smooth. Sometimes I forgot the time when Sam and I started playing outside, or I found one of Eunice's *True Story* magazines and got absorbed in a romantic story. Sam and I also got into fights now and then. When I'd remember dinner and check the clock, sometimes I had less than an hour to have everything ready and the table set. Then I'd rush like mad to build the fire back up and get the oven hot enough for the bread and biscuits. The old black farm truck would drive up in the yard while I was still elbow-deep in flour and Mama and Eunice would rush in to wash up and help me before the menfolk got in. Sometimes I was so late that it wasn't possible, and I'd see Papa coming to the house and the boys riding the mules up to the water trough by the well. All had to take a peep in the kitchen and know why "that gal" didn't have dinner done yet.

"Bet she had her nose in a book," one would say.

"That's all she's good for," from another.

Or, "She's so slow she works like dead lice are falling off her." (I never could figure that one out.)

Eventually, I'd get the table set with the bowls of vegetables, fried chicken, biscuits, cornbread, and always, *rice*. For Papa, a meal was not complete without a bowl of rice. I'd put large chunks of ice in the lemonade and dinner was ready. As the men and boys took their places, Mama, Eunice, and I went out to the end of the porch to cool off in the gentle summer breeze blowing from the south. Now and then one of us would peep in to see if anything was needed and fill up an empty bowl or glass. When they finished, the table was cleared of dirty plates, the bowls refilled, and the women and children ate. This was only when we had field hands for dinner. Other times, all family members ate together. The stomachs full, everyone found a cool spot on the porch or under a tree in the yard and rested and napped until time to go back to the field.

Only me, I had to do all those dishes; my rest would come later. That is, unless it was "fisherman day." Some man who was friends with Papa and the boys would come chugging up in an old truck with a large box of ice on back. He seemed to have every kind of fish in there. So the men would gather around to look at and discuss those smelly fish. I hated fish (except fresh creek perch) and hoped no one wanted to buy any, but of course that's exactly what everybody wanted. So I was sent to the kitchen for a dishpan. I'd take the longest time finding one, and it would be a small one. Then I'd have to make another trip for the largest dishpan in the house. How reluctantly I'd get that pan, hoping the man and the fish would have disappeared by the time I got back. But the dishpan would be filled to the brim and I would spend the rest of the evening scaling and slitting fish open while I wept. Sam was all sympathy and would volunteer to scale while I gutted and the cats sat waiting patiently for whatever fell their way. Finally the last fish lay fresh and cleaned, ready to be fried. Now it was my turn to be scaled. The scales covered my arms, clothes, and hair—and the smell! By dark I'd have two large platters of fish and a plate of bread in the middle of the table. How my family enjoyed those fish, and seeing their pleasure almost made the torture of cleaning them worthwhile.

One afternoon all had returned to the fields out across the highway. Sam had said he didn't feel good; his side hurt. I enjoyed being a nurse so I put him on a bed in the boys' room and got up behind him to read him stories and talk. We loved to talk about everything. All at once Sam told me to hush because he heard a noise outside. I hushed, watching his face fearfully for a sign of anything unusual. All at once there was a loud tearing sound on the outside wall directly behind my back. Even I could hear it. I jumped across the bed and grabbed Sam. We waited, but heard no more. Whispering, we started wondering what it could have been. Deciding it was one of the dogs, we ventured outside, after making sure nothing or nobody was lurking out there.

When we looked at the wall we saw two long, deep scratches slanted across the boards. Trying not to let Sam see how scared I really was, knowing we had no dog or cat large enough to have made those scratches that high up, I closed the door and told him to get on my back and hold onto my neck. Hooking both my arms around his legs, I set out running down the bay road beside the woods for Mama or whoever I could find for help. I wasn't that much taller than Sam, and his feet bumped against my legs, but the thought of that loud noise and scratch spurred me on to run even faster to get us to safety. After getting around the first curve, where I could no longer see the house, I set Sam down. My lungs about to burst, I heaved and panted awhile, then started on again. When we finally reached the barn, the family wanted to know what I came out there for, since Sam was supposed to be sick.

"He is," I told them. "But something scared us."

"What?"

"We don't know. We didn't see it; we just heard it."

"*You* heard it?"

Upon relating the story of the loud noise and the marks, I got skeptical looks, as usual, that said, "More of Mary's tales." They let us stay until quitting time though, and that night we had to eat warmed-up leftovers. The noise and scratches remained a mystery.

Thunderstorms were always a summer worry. One day after dinner, everyone took their usual noonday nap, and I lay across the bed to read but fell asleep. When I woke up and went to look for everybody, all had gone, even Sam. Knowing Mama and Eunice were supposed to be chopping peanuts in the corner of a field near the house, I wasn't worried about being alone, until I saw the edge of a black cloud through the trees behind the house. I started watching the road for someone to come to the house. I knew Mama would not allow anyone to work in lightning while around her, but no one came.

The cloud climbed higher and got blacker. Still no one in sight. I let down some windows and closed doors, peeping out every now and then, but saw no one. The sun was gone and now the wind was up; I could wait no longer. Slamming the last door shut, I set out running for the field to get Mama and Eunice. It was empty. By now, the clouds were all over, fat and dark, the wind blowing up dust.

I headed for the old house thinking they would have gone there to get out of the weather. At one point I stumbled through a rut in the road, falling on my face and stomach. Scrambling up and running on, I hollered for Mama when the wind would let me. Upon reaching the old house, I ran in. The people who lived there shook their heads; no, my Mama wasn't there. Someone else pointed over to William Boney's house, so I set out for there. I think the wind helped my speed; I know the lightning did. Just as big fat drops of rain began to fall, I reached William's porch.

There sat Mama and Eunice chatting away with Cousin Helen Boney (William's mama) and someone else. I fell into Mama's lap gasping. I know I was a sight with water streaking down my dusty dress and face. They were surprised to find I was alone. They'd left the boys at home because they were supposed to be plowing close by when actually I was the only one there.

This was just like the time I got lost in the woods when Mama let me go pick dog tongue with my older brothers and sister.* Everyone split up and each one thought I was with someone else. I had sense enough to keep the sun in front of me, so I finally saw the top of the crib and stumbled in that direction, finding the crib and home as well. Mama was surprised when I walked in alone and wanted to know where the rest were. I told her I didn't know and how I'd gotten home. When she heard them coming in some time later, she told me to keep out of sight.

Waiting until all had come in, she asked, "Where is Mary?"

That's when they missed me and looked at each other in surprise asking, "Isn't she with you?"

"No, I thought she was with you."

Then it was, "Oh my goodness! Come on—let's go back and find her."

Now I was enjoying this. Here I was home safe and my brothers and sister actually seemed worried about me, the pest.

Motioning for me to come out, Mama said, "There she is."

Then she told them how I'd found my way back home and to let that be a lesson to them not to let a small child out of their sight and how all should stick together in the woods.

My first summer of freedom was passing all too swiftly and the dreadful day was nearing again. I tried to ignore it as much as possible, even making believe I didn't really have to go back to

*This was a medicinal plant. Someone would come through our area, buying up all they could for a pharmaceutical company.

Raleigh, but would again be in the Iron Mine school. Miss Staten had left us and was now teaching in Jacksonville, a small town east of Wallace. Another plump, pleasant-looking lady from Warsaw named Miss Annie Allen had taken her place. I disliked her for that reason, although she seemed nice enough. Miss Beaty was still there.

Iron Mine opened before the Raleigh school, so for a few days I visited at my old school. Miss Allen once accused Sam of taking one of her songbooks home and got after him in front of the other children. That I could not stand. I tried to stare her into the ground but my eyes weren't that powerful. So I wrote her a note letting her know what I thought of her and her old songbook, and something about giving her a fat lip. Of course, Mama got the note and my legs got the switch. That ended my visits to my old school as long as Miss Allen was there. She and Miss Beaty both left not too long after that. Miss Allen got married and Miss Beaty transferred to Warsaw.

All too soon, the letter from Mr. Lineberry arrived with the opening date and my ticket and name tag inside. Again, Papa and Eunice took me shopping for new clothes. Mama cooked up more food for me to take, and you can be sure I did not throw this out the window. This departure was a repeat of the first one. Only this time I knew my schoolmates and could communicate with them. We always left for school on a Thursday so that we could have the weekend to get unpacked and settled for the new school year. I tried to shut out all thoughts of home and those dear ones I had left; thinking of them hurt too much. My schoolmates and I told each other about summer vacation, what we'd done and seen, and the trip back didn't seem so long this time.

9

Queen of the Fairies

I WAS assigned to a different bed, closer to Mrs. Mallette's room and near a window. This was much better. On Friday, after breakfast and morning devotion in chapel, we were told to report to the nurse's room in each dorm for something new. A whole bunch of doctors had come out from town to give us physicals. The nurses' rooms were converted into examining rooms with about three doctors to a room. We lined up in the hallway. While Nurse Stewart weighed and measured, the doctors had the girls strip to the waist and sit in a chair before them while they went over them. This was quite embarrassing. I had nothing to show, ten years old, but some of the girls were in their teens and fully developed. I'd never seen a grown person examined before. At first I was curious, but then I was so embarrassed that I shut my eyes tight and got out as soon as they turned me loose.

A truck brought all our suitcases and trunks out from town. These were carried into the sewing room where Mrs. Mallette and her helpers opened and inspected each one, then sprayed a very strong disinfectant over all our clothes. We could get our bags on Saturday and put them under our beds—no closets to hang our clothes in then. Most of the girls didn't bother another girl's belongings, but every group has a thief or two, and these would go back to the dorms when the rest of us were in class. They'd go through whatever bags seemed to have anything worth stealing. I lost a couple of dollars and some trinkets before I got wise and took my valuables to Mrs. Mallette to keep in her room for me.

Sundays were lonely: breakfast at 7:00, Sunday school at 9:30, dinner at noon, then a long afternoon of nothing until 4:00, when we had vespers, and then sandwiches for supper. One way of passing time was to stroll up and down the walks on our side of the campus or sit on the grass watching cars or whatever passed along the highway in front of the school. We had only two shade trees on the grounds and they were off-limits. One was located on the girls' side but too near the woods, the other halfway between the girls' and the boys' dorms. We might get near a boy there.

For me, Monday morning was a relief. At least classes gave me something to do. This year, I was in the sixth grade. Miss Laws was the homeroom teacher for the sixth and seventh grades. Spelling was taught by Miss King, and then we had classes in handicrafts downstairs; I wasn't old enough for sewing and cooking yet. Miss Laws proved to be a very nice teacher—strict, but nice in ways and looks. She was very light complexioned with long black hair and hazel eyes. She was also a missionary for her church. Most of the time, instead of punishing the children, she tried to tell them of Jesus to get them to behave for him. They tolerated her and watched her signs without any comment or expression, then went right back to whatever they had been doing.

Deaf people are very distrustful of hearing people. They're always suspicious that they're being talked about or made fun of for not being able to hear and talk. They sometimes resented me too because Nurse Stewart had told my teachers not to let me sign but to keep me talking to keep my voice strong. Therefore, when I talked or recited and they didn't know what I was saying, they told me my mouth was just flapping and they didn't believe I could talk. I got back at them by refusing to help them with homework or explain something to them so they soon left me alone. I was on my way to being accepted as one of them, but I wasn't quite there yet.

I was still a little kid and slept downstairs. All of my classmates were teenagers. One of the older girls, Minnie Applewhite, had also lost her hearing after she had learned to talk, so she and I became friends and spent a lot of time telling each other of our family life. Her mama was dead and she lived with an aunt who was mean to her. I told her she could share my mama, but she'd rather for me to talk about Frank. She'd get so tickled when I'd tell of some of the things he did and said.

Though I was still too young for kitchen duty or sweeping the halls in our dorm, I found other things to fill my time. Besides hanging out in Misses Kearney and Stewart and Hayes's rooms, I ran errands for them to different buildings. I convinced Mrs. Mallette I could run a sewing machine, so she let me sew hems in pillowcases a couple of evenings a week. Also, whichever older girl gathered the laundry on Sunday nights let me help her count the pieces and fill out the slips. Of course this gave me a sense of importance.

The woods and hills behind our school had a lot of hickory nut, walnut, and gum trees. They were something beautiful when the leaves turned color. The woods looked like pure gold with a little green. I'd gaze out of the third-floor classroom, longing to be out there. Sometimes the teachers had to come shake me to remind me of what I was in the room for. I asked some of the older girls if we could walk out there. They said, "No, no, no. And get beat? Locked up? Not me."

I had to get in those woods. I'd found a friend in another girl with the same love for the outdoors as I had. This was Maybur Richardson. She was a year or so older than me and taller. I never knew her race. Our school was for Blacks but she and all her family looked White—long, straight brown or blondish hair and blue or green eyes. Most of the other kids shunned her and said she smelled like White people. I never smelled her and didn't care what color or race she was; she was a kindred spirit. We slid down the stair banisters, played hopscotch on the walks, and raced each other. We finally found a young teacher we could talk into taking some of us for a walk in the hills and woods on a bright fall Saturday afternoon. Not too many wanted to go, but we got a dozen or so together.

We set out, passing the shoe repair shop, the heating plant, and the furniture shop. Turning west we passed the two shops where the blind boys learned to make brooms and mattresses, then the large yellow two-story house I had thought was the Sun-

Maybur Richardson, my playground buddy, in September 1937.

day school building when I first came. Mr. Whitney, the engineer, lived there with his family and the kitchen help and maids. Then we crossed the railroad tracks. Next came the school's dairy, and we stopped to see where our milk came from. The buildings were very clean. All the stalls had clean wood shavings on the floor and the building where the cows were milked had clean cement floors. I loved the smell because it reminded me of our cow at home. Some of the boys were about and asked what we were doing over there and where we were going. The teacher said, "Don't talk to them," and herded us out.

By now we were up the first of the hills and could look back down on campus. I could hardly stand my joy. At the top we were told to sit and rest awhile. Maybur and I couldn't. We found a smooth spot, lay down, and let go, rolling all the way to the bottom of the hill. We got to do that several times before the teacher whacked our bottoms, told Maybur and me to get in line, and told all of us to move. Soon we hit the thick part of the woods. It was a wonderland—gold, brown, and green. We ran about like squirrels, gathering black walnuts and hickory nuts to take back to campus. We were a tired but happy group of children when we dragged back late that evening just before the supper bell.

Maybur and I caught it from the second-floor girls. They accused us of wanting to go walk just to get close to the boys and talk with them. They told us what we'd get if we bothered their boyfriends. At first, I was too shocked to even answer. Boys were the last thing I thought about. At least, *those* boys. The only boys crossing my mind then were my brothers and Subud, Allen, and Leroy. At first we protested, but it was no use. Maybur's face turned red and she cried. I got mad and told them they were crazy and should be in the Goldsboro asylum instead of Raleigh and that nobody wanted their ugly boyfriends. I ended up offering to fight, but since they were all big girls, they knew they'd be punished for fighting one of the little kids. Besides, they needed me to explain some of their homework to them, so they backed off. Believe it, next time we went for a walk we had a very *long* line of girls.

Soon it was nearly time for the fair. We got our new fall clothes—coats, two pairs of shoes, hats or tams, underclothes, stockings, and new nightgowns. That year I was an old hand for the fair. I knew what to buy to stretch my spending money and which rides to go on. We saved up peppermint sticks and candied apples and popcorn to carry back to nibble on after lights-out. Right after the fair week came Halloween. The party was in the largest art room, which looked funny at night; we usually only saw it in daylight. Boys and girls mixed, but of course, sharp-eyed teachers were in the midst of them to make sure they didn't touch. We bobbed for apples and had great fun. Nell Kerr won the prize for the best girl's costume. Then it was Thanksgiving and we had the usual turkey dinner. I was doing well and making the honor roll each quarter but still getting in a little mess now and then— mostly for talking during study hour.

We didn't have an infirmary on campus then, so when it was time for the children's tonsils to be removed, both study halls in our dorm were turned into hospital wards. Beds were set up, and everything was scrubbed and cleaned. All who had been listed for the operation had to spend the night in there so they could be prepared early the next morning. By noon, the whole place smelled of ether and all was very hushed and quiet. The rest of us couldn't see our friends until the following day. Poor Hill. You might know she'd be a patient. After their tonsils were removed, the girls had to stay in bed for a few days.

Some of the older girls from upstairs got to be nurses' helpers. Their heads were tied up in clean white towels and they got to put on white kitchen aprons. They also got to carry the patients' food, help them to the bathroom, and comb their hair. How they flaunted their importance at us as we tiptoed in the hall, peering and peeping every chance we got, and scurrying like mice when Mrs. Mallette's door opened. The day finally came when the girls could get up, and their beds were moved back in place in the bedrooms. We welcomed them back as though they'd been on a long trip. For their part, the girls who'd had their tonsils removed hated to give up all the attention and petting, so they lay around as long as they could, asking one or the other of us if we'd go to the kitchen and ask Cook to send a bowl of cornflakes or whatever.

Being sick was the only time we were allowed such privileges. Even then, Cook grumbled and fussed. She hated pulling her heavy frame out of her seat by a window where she could keep watch on all the comings and goings on campus. From that seat, she also had a clear view of the large pantry door behind the kitchen where she kept all of her special foods and treats. The only one allowed in there, besides one or two kitchen helpers, was a girl from the second floor named Madgalene Williams.

Life soon settled back into our regular routine. This school year, too, was nearing its close and the teachers started reading various plays and drills for the school closing programs. The girls who'd be graduating were called in to look at patterns and white material for their graduation dresses. The girls wore long white dresses with ribbons and flowers in their class colors; the boys wore black suits and white shirts.

This year, Shakespeare's *A Midsummer Night's Dream* was chosen for the blind and deaf departments to put on together. The blind players would speak the parts and the deaf players would dance and be in the background. I was picked to be Queen of the Fairies. Naturally, I was thrilled to be in the play with the other children, but to have an important part was just beyond belief.

First came Easter with the boxes from home with our new

clothes, Easter candy, and other goodies. This year my outfit was a pale gray dress and matching jacket and gray-and-blue shoes. I also got lots of candy, cake, fried chicken, and fruit. I was given a speech to say in chapel for our Easter program. The Blind Glee Club was also part of the program. The club was well known for their beautiful songs. Thelma Freeman was especially good; she could sing "Ave Maria" in French. She and a few others were often invited to sing at churches in town. A group of six or seven older deaf girls signed the songs as the glee club sang. Gertrude Edwards was the leader. Being able to hear some, she would stand near the person singing and lead the signs while the other girls followed her. I'd never seen anything like it and sat there spellbound watching the graceful movements of Gertrude's hands and arms. Now I knew what song was being sung and when they started on "The Old Rugged Cross," I could just see our choir in Iron Mine and hear Mama's voice and Mrs. Annie playing the organ. My throat hurt and I wanted to cry so badly.

On Easter Monday we didn't have classes. The cooks and helpers boiled eggs and sliced ham, and fixed bag lunches while we paraded up and down the walks, roller-skated, or counted cars passing on the highway. Early in the afternoon we had a game of softball between girls and boys. Then all gathered at the large tree in the middle of our campus where tables and chairs had been set up. Of course, all matrons and most of the teachers were on hand to make sure we only *ate* and didn't touch or get touched by anyone of the opposite sex. One of the senior girls, Octavia, who considered herself a stylist and beauty queen, had put on a pair of blue linen bib overalls and a white lace blouse minus a bra. She was promptly ordered to go back to the dorm and take off that outfit and put on decent clothes (that is, a dress or skirt) and underclothes. She left in a rage and refused to come back rather than face humiliation.

Finally, the day of the play came. The fairies carried large white hoops covered in white crepe paper with pink and white roses. The dresses had fitted bodices and short full skirts, but not too short. For anyone to see our skinny or fat little legs above the knees was considered a sin. Crowns of pink and white paper roses sat on our heads. Thelma, the star with a singing role, looked very sweet in a long white gown with an armful of flowers. I don't remember what Ira, her leading man, wore.

I peeped from behind the shrubbery that served as backstage, my eyes glued on Mrs. Bass at the piano, thinking about how clumsy I'd always been. I prayed I wouldn't fall flat on my face first thing. One of the teachers lined my troupe up behind me, then laid a hand on my shoulder to restrain me just in case I got the urge to slip out ahead of the music. After what seemed an eternity, Mrs. Bass finally started playing, then looked at me and gave a slight nod.

"Oh my goodness," I thought. "Here I go."

Grasping my hoop firmly in front of me, I drew a deep breath and started counting one-two-three-four, one-two-three-four as I led the girls in circles, squares, turns, and straight lines, skipping and kicking the whole time. I didn't dare look at the audience. Stopping in a line facing the audience, we went through a drill with our hoops, then more skipping and kicking until I finally made the last count and mercifully got us all off the stage.

I peeped back to see the people's reaction. To my surprise, they were not laughing. They were actually clapping and we were told we'd done very nicely. I know all that anybody could see of my face was my teeth. How I wished Mama was sitting out there smiling and clapping for me! I wanted all my family, but especially Mama, Eunice, and Sam, to see me. Then I thought of the last play I'd been in at my old school and how the teachers didn't trust me to even walk on stage by myself and say one line. They should see me now!

And so another school year drew to a close—my last year on

the first floor with the babies. I'd be twelve and moved upstairs
to the junior department on my return. How grown I felt. To add
to that feeling, my group would be going home on the Greyhound
bus this year, a fairly new mode of travel. When the buses passed
on the country roads, people in fields stopped to gawk and say
such things as, "Look at that old bus go." So here was a whole
bunch of them, as well as Trailways buses, lined up in front of our
main building, waiting for the matrons and teachers to sort us
into various groups according to who would be going in the same
direction. Then we were given name tags to be pinned on the
front of our clothes. The drivers were given a list of the names of
all the children who'd be riding their bus and the towns where
they'd get off. Kids were running around hugging each other
good-bye and promising to write. Each was telling the other to be
sure to come back in September.

Soon buses started pulling out, heading in all directions. My
bunch was on the Wilmington bus. We headed south toward Garner and the first stop was Clayton. The bus driver stood up and
looked us over, trying to see who was to get off there. A lot of us
had removed our tags, saying we weren't cows. Since I knew all
the children by name, I spoke up and told him who all got off
there. He was a nice, friendly man and asked me to come sit by
him. He gave me the list, telling me to tell the students when to
get off. When I wasn't watching for town names and telling kids
to get off, I was watching girls flirting with whatever boy was on
the bus, whether it was their boyfriend or somebody else's. This
was their only chance to actually sit with a boy or get close enough
to touch one because there were no teachers on the bus. Freedom
already! Everyone seemed to be in high spirits. GOING HOME!
After nine months of jail life. After putting Kathleen Miller off in
Warsaw, I told the bus driver I'd be next in Wallace and soon we
were pulling into the Wallace bus station located at Miller's Drug
Store on Front Street.

As usual, my welcoming committee of three stood waiting: Papa, Eunice, and Sam. The driver helped me down the steps and thanked me for my assistance. When Papa came to get my bag he told Papa how I'd helped him and he didn't know what he would have done with those children if I hadn't been there to keep things straight. Papa kissed my cheek and Eunice hugged me, but when I started for Sam (who was about as tall as I was by now), he frowned and glared so I decided to wait until I got him home.

The house always looked small and strange when I first walked in, but I loved it dearly. And Mama—I couldn't get enough of looking at her. Now that we were home where other eyes couldn't see him, Sam was more than ready to acknowledge that I was his sister. "Come on, come on," he'd say and I had to go on a tour of the house, the yard, the crib, and the outbuildings to see everything that was new: puppies, Mama's little yellow biddies, pigs, whatever. Bennie, Frank, Willie, and Allen soon came in from wherever they'd been working. I jumped on each in turn to hug them. They didn't hug me back but patted my head and said hey. That was enough for me. I had enough feelings for everyone and then some to spare.

Eunice graduated from Wallace Colored High School that year. I think it was also that summer that she started taking nurse's training at Community Hospital in Wilmington. She had a boyfriend by the name of Brown, but I didn't get to meet him for awhile. Sam said he didn't have any neck, and that Eunice picked the worst boyfriends he ever saw. One was named Punk and he had a great, long neck, and now this one didn't have any neck at all. When I asked Sam what was between Brown's head and shoulder he said there was nothing, the head just set there. Sam had peaked my curiosity and I was anxious to see this neckless man my sister had met. I got my chance before very long.

One Sunday evening, Mama told me to start getting ready.

Bennie was going to carry us to the Sea Breeze. During the mid-1930s the beaches, like other public places, were segregated. The Sea Breeze was the beach that Blacks went to for entertainment. It was an exciting place with thriving Black-owned businesses, including motels, restaurants, and nightclubs. Since Blacks were not permitted to go to Carolina Beach, the beach reserved for Whites, the Blacks would ride the boat over to see it from a distance.

Sam and I rode in the rumble seat of the car, and Mama and Eunice rode up front with Bennie. It was indeed a thrilling time. We rode through Wilmington, and when we finally turned off the highway, I got a glimpse of the blue Atlantic Ocean that seemed to stretch as far as the eye could see. Oh, it was wonderful! Even Sam was awestruck.

Smells of food cooking filled the air, along with the sort of fishy smell of the ocean. We walked around to see the sights. There was a large white hotel that had a long porch facing the beach with rocking chairs, tables, and plants. We sat there for awhile, then noticed a long pier led from the hotel to another building out in the water. This was a restaurant and boathouse and Eunice suggested we walk out there. The pier was kind of narrow, and walking along made my head swim if I looked at the water. I had to fix my eyes straight ahead and walk by guess. We saw all there was to be seen. A large motorboat was tied up so passengers could get in and a very nice-looking Black lady, dressed in white pants, shirt, and cap, ran the boat as pilot. She would take the passengers on a round-trip across the sound to the White beach and back.

Eunice took me into the restaurant and asked if I wanted a hamburger. Of course I did. She ordered clam fritters. Yuck! I was surprised that my sister seemed so at ease about such things; I was flabbergasted. The hamburger was very good. We sat at a small table where the cool sea breezes could blow over us. I wished the kids at school could see me.

Bennie, Mama, and Sam came on out and Bennie asked if we'd like to ride in the boat. I was ready for that too, so he, Mama, Sam, and I got in the boat. As soon as it was full of people, it roared to life and away we went, bouncing over the waves. Oh mercy, I didn't know how much more excitement I could take without bursting wide open! The lady who was running the boat stood up at the controls, her hair blowing back. She had beautiful black hair like my sister and she got many admiring looks from her passengers. The spray rose up at the front of the boat and left a beautiful trail behind us.

Soon we were back at the pier and climbing out. Eunice had gone back on the beach. We decided we'd better think about getting home before dark, so we also started back. Walking over the water was a little easier this time. And what do you know? One of the first persons I saw back on the beach was David Mitchell from school, who had been among the first to befriend me my first year. How glad I was to see him and know how to talk in sign. He was a handsome young man and I was proud to introduce him to my family. Mama was just as proud that she could fingerspell well enough to also talk with him.

Leaving David, we went on to look for Eunice. When we did find her, a stocky dark-complexioned man was with her. I stared, and even before Sam could poke me in the side and mouth the word I knew: This was the famous Brown. He knew everyone except me. When Eunice told him who I was, he shook my hand and said, "Howdy, little miss," and smiled. I decided he was alright, even if his neck didn't show, so I smiled and said I was fine and glad to meet him. He seemed okay; at least I didn't see anything about him to rile me up.

The ride back home was just as thrilling as the one going. For days afterward that was about all Sam and I could talk about—the Sea Breeze and what we enjoyed best. The hamburger got my vote. Sam, on the other hand, loved the boat ride. The funniest happening for both of us was when we had met a group of men and women on the beach. One woman was sort of skinny and must have been drunk or something. She was quarreling with one of the men and took a swipe at him. She missed and fell in the sand, causing one of her breasts to fall out through the armhole of her red bathing suit. Mama looked horrified. Bennie looked mad and disgusted. Sam and I giggled until Mama told us to hush up and pushed us on.

This summer had another big surprise in store for me. Sometime before this, Bennie had bought a shiny new saxophone. I was fascinated. It lay there in a black leather case with a bright blue lining. Each time he took it out, I stood by hoping I'd be able to catch a note or two like I used to hear on the records he played. He'd blow a few notes that I couldn't hear, look at it, adjust some of the things on it, then back in the case it'd go and he'd put it on top of the wardrobe in the boys' room, telling Sam and me not to bother with it. Many times I climbed atop that wardrobe, opened the case, and stared in awe at that shiny instrument. Before I closed the case I just had to touch it with one finger. It felt cool and satiny. One Saturday morning Bennie got up acting very mysterious. Taking a washbowl of water and soap into his room, he scrubbed up and came out in splendor—white flannel slacks, white shoes, a pretty shirt and tie, hair all neat and shiny with little waves.

"Where's Bennie going, Mama?" I asked.

"Wilmington."

"What for?"

The more I was told, the more I wanted to know. It seemed he was going to trade his sax for something. Anyway, he put it in his car and left. Soon, I was about my usual Saturday morning chores of washing the breakfast dishes, scrubbing the kitchen and dining room floors, and helping to sweep the yard. Then I could have playtime. We didn't go to Wallace as we usually did on Saturday afternoon. Instead, Sam and I played outside until Sam suggested we go in the house.

As we entered through the kitchen door, we could see Cap Jack coming in another door carrying a fat suitcase. I stopped, wondering whose suitcase it was and why Cap Jack was bringing it in our house looking so pleased and happy. He waved at me and grinned. I had opened my mouth to start my questions when the door opened again and a nice-looking girl came in and stood still looking at all of us who'd gathered—Mama, Eunice, Sam, and myself. Then Bennie came in and stood beside her. I could see Mama and Eunice were talking to her. I just stood.

Cap Jack came where I was and told me, "That's Mable, your new sister."

"Huh?" was all I could say, not sure I had read his lips right.

He smiled and nodded, and Mama made it clearer by spelling, "Bennie's wife."

I was still too dumbstruck to know what to say or do. Bennie's wife?

Someone gave me a little shove. I took a step nearer, feeling excitement for a new happening in the family, but a little sad too, without knowing why. After acknowledging and greeting her, I fled back outside. Thereafter I peeped from a distance, still not used to the idea of a sister-in-law.

However, I was proud of the attention my family received at church the next day. It was the third Sunday, our day for preaching since our pastor was responsible for more than one congregation. Heads turned, eyes questioned who Mable was. It wasn't long before the word was passed around by whispers behind fans or hands, or openly.

"One of Ben Herring's boys got married."

"Which one? Bennie?"

They knew it would hardly be Frank. After church Bennie and Mable were surrounded with people wishing them good luck and wanting to meet the bride, someone they didn't know. Mable came from Pender County, near Burgaw. Being a farm girl, she fit right in with all our daily chores, and life went on until it was once again near time for that dreaded day of departure.

I'd tell myself I wasn't going to cry this time. I was over twelve years old, able to cook and keep house, crochet, embroider, and sew on Mama's machine without sewing my finger. I'd also be in the seventh grade. When the day to go shopping for school clothes came around, I was ready for that. I had my own ideas of what kind of clothes I wanted. I also wanted a trunk instead of a suitcase so I could carry more and keep it locked. Eunice, Papa, and I went to Collins Department Store for the trunk and I was allowed to pick out a good-sized one, large enough to serve as a bench for sitting on or as a table beside my bed. It had a divided tray inside that could be lifted out. How proud I was!

Because Collins was cheaper, Papa usually bought all of my clothes there, but Eunice persuaded him to go to Kramers and the Fashion Shop this year. They had the prettiest and latest things for girls and women. My dear sister; I couldn't believe it. She picked out a beautiful light-blue and white dress with a pleated skirt for my Sunday best in the Fashion Shop. She then picked out other pretty clothes, including shoes and a sweater from Kramers. Papa's face seemed to grow grimmer each time he unbuttoned the pocket on the front of his bib overalls and took out his worn wallet, but pay for them he did. Eunice could get just about anything out of our papa. She got cash from him to take me to the five-and-ten for toilet things. There, I loaded up with toothpaste, talcum powder, hairdressing, cologne, and this year, pink nail polish and sweet-smelling soap. We had only brown or plain white soap at school.

Back home I showed off my new belongings, feeling like a princess. Over the next few days, I spent my spare time sorting and airing my clothes and deciding what I could wear from last year. My favorite book, *Heidi,* always went as did my book of Bible stories and photos to show the other girls. I arranged and re-arranged the toilet articles in the trunk tray. I wouldn't let my mind dwell on how many days I had left at home, but it was always there, on the edge, until my last night at home came all too soon.

As I made my rounds telling all good night and pecking them on their cheeks, all was quiet and no one pushed or told me to go on. My resolve not to cry was what went. I kept thinking, *This time tomorrow night I'll be in Raleigh and won't be able to tell my family good night.*

As usual Queen sensed something and stuck right by my feet when I was standing, and when I was sitting down, she'd put her head in my lap, her eyes on my face. No one ran her out now. Time was flying by and I was soon on the Greyhound headed back to Raleigh.

10

The Old and the New

BACK at school there were changes. Our housemother, Mrs. Mallette, did not return; she had either retired or quit. We had Mrs. Holbrook from New Jersey, the very opposite of Mrs. Mallette. Mrs. Holbrook was young and slim with a short, boyish haircut and she wore bright red lipstick. She didn't know how old I was and put me back on the first floor. Here I was, twelve years old and still with the babies. Another new teacher, Miss Susie Morton, replaced Emma Bembury, a partially deaf student teacher who had gotten married. Miss Morton was also young. She dressed very stylishly just to go to the classroom, with never a hair out of place. She set about starting a campus club. She named it Dream Girls, and began to make plans for parties with both boys and girls, tennis games, and a drama department. We laughed and told her to wait until she ran into Reverend Williams's ironbound school rules and regulations. Miss Morton lasted for a few months, then she was gone and another took her place.

In the meantime, I'd been desperately trying to get transferred upstairs to the junior department. Maybe Mrs. Holbrook was trying to spare me some of the pains of growing up, but she finally gave in. One evening after school I came in to find she'd had another bed set up for me on the south side of the upstairs floor. Oh my! In no time I had one of the girls help me drag my trunk and other belongings up to my new quarters. After making my bed, I sat on it, bouncing with joy and smiling at whoever passed by. I was welcomed by Helen and Elizabeth and a few more, but mostly I was ignored.

There was one senior girl across the hall whom I admired. She was small and brown with beautiful shiny black eyes and very deep dimples, but what one noticed most was her neatness—her clothes always a perfect fit, pressed and spotless. She had a knack of staying out of arguments and fights with the others. She mostly kept to herself and tended to her own business. This was Dolly. Another senior I liked was Minnie Keaton. The opposite of Dolly, Minnie was strong-boned and very light complexioned, with shoulder-length brown hair that seemed to always be blowing in a breeze. Minnie always seemed to be amused about something.

Upstairs was very different from downstairs: More was happening since our housemother was down with the babies. She checked the second-floor rooms often, but someone always spotted her on the stairs and warned the others. After 9:00 inspection and lights-out, she was gone for the night. That's when the fun started. Someone would sneak food in from the kitchen—bread, wieners, sometimes twenty-five-pound cans of jelly and peanut butter. The food was only for a certain bunch who made up the "in" crowd. The rest of us weren't supposed to see or know anything.

The older girls could also talk to their boyfriends across campus. They'd turn a light on at a certain window in a corner. The boys would do likewise. A girl would stand in front of the window making signs to whoever was her guy. After they signed each other good night, another couple went through the same routine. This was done in the room I slept in since it faced south and the boys' dormitory. Never one to hide my curiosity, I lay wide-eyed, watching them. When they noticed, they told me to shut my big eyes or look the other way. I was new and they didn't know how trustworthy I was. I let them know my eyes were mine and I'd do with them what I pleased.

Soon my presence in that room and on that floor became a sore point for certain of the big girls, Hazel Gregory in particular, who was tall and quite pretty when she wasn't looking mean and sour, which unfortunately was most of the time. Sometimes I'd come on a bunch of them discussing me. They would say that they wished I'd stayed on the first floor with my short, big-eyed self, and some more names not that mild. I was the only twelve-year-old up there. The rest of the girls on my side were between fourteen and sixteen, and the older girls were on the north side. Hazel and her bunch didn't quite dare harm me though, for I had friends in high places. Dr. Vass still kept in touch, and Professor Rogers—who they thought was my father—was a regular visitor and always made sure I was treated well and taken care of. Also, Dolly and Minnie began letting me follow them around and would share treats with me. They took no foolishness off the other girls.

This year Mrs. Holbrook picked out our new winter clothes. Instead of the usual drab and cheap-looking clothes, we got pretty things. My coat was a pretty shade of burgundy and we each had black dress shoes and brown ones for school. However, we still got pink cotton bloomers, cotton stockings, and slips and gowns made by the sewing class.

It was soon time for the fair again and we were all looking forward to it. Mama had sent me a dollar for spending money. This year, when we got ready to load up the vehicles, Dolly told me to keep close to her and I was only too glad to do so. Once on the fairgrounds, she showed how really nice she was, looking after me as Eunice would have done and buying me whatever she thought I wanted. I wished she wasn't graduating. She also sat with me on the rides and bought me a long stick of peppermint candy for me to take back to campus.

Again the fair was behind us and Thanksgiving was ahead. I found out that being on the second floor meant you had to have a boyfriend. That was another reason I wasn't accepted by some and just tolerated by others. I was still a baby according to them. They looked at me in shock when I was asked if I got sick every month and I said no, that I'd already had measles and chicken pox. They told me that Mrs. Holbrook was crazy to put me up there with them.

Even Maybur was more acceptable than I was. We both loved the outdoors and she still took me to play on the swings and slides with her. She'd stand up in the swing and go so high it would almost loop over backwards. Several times, the chain came loose and she fell and got skinned up and bruised. Once she was even knocked out, and for a time we were forbidden to go on the swings.

The other girls still had meetings to figure out what to do about me. I had to grow up or get out. They finally decided to pick me out a boyfriend. Since William Davis was in my class and I'd been staring at him, he was chosen to be the lucky—or unlucky—man. It was his odd-colored eyes I'd looked at. I don't know what he said when they told him he had a twelve-year-old girlfriend; he was fifteen. Me, I rebelled and said I didn't want any boyfriend. It did no good. Hazel even informed me that I was going to marry him when I graduated.

"You're crazy," I told her.

"No, not crazy," she replied. "He'll go to Wallace and tell your mama and daddy he wants to marry you and they will tell you to marry William."

"My mama and papa would do no such thing," I signed to her. "They would not make me marry anyone."

"Yes, they will."

"You don't my know my mama and papa."

"I know your mama and I know your daddy. I see them come to visit you. They'll truly make you marry William."

I was speechless with rage. Presuming to know my parents and to even think they'd do such a thing—this girl was impossible! Falling on my bed, I rolled and cried out loud.

"Holbrook," one of the girls signed.

They scattered. Mrs. Holbrook came to the bed, smoothed my hair and asked what was wrong with me. I couldn't stop crying long enough to tell her. Finally she told me to go into the bathroom, wash my face, and stop crying. I think she questioned the other girls and found out Hazel had done something. When I returned, Hazel was on her own bed glaring at me but said nothing. The next day, Mrs. Holbrook brought me several *Daily Word* booklets and other little books and prayers for me to read to help deal with the hurts and injustices life hands us. I read them to this day.

I don't think I've mentioned our arts and crafts teacher, Mrs. Hagins. She was very short and sweet, but I'll never know how she became an instructor for any kind of crafts. For example, we were given stamped pieces of linen to embroider. She'd point to different flower patterns and say purple, red, blue—anything that came to mind. We'd end up with a hodgepodge of colors. The blind girls' knitting became knotted up as they tried to follow her instructions. Finally we just took over and decided on our own colors and followed book instructions for crocheting and knitting. I discovered a large old-fashioned loom across the hall in an unused room. I had never seen one before. I was delighted and asked permission to learn to operate it. I learned to thread it and fill the shuttle and spent many happy hours working the treadles and shunting the shuttles back and forth. I never made anything except rag rugs—odd-looking ones at that—but I couldn't have been prouder.

This year, Mrs. Hagins did not return. Instead we had Mrs. I. B. Free. She hailed from Alabama. She had gold-rimmed glasses and matching teeth. She was built sort of flat and squat, and at each step, her head and rear end gave a little shake at the same time and all the while she'd be grinning at you. She grinned even while whacking you. Her room was in the blind girls' dorm, but on her way from chapel or the classrooms, she'd walk with a bunch of us beside her, enter our building at the front door and pass through to the back, then on to her own room. None of the bullies who usually pushed a new (or old) teacher around to break them, ever bothered Mrs. Free.

She was fascinating. We gathered around her and followed her up and down the walks trying to discover what made her tick. The bags of old clothes and rags from the laundry room were sent to her department to be used in rag rugs, but she went through them first. Whatever was in her size and could still be put on, she set aside and really wore—holes and all. Her hair would be put in curlers each night, but the curls were never combed out. Some of the bolder girls would tell her something was torn or shrunk too small. She'd beam brightly and say yes or just go "hee" and hurry down the walk with us tagging right along with her.

One night, after a program in the chapel, we were escorting Mrs. Free back to her dorm and invited her to come in and visit with us awhile. She looked right nice that night, dressed in black. Up the stairs we went.

"Your bed?" she asked one of the girls.

Upon being told yes, she jumped in the middle of it, turned a somersault, and landed on her feet, grinning. She asked each of us in turn which was our bed, and did somersaults until all of us had been honored. Our mouths hung open, some covered by hands, and our eyes rolled at each other with the question: "This is a teacher?"

She looked at us, laughed, and signed, "Go now."

Her signs were her own and we had to learn them if we wanted to talk with her. She lasted one year and never returned; we missed her. The door to the room with the loom was locked up again and I missed it too.

Changes were beginning to take place. I had discovered the school had a library. The door was directly across the lobby from the office door. I noticed blind girls entering and leaving but did not know what for. I did know that older children were placed in there for punishment and locked in without food or water for a whole day. It was a while before I found that out.

On being sent to the office with a note for Miss Kearney one day and finding no one was there, I was about to leave when I noticed the mystery door was partly open. This being my chance to find out what was in there, I peeked around the door. I saw shelves and shelves of books and rows of black typewriters, each on its own small table. A blind girl was at each table, busily typing under Miss Kearney's instruction, but it was the books I wanted to get my hands on.

After delivering the note and returning to the classroom, I asked some of the other girls if they knew there were books in that room, and they said, "Sure." No one was interested. I couldn't forget and thought of those books all week. One Saturday morning after breakfast, I asked Maybur if she'd go to the office to see if we could go in the library. She didn't like being indoors and would rather be on the playground. The other girls I asked thought I was even crazier than usual.

"That's the jail room," said Maybur. "I'm not going in there."

I went alone and timidly asked Miss Kearney if I could please look at some of those books. She seemed surprised and a little doubtful but then nodded and told me to go ahead. I don't think anyone had ever asked to go in that room before.

I spent the whole morning exploring those books, some of

which I had read but most I hadn't, including *The Swiss Family Robinson* and lots of mysteries. Time flew by. Miss Kearney came in and said that it was time for dinner and to report to the dining hall. She also told me that I could carry two books with me and bring them back after I read them. I could have hugged her neck but she looked too forbidding—not the huggable type.

At dinner everyone wanted to know where I'd been.

"In the library," I said.

"What did you do to get in jail?"

"Nothing, I wasn't in jail. I asked to go in there to read books."

"Books? We have enough books Monday, Tuesday, Wednesday, Thursday, and Friday. Saturday and Sunday, no books! You're crazy."

What they said didn't bother me at all. I was already deep in a story and living in it with the people I was reading about. The library became my haven on Saturday mornings. I read the books on Sunday, only stopping if anyone went for a walk in the hills back of the school grounds.

With all this to fill my hours, time flew by. Thanksgiving passed with nothing outstanding. The girls who signed to their boyfriends at night were now telling them what they wanted for Christmas. One night during the courting session, a girl came and told me William wanted to know what I wanted for Christmas.

"To go home," I answered promptly.

"Oh, you know you can't go home. Stop playing and tell me what you want."

"Nothing," I said.

She relayed this message but William must not have taken it seriously.

He was one of the boys who worked on the truck with Mr. Council after school and weekends, hauling supplies from town to the kitchen and other places on campus. They were paid a few dollars and kept their girlfriends supplied with treats and fresh fruit. They slipped it to someone in the kitchen who passed it on.

I was coming in for my share of loot from "Mr. Blue Eyes," although I only saw him in the classroom and in the distance working with the truck crew. I still looked at him out of curiosity. Those blue eyes in a brown face were fascinating. He'd look back in a kind way and smile. One time he asked me why I always looked at him. But I just shook my head and looked away.

Christmas was soon upon us. We had the usual program in the chapel and Christmas bags were passed out. Back in the dorms, boxes from home were opened. As usual, my family had done me proud.

When the girls who worked in the kitchen got off and came upstairs, they brought more gifts for the girls who had boyfriends with any money. William had sent me a toilet set with talcum powder, cologne, and soap. Of course this attracted a crowd and mixed comments from, "That's sweet," to a lecture from Hazel telling me, "I told you so. He's your boyfriend for good now and you have to marry him."

I glared at her, ready to do battle, but Margie, being older and more sensible, stepped up and told Hazel to leave me alone. She then told me to calm down and not to be ready to fight, that it was Christmas and my mama wouldn't want me to fight on Christmas. That ended the argument for the time being.

The holidays over with, things settled back into the daily routine. Then one day, strange men started walking around the grounds with Reverend Williams and Mr. Lineberry. Afterwards, a large machine was moved in and began excavating a large area beside our dorm, between it and the administration building. Pretty soon other things started arriving and a little shack was set up to serve as an office. Reverend Williams announced in morning devotion that a new building would be added. The one starting would be a new dining hall and kitchen. Later, an infirmary would also be built. He'd also asked for a chapel and a gym but said there were not enough funds for those right now.

That was exciting news all right, but what excited the upstairs girls more were the men working so close to our dorm. We could stand by a window and look right down on them. I wasn't interested, but of course, my man-loving roommates found a new use for me. I was dragged to the window and told to call and ask them their names.

"Why? I can't hear what they say and they can't sign."

"Tell them to write on a piece of paper and throw it up here. Go on, open your mouth and tell them."

One of the men seemed to be better looking than the others, so the girls concentrated on him as he passed back and forth below us. We waited for him to look our way and finally he did. They waved and grinned and giggled. He waved back but kept going before I could say anything.

"Why didn't you ask him? You're so slow."

"Then ask him yourself," I snapped at them.

They backed down a little at that and promised me some apples next time the truck brought some in.

"He's coming! Open your mouth now and call him," I was instructed.

I opened my mouth and said hey. He looked up, waved again and again kept going.

I knew no name to call him by so I asked why they didn't write him a note and drop it to him. This had not occurred to them as most deaf people use sign language. One or two signs can say the same as a whole sentence in English, and the girls wrote the same way. Even though most had beautiful handwriting, hearing people couldn't understand their language.

"You write," they said.

So I wrote a note asking him to write a note telling us his name and to throw it up to the window. When he came by again, Ethel (called "Buckwheat" by us) got his attention and threw the note down. He read it, looked up and grinned, then found a pencil and wrote his name. He also asked the name of another girl gathered at the window. He folded the note and aimed it at the opened window but it wouldn't fly that high. Buckwheat volunteered to run downstairs and pick it up since she was the one most interested in him. We waited nervously for her to come back up safely without Mrs. Holbrook catching her. She came up, already reading the note.

"Whose name does he want to know?"

They read the note then looked at each other. No one knew who he meant, except that it wasn't me. Finally they gathered at the window and when he passed again each girl pointed to herself. He shook his head no until Odessa Baskerville's turn came.

"Yes," nodded the head.

So Odessa, a light-complexioned girl with curly black hair was the chosen one. She hadn't shown much interest in him beforehand, but now made good use of her new status by smiling sweetly and making motions for him to bring her something good to eat.

Poor Buckwheat was lost and I felt sorry for her. Ever since the first day she'd seen him, her whole talk had been of how handsome he was, his light complexion, his curly brown hair, and how she bet his eyes were green. However, she showed no resentment toward Odessa who was also her best friend. My usefulness in this budding romance had been served for the time being, so again I was told to go play with the other babies.

The cold rainy days of January and February dragged on. The library was my favorite place. I also took to visiting the blind girls' dormitory directly behind us. I'd made friends with several of the girls—some totally blind, others partially so. Some of them learned to sign and fingerspell. The ones who couldn't see at all learned to fingerspell by carefully feeling my hand as I formed each letter. I could talk to them and they'd spell to me.

Their dorm had pianos here and there so they could practice their music during after-school hours and on weekends. I would ask them to play some of the old tunes I knew and I'd stand close by or lay my hand on the piano to feel the vibration. Even that little bit of "hearing" made me very happy and very homesick. One song especially affected me:

> Lazy bones, sleeping in the sun
> How do you 'spect to get your day's work done?
> Lazy bones sleeping in the midday sun

I'd close my eyes, fitting the beat to the words, and remember back home: the soft-looking, white clouds scattered over the sky; the dust in the road, white and hot; the porch, shady and cool; everybody lying around drowsy; and bees buzzing over the flowers. Then I could just hear Papa rousing up and calling the boys to get up, saying it was time to get back to the field.

My blind friends would ask me to tell them about my home life, something I was more than happy to do. When I'd tell them I had on a new dress they'd ask to "see" it. I'd soon be surrounded by girls, their fingers going lightly and deftly over my dress while asking what color it was, and so on. It tickled at first and I'd squirm and giggle, but soon I sensed that it meant as much to them to imagine seeing colors and pretty things as it did for me to imagine hearing songs and my family's voices. So I learned to stand quietly and describe the colors of the dress and buttons. They'd "see" my hair also and even go down to my shoes and socks when I'd be dressed for special doings. They'd tell me my clothes and hair were pretty and to come back and see them again.

"Be sure now," they'd sign.

Back in the dorm, if my absence had been noticed (and most of the time it had), a committee would soon come up to ask what was I doing in the blind girls' dorm and to tell me I'd better stay out of there. They warned me I was going to get in trouble and said I was a short, crazy kid and must think I was blind too. They remembered that I wore shades when I first came there and threatened to run me over there to stay. I'd shut them out of my mind by remembering something I was reading or pick up a *Daily Word* and read from it. They held the Bible and anything related to it sacred and left me alone when I did that.

Spring was soon upon us again and teachers started planning Easter programs. I was included in the deaf chorale or glee club. I don't know what the teachers called what we did. We just called it signing songs. I was told to learn the words of each song and watch Gertrude's signs and follow her. They were mostly spirituals I had been hearing all my life, so I already knew them. However, I was a little nervous about being up there with the big girls, being the youngest and shortest in the group. I was told that I did well. That perked me up, so that I didn't even mind when the bullies found something to pick at me about.

The new building was nearing completion. Odessa had put the handsome carpenter down. For awhile he brought her candy bars and would throw them up to the open window where she could catch them. Then he started writing notes. I didn't see them, but shortly afterwards I noticed she no longer gathered at the window to wave and make signs at him. It turned out that Odessa had gone down to meet him and had seen him up close minus his hat. What a shock! The curly brown hair was mixed with gray and grew only on the bottom part of his head; the top was bald. His teeth were broken and stained yellow from tobacco. She said even his eyes were bleary. She'd turned and fled: end of romance.

This year for school closing we had a maypole dance and a sunbonnet drill. For the sunbonnet drill we wore large bonnets of different colors, matching gathered aprons with large bows in back, matching socks, and black patent leather shoes. I was to lead one line of girls and Percy (another short, plump girl) the other line. The drill was held outdoors on a low rise on the campus green between the deaf boys' and girls' dorms. They had timed it so the drills would be just at sunset and silhouetted against the evening sky.

The maypole dance went well, but some of us had to change for the sunbonnet drill and something else delayed it for a while. Anyway, we came marching out, but by then it was nearly dark and we started stumbling—both Percy and I were night-blind. Mr. Lineberry, trying to be helpful, drove his car out on the green behind the audience and turned his brightest beams smack in our faces. That really fixed us both as well as the rest of the girls. Before, we'd been just stumbling a little, now blinded by bright lights, we panicked and went wild, skipping drunkenly in whatever direction our feet carried us. The rest couldn't tell the difference between me and Percy and didn't know who to follow. So they took off after first one, then the other, whichever they saw passing. Bonnets fell back, apron bows came loose and trailed along behind us. I was thankful that it was dark by this time and that I couldn't see anyone's face. I hoped desperately they couldn't see mine. Some of the teachers who'd been waving frantically at us finally herded us off.

Back in the dorm that night the girls just looked at us and fell out laughing—friends as well as bullies. Margie did try to defend us by saying Mr. Lineberry shouldn't have shone the headlights in our faces; nobody could see like that. But even she laughed when Jessie and Buckwheat got up to show how funny Percy and I looked when we skipped headlong into each other. I thought I'd cry, but thinking back, it was funny and I laughed too—going home had a lot to do with that.

11

Changes, Worries, and Adventures

BEING at home this summer was about the same as usual, except Bennie and Mable had moved to Pender County near her family. Being home felt odd without Bennie. He'd always been there except for one summer he had spent in Norfolk. I'd look at his place at the table that now seemed lonely and empty. I hadn't really had time to get used to Mable being with us, because I had had to leave for school shortly after they married. I had enjoyed riding with them over to her folks' farm where they had lots of apple trees, other fruit trees, and peanuts. Mable was a very smart, hardworking farm girl and nothing seemed too hard for her to tackle. Allen moved with Bennie and Mable to help them on their farm. I missed him also.

This summer was pretty quiet. About the biggest event was going to Jones Lake over in Bladen County. The lakes, like the beaches, were segregated. Jones Lake was a park built by the state for Blacks. When Papa announced that he was taking us to Jones Lake for a picnic one Sunday, we anticipated the trip with a great deal of excitement. Eunice and I went to Bennie's that Saturday to spend the night. We'd go with Bennie and Mable to meet the rest of the family at Jones Lake the next day. Mable was up late that night baking a chocolate cake; she also made potato salad and fried chicken for the picnic. We got up early Sunday morning and were soon on our way. I don't remember the exact route we took but I'll never forget my first ride on a ferry. We drove right up to a river and seeing no bridge, I wondered if Bennie intended getting the car to float across, but I didn't dare ask. We just waited. Finally I saw a long, flat, queer-looking boat coming our way. Slowly it edged up to the riverbank and stopped in front of us. Next thing I knew, our car and some more cars behind us were parked securely on the boat and we were moving across the river. After reaching the other side, it wasn't long before we arrived at Jones Lake.

Finally we were at the "big-time" place for Blacks that I'd been hearing so much about. I had pictured lots of rides, refreshment stands, picture-taking booths, dancing, and games, but it was nothing like I had imagined. Instead, there was lots of light gray sand and long leaf pines and scrub oaks. I only saw two buildings in addition to the sheltered cooking grills with tables and benches that were scattered about. The lake itself looked to be newly built as there were still roots and fresh earth about the edges. A long boardwalk or pier led out into the water.

After walking about a bit and getting our bearings, Eunice told me to come with her. She headed for the larger of the two buildings. Inside she was given a wire basket with a bathing suit, a large pin with a number, and a towel in exchange for fifty cents. When I was asked if I wanted one too, I could only shake my head. *Me* put on one of those things in public so people could see how fat I was? No way!

Next we went into a little stall where she changed into the swimsuit. Looking at it, I was very glad I didn't have to put one on. It had moth holes and was made from what felt like wool.

Then we went in search of Mama and Papa and the rest of our family. We found them under a picnic shelter with the boxes and baskets containing our lunch sitting on the table. Eunice soon took off for the water and to meet new friends while Sam and I begged our parents for money to go to the concession stand for ice cream cones. We were told to wait until we'd had lunch. I guess they hoped that the food would fill us so full there'd be no room for ice cream. We found a bench near the water to sit and watch the array of bodies passing us. They were clad in all shapes and colors of swimsuits, shorts, and pants, all wet and stuck to them. Some were fat, some skinny, some right nice. We stared and giggled until Mama sent someone to tell us to come eat. She was passing out plates of food piled high with fried chicken, potato salad, ham, butter beans, and corn.

Around us, other people were making use of the grills, roasting hot dogs and hamburgers. The air smelled delicious and did we eat! Satisfied with food, Sam and I hadn't forgotten the ice cream cones, but again it was "wait and give your dinner time to digest." Put down again, we ventured farther out and discovered an artist doing an oil painting of the lake. We were fascinated, watching him make deft strokes of color as he sat on a little stool behind his easel. His picture looked exactly like the scene before us. Mama and Bennie came by and moved us out before we started breathing down the man's neck.

Finally we were given permission and money for the long-hoped-for ice cream cones. Finding the concession stand beside the boardwalk leading to the lake, we stood trying to make up our minds what flavor we wanted. It didn't take Sam long; he knew he loved vanilla. Me, I loved them all. When I'd about decided on vanilla too, another customer ordered chocolate. I stared longingly at the big cone piled high with delicious-looking chocolate and opened my mouth to say chocolate when someone else was handed a lovely pink strawberry cone. All the while Sam was nudging me to say what I wanted. I still stood there thinking: vanilla . . . chocolate . . . strawberry . . . peach . . . or maybe something else. I just could not decide. Just then Eunice came up to see what was taking us so long, and seeing what the problem was, she solved it at once by ordering a chocolate cone for me. She knew my taste as well as I did. Back at the picnic area, all was packed and ready to go. Eunice and I said good-bye to Bennie and Mable and got in the back of Papa's pickup with the rest of the people he'd brought from Iron Mine.

Like the trip to the Sea Breeze, this trip was talked about for a few days. Then we laid it aside for newer happenings and the business of everyday farm life. The hot, dusty days of August were upon us and Sam and I carried dinner to whoever was tending the tobacco barn. One barn was near the Powers farm over across the bay from our house. I loved the feel of the soft hot dust squishing between my toes as we walked along to the field every day.

Probably because we were usually alone on these journeys, Sam and I felt close and didn't argue when we carried the dinner. He could fingerspell and we talked of many things. Mostly he asked me to tell him about my school and the deaf and blind children. Then he'd tell me bits of gossip he'd overheard or some family business I didn't know about. Thus he informed me that Papa was considering selling our farm and buying another place down at Rocky Point, northeast of the Cape Fear River. I was horrified and stared at him with my mouth open.

"Oh no! What for?"

"A better place," I was told.

"It can't be better than Iron Mine. I bet it's not even as good."

According to Sam it was better because it was near the river and the house had two stories.

"A big house," he added.

"I don't care. I don't want a big house. I'd rather have our house," I argued.

Gone now was the peaceful togetherness we'd been feeling. I was worrying myself into a lather and couldn't wait to get back home to run to Mama and ask if this disturbing news was true. I went in search of her as soon as we arrived back home.

"Mama! Mama! Is Papa selling our home and moving us away?"

I was almost screaming.

"Oh, he just discussed it with Mr. George King," she told me. He was a friend as well as a land agent for farms.

"Please Mama, tell him not to sell. I don't want to move to Rocky Point," I begged.

I'd never seen Rocky Point but was sure it was a horrible place: in a swamp beside the river and full of snakes and mosquitoes. Leaving Iron Mine for nine months to go to school in Raleigh was bad enough, but to leave it for good and never have it to come home to—I just couldn't bear to even think of that. I looked at the fields, the woods, the pond behind the house, the twin oak trees at the end of the porch, the big pine I used to hear the wind blowing through, and the house itself. I loved it all and although I no longer attended Iron Mine Elementary, it and the little white church beside it were still very much a part of my life. I loved them all so I worried that summer.

I could leave my worries behind each Saturday evening when Sam, Willie, and I would go to Wallace. We'd sit through three cowboy movies, a couple of cartoons or the *Three Stooges*, and see next week's coming attractions, all for fifteen or twenty-five cents. Hot dogs and popcorn were ten cents and Cokes were five cents. Willie never associated with Sam and me once we got in town, but I knew he was up there someplace. How I loved to watch

Johnny Mack Brown, Roy Rogers, Charles Starret, Hopalong Cassidy, Gabby Hayes, and the rest of those hard-riding cowboys.

One evening we arrived late and the place was packed. Some people were even standing. Sam and I finally found two seats together way in the back. We sat down gratefully, then found we couldn't see over the grown-ups in front of us, so we stood up. I still couldn't see so I stood on my seat. The view was good. I got so carried away with what was happening before my eyes, I forgot about my feet. During a really exciting scene, I jumped and clapped. The front of the seat went up and the back went down and so did my feet, with a loud BANG! There I stood with my feet on the floor and my legs in the crack. Necks craned, heads turned to see what all the commotion was. Sam refused to even look at me, trying to pretend he'd never seen me in all his life. He couldn't stand it for long. Knowing I was trying to free myself and probably afraid I'd do something worse, he helped me free first one foot, then the other. For the rest of our time, I kept my feet fixed on the floor. After that, I just caught a glimpse of my heroes when I was lucky.

So another summer at home was drawing to a close and "back to Raleigh" loomed large and dark on my horizon. Time spent with Queen and my family became more precious to me. I tried to avoid arguments with anyone, where before I'd jumped in headlong. One Saturday night, Mama told me to get in the truck, we were going someplace. We all piled in except Frank and Subud. They'd already left in Frank's car. We headed down the dirt road toward the Katy Ford.

"Where are we going?" I asked Mama.

"To Mrs. Stella Johnson's house. They're having a birthday party for her and we're all invited," she told me.

The Johnson girls as I remember them were Ira, Etta, Eulah

Mae, and Allie Dee. Eulah Mae was one of Eunice's best friends and also a play mother to me. I loved her too and was happy to know that's where I was going. The house was primped up and looked really nice. I settled down to enjoy the party, hoping there would be dancing. I loved to see people dance. My pleasure was short-lived.

I sensed a commotion going on outside and upon looking, saw the yard was full of other Iron Mine people. Papa came and spoke to Mama, whereupon she hastily gathered all of us up and into the truck.

"Why are we leaving, Mama?" I kept asking.

"Hush," was the only response I got.

Papa headed back home with Eunice, Sam, Mama, and me in front with him. Willie, Allen (who was back with us for awhile), Evander Murphy, and some others rode in back. We had reached Jean McKoy's house when another car stopped us. I saw it was Frank's car. Everyone else got out of the truck, but I was told to stay there. Knowing something was happening, I looked around wildly trying to figure out what. Where was Sam? And where had Mama and Eunice disappeared to? I was just fixing to stick my head out of the window on the passenger side when I saw Frank in the headlights of the car, coming out of a butter bean patch with a long-barreled shotgun. I screamed and someone reached their hand in the window and covered my mouth. I slid away to the other side and jumped out, determined to find Mama, Sam, and Eunice.

Just as I got my feet under me, I saw Allen running along the ditch bank reaching for something inside the ditch. Wondering what it was, I watched a few minutes, then turned toward Eunice who was standing a little ways farther down the ditch.

"Eunice what's the matter? Where's Mama?" I screamed.

"Hush."

She motioned toward the ditch. Looking again, I saw two

My "adopted" brother Allen and my brother Willie, *right*,
playing around at Northeast River.

hands stretched up out of the ditch waving back and forth. I stood
and stared. Allen was trying to grab the two hands. Going closer
and peering through the dark, I saw it was Mama. Sitting next to
Papa, she'd gotten out on the side by the ditch. While trying to
get to Frank, she'd fallen in it. Not knowing how to get out, and
being nearly hysterical with worry, she was marching up and
down, praying and flailing her arms while Allen tried to rescue
her.

I ran beside Allen, crying and calling "Mama! Mama! What's
the matter, Mama?"

Papa came to help, and along with Allen, lifted her out of the
ditch. She ran at once to look for Frank while Papa got a hold on

me and put me firmly back in the truck along with Sam. The rest
gathered in a bunch in the darkness while I shook and shivered
with fright. Sam was huddled down too. I asked him what was the
matter. The only thing he knew was that Frank wanted to shoot
Vander. Finally the crowd broke up and everybody started getting
in the truck again. We proceeded home with Frank's car following.

As soon as we got inside the house and a lamp was lit, I pounced
on Mama, wanting to know what and why. It seemed Subud had
gotten into an argument with Vander and some more boys outside
Mrs. Stella's house. He then told Frank they meant to harm him
(Subud, that is). Frank, being high on white lightning whiskey,
was determined to protect Subud. The two of them had gone
home and gotten one of Papa's shotguns and come back to shoot
them up. They'd stopped up the exhaust pipe on the truck with
dirt to keep everybody there, but Willie found it and cleaned it
out, so we'd met them before they got all the way back. Mama
and Papa had gotten on Frank, and on Subud for putting Frank
up to it, knowing he was high. They'd talked it out, there in the
road, and it ended up with Vander getting in Frank's car and riding
home with him and Subud, and spending the night. For the next
few days, Subud was all apology for his share in the mishap and
vowed he was going to join the church the next third Sunday and
be a good boy for the rest of his life.

"That's right, son, you do that," Mama encouraged him.

He did join the church and was baptized with me two or three
years later.

This was the summer I saw a change in all the little girls I was
friends with. They'd paired off into sets of best friends and just
had time for each other. At church they sat together giggling and
whispering until Cousin Archie would go back and threaten them.
The little boys also acted curious. They too formed little groups
and stared boldly at the girls and snickered. No one seemed inter-

ested in playing house, tea party, or any of the yard games I'd
loved to play. Thelma would still be willing to walk out to my
house but not to play, so I sought Doris's company. She was still
young enough to enjoy what the other girls used to, so she, Sam,
and I played together.

My folks bought me a really pretty dress since it was getting
near time for the dreaded trip to Raleigh. When I put it on with
my usual socks and patent leather shoes, Eunice said the dress
would look better with grown-up stockings and low heels. I was
flabbergasted. *Me* put on long silk stockings? Not on your life! I
could still remember Sis Ette's funeral. We argued back and forth
with her telling me all my friends were wearing stockings to
church, and asking why I couldn't be like them?

"Because I'm not them. I'm *me* and I'm *not* going to wear those
things."

She said I was odd. All the other thirteen- and fourteen-year-
olds had boyfriends and she wanted to know if I had one.

"Naw. I don't want no old knotty-head boy."

I hoped that would be the end of it but no, she said all the
girls from town and from Rockfish (a nearby community) were
wearing heels and stockings and had boyfriends too.

So that's what's wrong with everyone, I thought. *Who wants a boyfriend? If I did get one, who would it be?*

I let the boys I knew pass through my mind, rejecting every
one.

Maybe, I thought, *Thelma and I could swap brothers. She could
have Willie for her boyfriend and I could have Leroy. Then we wouldn't
be odd but we also wouldn't have to put on and act silly.*

When I put this idea before Thelma, she acted like she never
heard me and made no comment. So I tucked that idea away for
the time being.

However, much to my surprise, a new boy in the neighborhood, whom I'd noticed at church and Sunday school, showed up at my house right after dark one night. He handed me a large brown paper bag then helped himself to a seat. Opening the bag to see what was inside, I found fruit: apples, oranges, grapes, and bananas. Mama told me to say thank you.

I found out his name was William DeVone and that he was from Shanghai. I sat there tongue-tied while Mama and Eunice did the talking. It didn't take me long to go to sleep. When I woke up a good while later, he was gone and it was time for bed. Eunice said I should have talked to him.

"What about?" I asked.

She said he seemed nice and had a brother named Erwin who was going to see Gladys.

Gladys could have them both. I was only interested in the fruit. Anyway, it was time for me to start worrying about leaving my home again, and all those dear to me.

12

Coming of Age

I'D NEVER be able to face the time of year when school started without a feeling of great loneliness and loss at being separated from my family and home. Once back on campus, it was a little easier since I had friends and could communicate with them. We went about getting settled in, seeing who was new, showing off new clothes and trinkets. I still had the same homeroom and Miss Laws, but had to take English under Mrs. J. D. Mask. Mrs. I. B. Free was gone and a Miss Leach had her place. Mrs. Holbrook was back and Mrs. Alston was still matron for the blind girls.

As usual, we had a bunch of new students, but the outstanding one as I remember was a girl named Gracie; I never knew her last name. We found her sitting on a bed in the junior girls' room one day when we came in from class. She had a brown complexion and pretty hair, but she was thin with very large black eyes that just stared at you with no expression. We gathered around and waved at her.

No response.

Each of us took turns making motions trying to get her to at least nod her head or something.

She just sat and stared.

Next, "Hazel the Horrible" stuck her face close up to Gracie and started trying to ask her name, thinking she might be able to hear a little. The girls told her to stop before she scared the girl to death and that Gracie knew she couldn't talk.

"I too can talk," she told them, then started shaking the poor girl to make her talk, laugh, or cry.

But Gracie never did. We wandered away, but went back when the bell rang for supper and tried to make her understand that it was time to eat.

Nothing.

I was told to "open my mouth" and tell her to go eat.

Still nothing.

The rest of us went. By the time we got back it was near dark and she still sat there. We had study hour, then started preparing for bed. We gathered around Gracie again and told her to put on her gown and go to bed. When we still got no response, one of the girls picked up her suitcase, laid it on the bed, took the key from around Gracie's neck, and opened it. It wasn't even half full: a couple of brand-new cotton dresses, a nightgown, and a pile of Kotex. We took the gown and went through the motions of pulling off a dress and putting on the gown, but it was a waste of time. Hazel grabbed the gown, pushed her face close to Gracie's, looking as mean as she could—which was mean indeed—and tried to pull the dress over her head and dress or undress her by force.

No go. Gracie hung onto her clothes and her dignity.

Finally giving up, we went to bed and left her sitting there in the dark.

Upon awakening the next morning, we expected to see her either asleep or still sitting there. Neither was the case. Gracie and her suitcase had disappeared with the night. Since both hall doors were always locked at night on both floors, and all window screens closed and locked from the inside, where was she? Margie thought that maybe Mrs. Holbrook had come up and moved her downstairs or something. However, upon being informed of the happening, Mrs. Holbrook was shocked. She said she knew no more than we did and hurried to call Reverend Williams. He hurried right over, examined the door locks, and questioned all of the upstairs girls. After going to bed and lights-out, no one had seen Gracie. So that was the talk at breakfast and in the classrooms.

"Wonder where Gracie is?"

"How did she open the door and get out?"

"Maybe she was really a ghost or a magician."

I hoped she wasn't a ghost. When I thought about Snooks on that windy March night years before, I still got the shakes.

"You all are crazy," Margie said. "I had my hands on her and she was warm. Ghost, nothing."

So it remained a mystery until a day or so later when we got word that she'd been picked up walking along a highway right outside Raleigh. Reverend Williams or Mr. Lineberry had gone after her and returned her to her home without bringing her back to school at all. That was Gracie's time at our school.

The new dining hall and kitchen had been completed during the summer. Some of us didn't think it was really completed as the inside walls were exposed brick and the building had exposed overhead beams. The floor in the dining room was a very pretty parquet design, and instead of the long tables, we had brand-new tables that sat eight children each. A huge white refrigerator with double doors stood at one end of the dining hall. Swinging doors led to the kitchen, which was bright and sunny with tile floors, a brand-new dishwasher, and two large steam cookers, plus the same long black coal range we had had before. It also had two shiny steel double sinks—one for scrubbing pans, one for vegetables—and stainless steel worktables.

Down below on the basement level was a large storage room for food supplies, a cooler to keep the cans of milk from the dairy fresh and cold, and a bakery with long mixing and kneading tables and an oven with lots of racks. We were supposed to start having baking classes here. A pretty, young, home economics teacher had been hired to teach it: Miss Perry from New Jersey. She had long shiny black hair and wore new white uniforms. However, our regular cook thought she was new kitchen help and put her to work along with the rest preparing vegetables and meats, waiting tables for the teachers, scrubbing floors, and so on. It was more than Miss Perry could take and one morning she fainted. Two of the senior girls carried her to our dorm and went for Nurse Stewart. Miss Perry left the next day.

Another pretty, young teacher was hired for PE. The school now had a tennis court on the playground, so Miss Bowden got busy organizing teams and had us send home for gym shoes and shorts. She also got a girls' softball team together. Mama and Eunice sent me brown and white gym shoes that made me feel so springy, like walking on air. I took to tennis right away, but never got to even halfway learn the game. We weren't allowed to wear anything above our knees outside of our bedrooms, so when Miss Bowden was seen out on the tennis court, not only in shorts herself, but with us girls dressed in them too, that was the end of gym and sports for us. The older teachers talked of how fast these young teachers right out of college acted.

"Carrying you girls out there with shorts on for men to see your legs."

They turned their mouths down and shook their heads.

"Bad."

I tried to defend her.

"She's nice and she's teaching us to play tennis and other games," I said.

"Stop talking and get your books out," I was told.

Miss Bowden stayed for the balance of that year, but said she wouldn't be back. As long as she was there, she took us on hikes, and helped us gather black walnuts and hickory nuts from the woods. We'd dry them out, then sit by a warm steam radiator on cold rainy days, eating them and reading or gossiping. She did what she could to relieve our boredom and help to make our lives more enjoyable.

During my visits to the blind girls, I'd noticed Mrs. Alston didn't look too well and was quieter. She didn't glare at me every time she saw me coming or going in her place of business as she once did. Some of the girls had said that if they'd be on the walk when she was passing our dorm, she'd pinch them if they didn't move fast enough, so we avoided her and Mrs. Smith—another pincher—as much as possible. One morning just before the first breakfast bell, a long black ambulance pulled up and stopped between the two dorms. It was really a hearse but was used then to transport both the sick and the dead. Everyone was all agog at this latest happening, rushing to the windows and outside to see who it had come for. A stretcher was rolled into the blind girls' dorm.

The first breakfast bell rang to get ready; we stayed where we were. By the second bell, we knew it was Mrs. Alston. They rolled her right past me and I was shocked at her appearance. Her face was a nasty gray and her eyes were half-closed. I felt like crying and wished I hadn't seen. If she hadn't been exactly loving, she hadn't done me any harm either and had always let me visit over there.

We went on to breakfast very quiet, except Hazel. As usual, she knew everything there was to know. She knew Mrs. Alston had been sick and what was wrong with her, and on and on. I wished she'd hush. In morning devotion, Reverend Williams announced her illness and that she'd been carried to the hospital in town. She lingered there for a day or so before he announced that she had died. This saddened all of us, as she had been there for years and seemed to belong—she was one of us.

Even Hazel shut up until Mrs. Alston's nephew, his wife, and his niece came to gather her belongings. They took time to visit with us and get acquainted. All three were handsome people. The niece had long, thick dark brown hair and a lovely brown complexion. Naturally, Hazel got right in their faces and started running her mouth—or hands rather—about how good she'd loved Mrs. Alston, and about what she had said and done. We raised our eyes heavenward and wondered why Hazel didn't drop dead right then. Before they finished and were ready to leave, the nephew decided to sing for us during morning devotion. He told us that when he was a small boy his aunt used to sing a special song for him that he'd never forget, so he'd like to share it with us. One of the teachers signed as he sang it. All who could hear said he could really sing and I wished I could hear him.

Hazel raved for days about how pretty they were, how nice, and that they loved her and hadn't paid the rest of us any mind.

We said they couldn't see anyone else with her right in their eyes. Then looking at my head, she sneered at me and said I thought I had pretty hair but that the niece had "good" hair for sure, like White people had. Mine wasn't nothing. Then to get in a last lick she added that I was short and big-eyed and couldn't talk like she could.

I didn't even attempt to answer. Someday I was going to get ahold of that girl.

The bulldozers and other machines were back on campus, scooping out a place for the school infirmary. This was to be built a little to the rear of the heating plant and the shoe shop, beside the blind girls' dorm. Thank heavens it was far enough away that my roommates couldn't see how the men looked or what color their eyes were so I didn't have to "open my mouth" and say foolish things for a bunch of man-starved females.

I was busy going to the library and trying to teach myself to type on the blind girls' typewriters. The keys were unmarked so I had to use a key to see what it was and then remember where to find it—not an easy thing to do, but I was coming along. My blind friends were also teaching me to read and write in braille like they did. I never learned to read by touch but learned the letters and could read and write them by sight. One of the blind boys who had partial sight even started writing me notes in braille. How proud I was to be able to read it. I borrowed a slate and point and wrote him back, my first note to one of the opposite sex. His name was Thomas. Thank heaven Hazel's prying eyes couldn't read braille.

The hazy, warm days of early autumn marched on. I was taking English and geography under Mrs. Mask. I had admired her from a distance for a long time. She'd be standing in her doorway when classes changed or started, and I always smiled at her in passing and it was always returned. Now I had her for a teacher. Some of the older girls had told me I wasn't going to be smiling long because she was a warhorse for sure, but I didn't believe them.

The first day I reported for class I sailed in wearing a big smile and wishing her a good morning. She returned the smile, but after we'd all been assigned seats, she stood before us minus her smile. She explained her rules and re-explained them. Sit straight; no talking—or signing rather; no copying; keep work neat; use plain handwriting; use periods, commas, question marks, and other punctuation where needed; no eating in class; keep all books, papers, and tablets under the desk and out of sight except while in use. That was English. In geography, we found she considered it a small world indeed: We were expected to learn the whole globe like our own backyard. Because I still had my voice and speech and understood sometimes, I'd been breezing through my English classes and snagging an A almost every time. The first test we had under Mrs. Mask, five points were taken off for every *e* I made that looked like an undotted *i* and the same for every *i* I forgot to dot. I took it and tried to act like it was no big deal at first. However, when my A on the honor roll turned to a B I really tried to be more careful. I didn't want Mama to be disappointed in me, and our report cards were sent home quarterly.

On one test, I'd gone back over my papers to be sure I had everything perfect, to no avail. She'd found an *e* that she said looked like an *i* and marked it wrong. I laid my head on my desk and cried. All my frustration that I'd been holding back poured forth. I wanted to run where Mama was and put my head under her apron where I couldn't see the class laughing. A big eighth grader, crying in class. Minnie didn't laugh. I could tell she wanted to say something but didn't dare. I was sent to the bathroom to get control of myself and wash my face.

Years later, after my school days were over, I found a letter she'd sent Mama with my report card, telling her of the incident and how she was trying to teach me all she could. She said I had a lot of potential and that she wanted me to do my best, but that I was sensitive and proud and hated to be brought down. She also gave me compliments and let Mama know she cared about me. That's when I found out what a really good teacher she was.

Algebra and history were Mrs. Edmondson's subjects, but her room was also homeroom for the senior class. Her classes were a breeze. She'd tell us what pages to study, put a sample of algebra on the board to show how it was done, then start telling us what she'd had for breakfast, how delicious her hot biscuits and grape jelly had tasted, and then ask if we thought she was gaining or losing any weight, that she didn't want to be fat and was going to start exercising. We were then treated to a show of how she could kick her leg. Her girdle or corset wouldn't let the leg rise much. We smiled and nodded, agreeing with all she said. While she talked, the rest of the girls would be either copying my algebra or simply doodling and marking time 'til our next class. I learned algebra because I was curious about all those xs and ys and wanted to know how it worked. By the time we came back for history after lunch, she'd be full of gossip.

I was also taking machine sewing this year, learning to make simple things like pillowcases, sheets, straight nightgowns, and slips. Soon the year was nearly gone. We'd been to the state fair, had Halloween, all about like the year before and the year before that. I had helped pluck turkeys for Thanksgiving, eighteen or twenty of them, and the older girls and the kitchen staff cleaned them out. Some of us snitched a bunch of livers and fried them up nice and brown for a pre-Thanksgiving feast.

By now, I was more or less one of the gang. However, "Hazel the Horrible" didn't accept me. A bunch of us sort of hung together: Madgalene (or "Madga"), Buckwheat, Jessie, Odessa, Cora Lee Andrews, Cora Lee Ross, Rena Mae, Beulah, Minnie Applewhite, Louise Clayton, Rosa Lee Eatman, and Percy Foy. Bonnie McCullough, a short-haired tomboy type was also part of our group. The teachers, one by one, found out they couldn't whip Bonnie. She whipped them instead, male and female alike. In playing softball, she could hit clear out to the highway. However, she was a kind and generous person with the rest of us, always willing to share her loot from the kitchen.

Buckwheat acted somewhat like the one on Little Rascals. Jessie was quite tall and forever using us shorter girls for a prop and leaning on us. Rena had the best build and a cute babyish face and was always in hot water with someone over their boyfriend. Percy was clumsy and bumbling and Louise was the clown.

Left to right: me, Minnie Applewhite, Louise Clayton, and Jessie Cooley
standing outside our dorm in 1938.

Madga, on the other hand, was the indisputable queen of the
campus. She had average looks, but she had a style and way of
her own. If she liked you, you knew it and you were "in." Otherwise, she paid you no mind. Her parents were divorced and she
lived with her mother, who never came to see her in all the years
she attended school—from the age of six on up. This year was
her junior year. Knowing already about queens from the Iron Mine
school, I never even tried to get to know her. She slept across the
hall with the senior girls anyway and I had little contact with her.

Margie, Flossie, and Maybur didn't really belong to any group;
they were just friendly to all. No one knew how to classify Hill.
She seemed always to be on the edge of a group staring at us, but
if anyone asked her if she wanted to say anything, she'd smile a
little and say no. With her proper skirts and suits and motherly
shoes and stockings, she seemed more like a teacher watching us,

so the girls would drift away. She had wanted to be a teacher like the rest of her family but lost her hearing when she was about eleven. Although they had a nice home on a quiet street in Williamston, it sounded like no one went any place except school, church, or to visit friends and sit quietly while sipping coffee, tea, or a fruit drink. I felt sorry for her, thinking of my own large, noisy family. I spent many hours with her, becoming well acquainted with her family, as talking about them seemed to make her happy.

Hazel would often notice us and stop to ask what and who we were talking about. I'd tell her not to worry, that we wouldn't waste time talking about her. She'd become enraged and tell me about my little, short, fast self and that she was going to tell all the other girls we were talking about them. Hill would become frightened and beg me to stop fussing but I never did. I couldn't abide Hazel.

On Thanksgiving Day the cooks and kitchen help got busy with dinner right after breakfast was out of the way. We could smell roasting turkey and dressing all over. Visitors started arriving, some bringing their children boxes from home. My box had come by mail and I'd get another after the weekend. Mr. George Byrd from Raleigh knew my papa and often went to hunt with him, so Mama would send some things by him. The kids couldn't mistake him for my parent since he was White and blue-eyed. They did ask why he came to see me.

I was just going down the back stairs of our dorm when Bonnie came racing down past me. She went through one glass-paneled door at the foot of the stairway, but when she got to the second one opening into the lower hall, she couldn't slow down in time. Her face slammed against a pane right before my horrified eyes. I leaped the rest of the way downstairs to her. The blood was spurting from the side of her face where the glass had opened a gash from just above the corner of her left eye almost to her chin. I grabbed something from the sewing room for her to hold against her face, then ran for Mrs. Holbrook.

Mrs. Holbrook was already on her way out. She called Nurse Stewart and Reverend Williams and we got Bonnie to the nurse's room at the end of the hall. By then a crowd had gathered and Bonnie's mother was there. She lived in Asheville and hadn't been able to visit Bonnie before because of the distance. This year she'd had a ride and decided to surprise Bonnie who, having seen her mother arrive from upstairs, was rushing down as fast as she could to greet her when she ran into the door.

It was a very bad cut. Dr. Delany had to come out from town and sew it up.* As soon as she could, Hazel got ahold of the mother to introduce herself as Bonnie's best friend. She said she'd tried to help her when she got hurt, and so on. After she'd thought about it, she even tried to hint that I'd pushed Bonnie into the door. Bonnie told everyone that was a lie, that I wasn't even close to her and had been the first to help. Margie told Hazel she should be ashamed.

So an exciting Thanksgiving Day passed on into Christmas. It was as usual with the exception that some of the upstairs girls, including me, got to go into town and see a movie. Being off campus and among other people was very exciting, even though we were herded along like a bunch of dim-witted sheep. The movie wasn't that much. The building was located in a run-down part of town and the picture itself was about circus life. Christmas gone, we settled again into our daily routine—up at 6:00, breakfast at 7:15, devotion in the chapel at 8:00, classes at 8:30, lunch at noon, school out at 2:20, vocational classes from 2:30 to 4:00, sup-

---

*Dr. Delany was our school physician. He seemed quiet and was very nice. His two sisters, Bessie and Sadie, wrote *Having Our Say* and *The First One Hundred Years*.

per at 5:00, study hour from 7:00 to 8:30 (a change from previous years, to give us time to get ready for bed), and lights-out at 9:00.

Work on the infirmary was progressing. We certainly needed it. Every year at this time girls got the flu or measles. Each nurse's room only had two beds, so the rest had to stay in the same beds they always had. The nurse visited them each day, bringing doses of castor oil and a bitter-tasting cold remedy named 666 that we called "three-sixes." Yuck! I can still taste both. The castor oil was mixed with a sweet brown liquid that was supposed to make it taste better. It didn't. Not all the patients had flu; some just wanted to play hooky and get lots of cornflakes from the kitchen. That was standard fare for all sick people, no matter what the ailment. That was the only time we got cornflakes, which were usually reserved for teachers and staff.

13

Boys and Other Trouble

JANUARY passed slowly. I still had my periods of despair in Mrs. Mask's room but not as often as before. Two new boys had been enrolled since Christmas. One, husky and happy-go-lucky like a friendly puppy, was Lorenzo Brandon (Brandy for short). The other was sort of short for a boy, very light-skinned with shiny, black eyes that looked directly at you without blinking. This one was Leon Wright Davis. They'd both lost their hearing recently, Leon from spinal meningitis. They both had good speech; in fact, Brandy seemed to still have his hearing as well. He heard everything said to him, or to anyone else for that matter. Brandy livened things up considerably by singing at the top of his voice as he walked about campus. Two of his favorite songs were "Big Leg Woman" (I'd never heard that one) and "Blues in the Night." That one I knew. Some teachers told him to be quiet and slammed windows down while others laughed. Leon, however, was very serious and intense.

I became friends with both after they found out I could speak well too. They had difficulty understanding the way the other deaf children phrased their words. Since they were both nice-looking boys, it wasn't long before my match-making friends had chosen a girl for each of them. Buckwheat was presented to Brandy and Maybur to Leon. He protested that he didn't want a "Whitey," and furthermore, he'd pick his own. For awhile he seemed to like a timid, big-eyed girl named Ruth, then he tried different ones, Cora Lee Andrews and others. None seemed to get along with him. He told me he didn't know what their notes meant and he didn't understand their sentences.

Another boy came in a little later. He'd also recently lost his hearing. This was Clifton. He became friends with Leon since they could both speak and understood each other. If Brandy didn't understand the other deaf kids, he never let on, but would grin and bumble about and act just as happy. He was placed in the same class as Hill. After noticing how prim and proper she was, he got a kick out of shocking her. He asked her to be his girlfriend. She looked as proper as she could and said she wouldn't have him. That seemed to encourage him. He wrote notes and slipped them to her and blew her kisses across the room when the teacher wasn't looking. He even started singing one of his songs outside so the blind girls could tell her about it.

> My mama done tol' me—son . . .
> A woman'll sweet-talk, and give ya the big eye,
> but when the sweet-talkin's done
> A woman's a two-face, a worrisome thing
> who'll leave ya t'sing the blues in the night

Hill was horrified.

We all had a good laugh over Hill and Brandy. The girls gave Jessie to Cliff. He was also short and loved to dress to a T. He wore suits and ties to class. Jessie told him she didn't want him with his short, preacher-looking self. He was quite smitten with Jessie and wouldn't give up. She at least kept all the candy and other treats he sent her.

There was another more serious romance on campus. I'd noticed one young deaf man with much interest because he bore a striking resemblance to Clark Gable. He was very tall, with dark brown wavy hair, sideburns, a small mustache, and green eyes. This was Claude Lyles. I stared every time I saw him. He was in charge of the older boys' activities and was the assistant instructor in woodworking. He and Thomasina had started school the same time, age six, and now they had both graduated and worked as student teachers. Thomasina assisted with the first-floor girls and taught beginners.

They were a perfect pair. She was tall for a girl, neat and gentle, always kind and smiling and trying to tell the children how Jesus wanted them to live when they misbehaved. The other two girls who had graduated and come back to work for the school, Lillie Bell and Emma, had married and quit work, but Thomasina was trying to buy her mother a home. Her dad had left them and gone to live in Washington, D.C. Her sisters had gone to live there also. Claude wanted Thomasina to marry him, but she wanted to wait until she'd finished paying for her mother's house. So there they were, two lovely people, in love, but couldn't marry. It was so romantic, like a story.

I'd think of some of the sweet love songs I used to hear on the phonograph at home, one in particular: "Goodnight sweetheart, till we meet tomorrow, / Goodnight sweetheart, sleep will banish sorrow." I'd hear that song and others, close my eyes, and be back home sitting by the heater seeing Bennie over in the corner keeping the phonograph going and playing record after record. My throat would fill up and so would my eyes.

Come February, just about everybody had the flu, and wasn't able to eat Valentine candy. I received a box from William as well as some from home. The teachers also bought small candy hearts with words on them and tied a handful up in white or red paper for each of their students.

For special occasions, three teachers planned the songs and programs: Miss Mann (the voice teacher), Mrs. Bass (the piano teacher), and Mrs. Edmondson, who interpreted for the deaf girls. They had picked me to replace Gertrude in leading the signs. Gertrude could hear well enough to be able to sign each word as it was sung by the blind chorus. I had to rely entirely on speech-reading and the fact I knew most of the spirituals. I still heard them in my head.

We started practicing for Easter. As long as it was just practice I did fine, never missing a word. However, the first few times I had to stand up in chapel and face the entire student body as well as staff and visitors, I got stage fright and glued my eyes to Thelma Freeman's lips, afraid to even blink for fear of missing a word and falling behind in the signs. We usually signed such old favorites as "Swing Low, Sweet Chariot," "Steal Away," and "It's Me, O Lord." My favorite was "Ev'ry Time I Feel the Spirit." I never missed on that. So now we started on the Easter songs—"He Arose" and "Were You There?"

The other girls had to get used to me because I was so much shorter than Gert. Some said they should stand me on a box directly in front of them so they could see me. My group consisted of Madga, Buckwheat, Jessie, both Cora Lees, Louise, Minnie, and Flossie. Mr. Lineberry complimented me one Sunday evening after seeing us sign "Swing Low," which was his mother's favorite. Following that gesture, I grew more confident and it was much easier.

Toward the last of March, there was a sort of change upstairs. I couldn't say just what it was. Some of the senior girls across the hall acted differently. They didn't seem to play and kid around as much, and seemed to have more candy and snacks than they'd been having. Some became quite snappy if they noticed any of the juniors looking at them. They asked what we were looking at and to look the other way and quit gawking at them. Although Hazel wasn't a junior (she was about twenty at that time), she still slept in our room about three beds down from mine. I had a nice corner by a window and had flowers on the sill and pictures. Anyway, I was sort of surprised when she came up with that crack about not looking at her, so I informed her a cat could look at a king and I could look at her if I wanted to, for they were my eyes. Then I closed them so I couldn't see what she had to say.

Percy also slept in my room and one night as we were both washing up for bed she asked me if I had slept well the night before. I nodded yes.

"You never think you see anybody?"

"See who?" I asked.

"I don't know. I thought I saw somebody shaped like a man or boy last night."

"Oh, my goodness." Right away I thought of Snooks and turned cold.

"Maybe I'll sleep with you tonight," she said.

"OK, come on."

I'd be only too glad of some company since Snooks had found me way up here. After lights-out and Mrs. Holbrook was downstairs again, Percy crawled in my bed and we both slept peacefully through the night. Anytime after that if she got uneasy, she'd show up and we'd spend the night huddled in one small bed.

Then things got worse. Some girls would gather in a little bunch signing away like mad, then stop quickly if anyone got near them. I just figured they must be talking about me, so I thought, *Big deal, I'm used to that.* No one else mentioned anything strange so I went on about my business.

Every Sunday night, Mrs. Holbrook posted a paper on the upstairs hall door listing each girl's work duty for that week. Four had to go to the kitchen at 6:00 to help make biscuits for breakfast and get other things ready. Two had to wait tables for the teachers. Four had to sweep upstairs bedrooms and hall floors before time for devotion. A whole bunch, four to six, had to help clear tables and wash dishes. I had never been on the list for anything, and I wanted to be on the kitchen list so bad. I'd asked Mrs. Holbrook several times if I could but she hadn't put me on so far.

"That's for older girls," she told me.

"But I'm fourteen this year," I protested.

Of course Hazel didn't want me on the list for kitchen work.

"You can't cook, you sweep," she told me.

"You don't know what I can do," I snapped at her. "I cooked at home."

The more I saw of the girls going on kitchen duty with starched white aprons and little white caps, then coming in the dorm with all kinds of goodies from the teachers' tables and leftovers in the kitchen, the more I envied them. They passed out tasty snacks along with kitchen gossip. At least they shared with their friends; their non-friends were told to get on about their business and stop looking. Percy and Maybur always divided with me, so I fared well. I still pestered Mrs. Holbrook to put my name on the duty list, and I finally made it to wash dishes. It wasn't what I wanted, but at last I was in the kitchen and I liked running the dishwasher. One girl scraped plates, another filled trays, and I'd push them into the washer, slam the door, and turn on scalding-hot, sudsy water to wash, then push a lever for clear water, just as hot. When I'd finally open the other door and push the tray out, they'd be so hot, they dried in seconds. Other girls stacked them, piled them in carts and pushed them in the dining room and set all the tables for the next meal. All of this was accomplished within an hour.

I also had to report to the dining hall at 1:30 with the rest of the eighth-grade girls to sweep the floor. For us this was fun and a time to snack. The teachers' leftover food, along with other goodies, was stored in the refrigerator. We swept the floor to where we could finish it in a shake, peeping into the kitchen to make sure the staff, especially the cooks, were still on their afternoon break, then opening the doors carefully, we inspected the contents. There'd be deviled eggs, salad, Jell-O, pies, and hot dogs—the old-fashioned kind, little and red in long strings. Once, Louise was snitching a string of them when somebody saw Reverend Williams headed toward the kitchen. We signed to Louise and snatched up our brooms and started sweeping busily. Lou, having no handy place to hide her loot, stuffed them in the front of her dress. Being fat with a large bosom already, you couldn't tell anything else had been added. By the time Reverend Williams appeared at the kitchen door, all were working industriously. He eyed us suspiciously, nodded, and left.

March was passing into April, things were turning green, thoughts were turning homeward, but something still wasn't quite right about our campus. I went over to the blind girls' dorm for one of my Saturday visits and found the crowd I buddied with had gathered in one of the music rooms for a meeting. They pounced on me and started asking questions so fast I couldn't get what they were saying. I told them to cool down and come one at a time so I'd know what they were asking me.

"What do you think of this school?"

"Why can't we go uptown and shop?"

"What do you see going on around you?"

They said they were fed up with being treated like prisoners and wanted a new school system. They told of injustices by teachers and for me to tell the deaf girls and boys what they said, so we could all protest. One girl, Ruth, was from a well-to-do family right there in Raleigh, and her people visited her every Sunday. They knew newspaper reporters and said they would send them out to investigate. An investigation did occur after I finished school and Hill and Flossie wrote and told me about the changes that took place, including the firing of some of the staff.

This was my introduction to politics and it turned out to be quite a meeting. I was appointed chief reporter (or spy) for the deaf girls. I was to be the group's eyes and report every important thing I saw. They'd be our ears and report all they heard. I agreed, but wondered how my dorm-mates would respond. I hadn't long to wonder. When I mentioned it to some of them in a roundabout way, most were indifferent and said let the blind girls tend to their own business, best thing to do was whack the teachers and hearing people over the head if they bothered them. Margie advised me to leave it alone, or I'd be in trouble. Only Hill and Flossie were interested.

Once, we went to a program in town at the school for the White blind children. Afterwards, we were given a tour of their campus and the differences between their school and ours were unbeliev-able. Instead of long rooms with rows of beds, all with white spreads and only shades at the windows, they lived in family-type houses with only a few bedrooms to each building and two or three to a room. Each house had a nice homey living room, a dining room with white tablecloths, and china, silver, and glassware in-stead of the bare tabletops and metal plates and cups we were accustomed to. The bedrooms had pretty colored spreads and ruf-fled curtains. The auditorium was beautiful with a sloping floor, comfortable individual seats, and a stage with rich red velvet cur-tains and floodlights, plus a heated swimming pool and gym in another wing. Ours was a level floor with hard wooden benches and no stage or curtains.

Mr. Lineberry had meant to give us a good time by inviting

us to attend the play put on by some Meredith College students. We did enjoy that, but seeing such a difference in how the White children were treated and how we were treated at the Black state school left us depressed and angry. That's why Flossie and Hill and a very few more were willing to help the blind girls with their protest. Some of the girls couldn't get over seeing a heated indoor swimming pool while we didn't even have a bathtub in our bathrooms—only lavatories and showers and commodes. When we told this to the blind girls at the next meeting, they were mad! Thelma and Catherine, the leaders, promised they would get them all, and get them they did, but not right away.

Other things were afoot that I didn't know about at the time. One night, just before lights-out, Percy followed me to the bathroom again and after making sure the door was shut good, asked me if I ever saw anything at night.

"Like what?" I asked.

"Like a man," she answered.

"A man!"

I stared at her in horror, thoughts of Snooks again rising up before me. He'd found me again after all.

"A dead man?" I asked.

"A live man. Boy. Whatever, a *he*."

"But how, where, when, and who?"

"I don't know who. I saw him, or his outline, last night, standing in front of a window near Hazel's bed."

Percy's bed was against the inside wall, and she could see anything between her and the windows. My bed was in a corner under a window so I didn't have such a view. We both stood there frozen with fear, wondering who and how he'd gotten in. We thought of Gracie—she'd gotten out so it was quite possible someone could get in. We'd felt so secure in our rooms upstairs at night, knowing the heavy doors at each end were locked and the night watchman was making his rounds every so often. Now Percy had seen a man right in the room, only a few feet from her bed.

"You'll have to sleep with me tonight, Percy."

I wished I could close my eyes and open them to find myself at home where I could hide under Mama's apron knowing Papa and my brothers would surely fill anybody who dared break in on us full of buckshot.

"No, you sleep with me. Your bed is near the door," Percy told me.

We stood there and kept wondering who and why and how anyone could get in. Finally I asked if we shouldn't go spread the word so all the girls would be alert. But Percy said no, she wasn't going to bother with them, some of them might already know, and for us to just look out for ourselves. Remembering how everybody scoffed and said I made up things, keeping quiet made sense. As soon as Mrs. Holbrook had been up and turned the lights out, I moved to Percy's bed.

I don't know how long I'd been asleep when Percy jerked upright, grabbed my hand and signed, "Run!" And run we did, still holding hands to stay together. Instead of heading for the bathroom, Percy steered me to a hall closet where extra blankets and towels were kept. After scrambling in, we found the switch and turned the light on.

"What was it, what are we running from?" I asked.

"Somebody, I don't know who, was feeling my head."

"Maybe one of the girls was waking you to go to the bathroom with her."

"I don't know. The hands felt funny, not like a girl's."

I thought on this awhile, unable to even consider a male hand could actually have touched Percy in her bed, and in the nighttime too. So we huddled there among the blankets wondering what to do. Finally I suggested we go back in the room, turn on a light, and see if we saw anybody who wasn't supposed to be in there. She wasn't happy over the idea, but by this time we were both sleepy and longing for our beds. Turning out the light, we opened the door and peeped out but the hall was really black so we couldn't see anything. Feeling our way back to the door, I reached in and pushed the switch. The end of the room was flooded with light and flooded with Hazel. Her bed was midway down on the window side and still dim, but we could see her arms waving wildly, signing something. Thinking she may have seen somebody, I went closer to see what she wanted.

"Turn that light off right now," she was saying.

"What for? It's not your light."

"I'm going to tell Mrs. Holbrook you turned the lights back on after 9:00," she told me.

"I'll tell her I had to go to the bathroom. You're just mean and furthermore . . ."

But Percy had cut the lights off again. I found her in my bed after stumbling about and feeling my way back. The night passed without any further disturbances.

By now the weeks before going home could be counted on one hand and we started practicing for the closing program. After last year's disastrous show, they'd decided we'd have no more outdoor dramas. It would be just an indoor program, this time with piano recitals and singing by the blind students, signing and speeches by the deaf students. I was learning a poem that went, "I shot an arrow into the air. . . ." I thought I'd rather shoot one in Hazel's rear end.

Then one day Mrs. Whitaker called a meeting for all second-floor girls, both juniors and seniors. She came upstairs in her usual black skirt, white blouse, glasses hanging from her neck on a black ribbon, a little hair straggling from the knot on the back of her head. Smiling and greeting all of us, she told us to gather around and pay close attention to what she had to say. We all wondered what it was.

"Now all you girls have 'special days' each month, don't you?" she began.

No one answered, but she didn't seem to expect us to and went on.

"That means you're all getting to be young women, and young women marry and have children."

Some girls giggled, some poked each other and said, "What's she telling us this for?"

I was uneasy, wondering what this was leading to. She went on to say that perhaps some of our mothers didn't know how to talk to us and explain about life so she was telling us before we went home. Then she really got down to bare facts about what was expected of a wife, how babies were started, and how they were born. She finished by telling us to be good wives and that it was right for wives to be meek and obedient.

I'd already decided I wasn't going to be any kind of wife, meek or otherwise. I felt nasty and wanted to cry. I'd seen love scenes in the movies and thought them thrilling and romantic, but this other stuff Mrs. Whitaker was telling us about? Never! I didn't want any babies if that's the way they came about. In fact, I'd never even considered myself as a mother. She brought up about the birds and other animals and it being natural. I thought about Mama's hens running and squawking over the yard with the old rooster hot on their heels dragging his wings.

I looked up to see Hazel smirking at me and saying "William." I glared. Soon the meeting was over and I fled. I tried to forget the whole thing but it stuck in my mind. I felt my ideas on love and marriage had been ruined and it was all a bad business, but then I'd think of all the beautiful songs I used to listen to like "My Blue Heaven" and "Goodnight Sweetheart." Didn't they mean anything? I was confused.

Not long after this, we'd been having a peaceful period, Percy and I. We each slept alone again, so I was caught off guard when one night I woke up to find a hand on my head and another shaking me awake. I came up fighting using a stuffed giraffe to hit with. The hands turned loose and a second later the light near my bed came on. It was Cora Lee Andrews.

"Stop fighting. I'm telling you something," she signed to me, then turned out the light and came back, telling me to feel her hands in the dark.

She said for me to go out on the landing at the top of the stairs with her.

"The door is locked," I said.

"No, it's not."

"What's to go out there for?"

"Somebody wants to see you."

I think I knew what was coming next even as I asked who.

"William," I was told.

"No, no. I'm not going out there."

"Oh, come on."

She pulled at me. I went under the covers, holding them tightly over my head. She gave up and left. No further disturbance, but I was still fearful the rest of the night. When I told Percy the next morning, she wasn't surprised. She'd found out that a number of the senior girls in the other room were jamming the hall doors both up and down stairs so they weren't really locked. Their boyfriends had been meeting them out by the stairs for a good while. She said the boys would bring the girls candy and treats and they'd all party, but for me not to let them know she'd told me that, for they'd kill her.

I was shocked and decided to keep my mouth shut and tend to my business but they'd have to leave me alone. I told Cora Lee and she said she'd do that, but why didn't I come out and be with the rest of them, that they had a good time eating, playing, and talking. She also said that Rena was out there and that she liked William and would take him if I didn't go to talk with him.

"She can have William. If Mrs. Holbrook or the teachers come up and see you all you'll be in trouble," I said.

But she assured me they had a foolproof way of doing it and wouldn't get caught.

One morning after that, Hazel told me at breakfast that William said for me to send back his watch that he'd let me keep. I said he could have it back anytime.

"Give it to me and I'll give it to him," she said.

"No, I'll give it to him or send it by somebody else."

I didn't trust her a bit. I passed on, and seeing a girl I knew to be on kitchen duty, I took the watch off and asked her to give it to William for me. I figured he was angry because I had refused to meet him that night and wanted nothing more to do with me. I was a little sad too, because he seemed to be a really nice person and was cute in an odd way. However, I told myself I wasn't going to get in any trouble and get expelled. It would hurt my family, especially Mama. I thought of the lines from a song: "I would be true, for there are those who trust me, / I would be pure, for there are those who care."

When I returned to the bedroom Hazel was telling a bunch of girls how I had tried to get her to give William his watch because I was afraid of him, but that she wouldn't do it. She said I was too fast and had no business getting involved with him, and on and on. My blood started boiling. I'd had enough of Hazel and I marched straight up to her.

"You lie!" I screamed in both speech and sign. "Why do you have to lie? You ought to be ashamed."

"It's true, it's true. Ask Flora. She was right behind me."

When asked, Flora shrugged and said she'd seen nothing. Hazel kept swearing she was telling the truth. Snatching up a Bible from a nearby table, I dared her to put her right hand on it and say she was telling the truth.

Snatching it from my hands, she held it up and said, "Now see, I'm telling the truth."

I could stand it no longer. To actually see someone who I *knew* was lying swear to it on the Holy Bible was more than I could take. I slapped her full across the face and she came after me. I didn't even feel her hitting me. Recalling a hold Frank had taught me, I grabbed her arm, carried it around her head and forced her up against a steam radiator, where I proceeded in trying to choke her tongue out.

Hands were pulling at me. When the girls finally got me off her, she was through fighting. I'd left red marks and scratches on her face and neck and her hair stood on end. Ignoring us, she headed for the bathroom. Jessie was crying while Margie was going over me to see if I was hurt but found nothing. I asked Jessie why was she crying and Flossie was about to. They said I was so little and Hazel was a grown twenty-year-old and they thought she'd hurt me.

"Oh, shoot," I told them. "My brothers taught me to fight long ago and I'll take her on again if she comes back and tells lies on me anymore."

Margie told us to all get on about our business now and let Hazel go. She said everybody knew what a troublemaker she was and for me to stop fighting. She was surprised at me, thought I was a sweet little girl, and that my mama wouldn't like it.

"My mama didn't teach us to be cowards. She'd understand."

But I wasn't really sure on that score since I'd slapped Hazel first. I did think Mama would approve of me defending what I believed in: the Bible.

Anyway, Hazel left me alone, at least to my face. Plenty was said behind my back, I knew. One day her boyfriend, Raymond, passed me in the kitchen and told me I wore pretty nightgowns.

"You know nothing about my nightgowns. And don't talk to me. Talk to Hazel about her gowns," I snapped.

He just laughed and said something about "already."

I walked on, paying him no more mind. Spring departures were almost here. We'd had our Easter program and made dresses and other things for exhibits for school closing. My mind was on better things than Raymond. He always reminded me of a hairy ape.

The smell of honeysuckle and other spring flowers was in the air. I loved walking across campus going from one building to another. Sometimes I'd pass William, and he'd smile and wave and ask where I was going. He had such a kind smile and those odd blue eyes. I felt friendlier toward him now and wished we could be like "outside" girls and boys who could talk and laugh with each other and just have fun, like I did at home with my brothers and their friends.

Here it was a crime just to speak to the opposite sex if a teacher or houseparent saw you. The older girls often talked of other girls and boys who'd been there before me and been expelled for being caught talking or hugging each other in isolated places. Some used to meet in the forest behind our dorm, I was told. For me, that was really strange. I was more used to male companions than female and saw nothing wrong with it. It was this marriage talk from Hazel and Mrs. Whitaker that turned me off.

Things were still going on peacefully until again I was awakened late one night, this time by a strange but rather pleasant odor. It wasn't perfume or flowers, more like the fresh, clean smell of soap. I also sensed a presence. When I looked up, there between me and the nearby window was a shadow. I wasted no time leaping out the other side of the bed. I headed for Percy, stopping only long enough to grab her hand and pull for her to come on. We went straight to the linen closet. After closing the door, I told Percy what had happened. Who it was I didn't know and didn't wait to find out. I was tired of running so we spent the better part of the night huddled among the blankets and towels, only going back in the bedroom when it was light enough to see what was around us.

I had about decided to ask Mrs. Holbrook if I could transfer my bed to the far end of the room but Cora Lee got me alone and asked me why I had run.

"Was that you?" I asked.

"Yes, me and William."

I gaped at her.

"You brought him to my bed?"

"Yes, he wanted to give you back his watch and some candy. He didn't say anything to Hazel about you. He said he was sorry and wouldn't be back anymore."

Cora Lee also told me none of the boys would be back because the night watchman saw one of them and almost caught him, but didn't know who it was. I was glad we would soon be leaving for home.

This year, after the program in chapel, we had a social of sorts. We could mingle under the watchful eyes of teachers and other staff, nibble cookies, and drink punch. I did get to talk with William. He came and stood by me saying he was sorry about everything and about scaring me and for me not to be mad with him.

"I'll be leaving early in the morning, before your bus, because I live farther away in Concord," he told me.

We talked of home and what we did during summer vacation.

He was a city boy. The housemothers were beginning to round up their charges, so William told me he'd write me and to be sure and answer. There was nothing else to say so we just stood there looking at each other until he saw Mrs. Holbrook headed my way.

Then he said, "Good-bye, Herring."

I said bye and that maybe I'd see him again before his bus left. I did see him next morning at a distance, while all were gathered in front of the administration building waiting for the buses to come. He waved and that's the last I saw of William. He never came back to school.

14

More Changes and a Difficult Decision

THIS summer at home started out like the rest, but now Frank was married. My new sister's name was Lattice and she came from Cross Road. I'd seen her a couple of times but only knew her as Mr. Jim Marshburn's daughter. It was fun having another sister in the house, but I often mistook her for Eunice. They were both slim and straight, taller than I, and wore their hair the same length and style. Sam was taller and Willie was a senior in high school, driving the one bus that now came out as far as Iron Mine. All ages rode it from beginners on up and it was packed.

Eunice was working as a cashier in Little Harlem, a new entertainment spot on Back Street. Queen was glad as ever to see me home again and stuck to my heels like always. We had another little dog named Bobby—a hunting dog but small and very lovable. Some days when it was too hot to work and Papa loaded us and his fishing poles in the truck for a trip to the creek, Bobby went too. He loved to jump in the water and paddle about.

It had taken me a little while to get adjusted to being home this time. All that "facts of life" talk from Mrs. Whitaker had made me feel I was different—that somehow in knowing such things I was soiled. I now felt a lot older. When Mama brought up the same subject one day, I begged her not to talk about it and told her I already knew.

"Who told you?" She asked.

"A teacher."

She seemed doubtful.

"Well, if you need to know anything else come and ask me."

"Yes ma'am."

I fled, having no plans to ask anything, at least not anytime soon.

When I went to town or around the neighborhood, I saw boys looking at me who'd paid me no mind before. I'd cross my arms over my chest and frown them down. When Eunice suggested again I wear long stockings to church, I rebelled. Mama said I was old enough now and they'd look nice.

"No, ma'am. I don't want to wear any old stockings anywhere," I told her.

It didn't matter to me that all the other little girls were wearing them and heels too. I didn't know why, but I did know I had no intention of wearing long stockings or make-up.

However, I was soon comfortable with my family and other friends. I felt especially close to Thelma, Gladys, Berthena Hayes, and a new girl, Lena Mae Spencer. Frank had a blue convertible and on weekends and sometimes weeknights, he rode Eunice, Lattice, Willie, and me around to different nightspots. As a result, I became interested in some of the popular tunes of the summer of '39. Among my favorites were "I Dream of You (More Than You Dream I Do)," "Song of India," "Small Fry," "Hold Tight," "Wings O'er the Navy," and "Pistol Packin' Mama." I would learn the words from hit song magazines and catch the beat from the jukeboxes or the records we played at home. Music always made me foolish and I'd dream.

The war had started in Europe and they were building Camp Davis not far off. Iron Mine, however, paid it no mind except when there was news of some local boy being drafted. Life was becoming exciting. I was allowed to spend Saturday in Little Harlem with Eunice. I had a comfortable chair behind the counter and all the Cokes, ice cream, gum, or candy I wanted. I'd help Eunice wash beer mugs and wipe the counter while Dave Wells guarded us. He sat up front, and if the crowd started getting noisy and out of hand, he'd yell them down. When they refused to obey, he waddled out of the shop and over to Front Street to reappear with a cop. If the cop couldn't control the person, he'd lock them up in the nearby jail. When word spread that so and so was locked up, everybody had to run and peep through the window so they could see how the person looked behind bars. If I tired of Little Harlem, Eunice or Dave would give me change and I'd head for Front Street and the five-and-ten. A lot could be bought for a dollar then—headbands, hair ribbons, talcum powder, nail polish, funny books—all about ten to twenty-five cents each.

A cute boy that I liked to look at worked in one of the stores. He noticed me too. That summer I learned romantic songs and thought of someone to fit them to and admired any likely prospect from a distance. Yet if they got near me and spoke, I froze. I didn't know what to say to them and they didn't know how to talk to me, so there it ended.

One or two turned out differently. Joseph didn't let deafness stand in his way. He was tall and very cute. Seeing me in a crowd, he'd push his way through and tell me hi, kid around, and treat me to a soda or an ice cream or something. We became good friends and it's lasted through the years.

Another was Jack Bennett. He was quiet and studious. He worked across the street from Little Harlem and during breaks he'd come over, sit beside me, and like Joseph, learned to talk to me so I could understand. We discussed books and other happenings. Sometimes, he'd walk on Front Street with me and window-shop. He also became a good friend. When he finished high school and entered Shaw University in Raleigh, he'd come out to our school to see me. We remained friends until he moved north to New York.

Through the week, it was the usual farmwork, only I had Lattice to help me cook and did we have a time! She never bothered to learn sign or fingerspelling. She said she didn't need to because we could talk anyway, and what I couldn't understand, she wrote. I learned all about her family: her mother and dad (Miss Leatha and Mr. Jim), two brothers (Carl Henry and Lenton), a grandmother (Miss Tobe), and her Aunt Wilma. I brought her up-to-date on the Herring family, past and present. We told each other of all the neighborhood happenings, and of course, talked about my school days in Raleigh.

Oftentimes, we got so carried away we forgot to watch the clock and before you knew it, our hungry people would be coming in for dinner. We'd scramble around trying to do an hour's work in fifteen or twenty minutes. They knew we'd been gossiping but no one said much, maybe because Lattice was still a bride. Sam had joined the field workers, now that I had someone else at home with me. Lattice and I both loved sweets and tried to have something good for dessert every day. The busy fun- and work-filled days of summer seemed to fly by.

I was having a different kind of fun this year of '39. I'd always been happy to be home and roam the fields and woods, play with Sam and Willie, read, and follow Mama and Eunice. Now, for the first time, I was going where the other girls and boys went, seeing them dance and horse around with each other. I knew all the dances and lots of guys who didn't know me came up with their hand out for me to dance, but I'd shake my head. I'd only go out on the floor with someone who knew me. For one thing, I was afraid I'd lose step with them if I missed a beat. For another, I didn't want them trying to talk in my unhearing ears or get close to me. Yet, I enjoyed just being there and catching what I could of the jukebox music. The next day, I'd go through all the steps and sing my version of the songs to Sam or to Queen and the other dogs. They listened. I never knew whether my baby brother just pitied me or had no ear for music. The dogs and cats seemed to like any sound coming from my mouth. On the Fourth of July we didn't have to work, so Eunice and I went down to Back Street. The building that Willie Smith's barbershop had been in was now a cafe. Eunice and I stopped in for her to chat with friends. I noticed a stout, pleasant-looking waitress busily waiting on people. She wore a uniform similar to that worn by waitresses at school and it reminded me of Raleigh. Leaving there, we went next door to Bro and James Pearsall's shoe repair shop. They had been Eunice's schoolmates, or at least James had. They kept a record player in there and the latest records. Eunice loved music too, and liked to listen to the music and talk.

Someone came to the door and said something. Everybody looked startled and Eunice told me to come on. We hurried to the cafe that we'd left just a short time before and there lay the waitress on a bench. She lay on her back, eyes closed, very still.

"What's wrong with her, is she sick?" I asked Eunice.

"No, she's dead."

Dead! I couldn't believe it. I'd just seen her carrying trays of food to tables, but there she lay, hands still, never to wait on anyone again. All the joy went out of the day for me. I wanted to cry and I wanted to go home where Mama was so she could talk to me about Jesus or just rub my head and I'd feel better. It was near night before my sister was ready to head for home and a long time before sleep came to me. I kept thinking of the waitress' hands: They were so still where before they'd been busy.

Another tragedy that happened this summer was to Mrs. Mary Lou's son, Stephen Allen, age fourteen. They were coming from Wallace one Saturday night on Mr. Pat Murphy's or Mr. McKinley's truck, when they stopped at a store at the fork of the road this side of Rockfish on Highway 41. Stephen Allen went in the store for an ice cream cone. He was returning to the truck, enjoying the ice cream, when a speeding car hit him, knocking him into the air, and kept on its way. They said he was dead with a broken neck when he hit the ground. Ice cream lay melting, never to be licked and savored by him again.

Frank took Lattice and me to the funeral that Sunday evening. Because it was summer, Stephen Allen had to be buried as soon as possible. Someone had made a wooden coffin covered in black and Stephen Allen was dressed in a black suit and white shirt. White cotton was stuffed in his nose and even as we looked at him, the cotton colored with fresh, bright red blood. It was sad and frightening, and we left. His blood seemed to still be flowing, so I don't know if he was in a coma or really dead.

Well, life isn't all sadness; we had fun times too. Queen and I still played and went for walks early on Sunday mornings while the family slept late. It was again tobacco-curing time, so Lattice and I cooked for the family and field hands. Lenton was somewhere near my age and often came over to visit Lattice for a few days. He was a lively person and liked to play with Sam and me. We would fit ourselves into old tires and roll about the yard, or play marbles and other games.

Lenton would just as happily go off with Frank in his convertible with the top down and they'd have a ball. One night, they were supposed to spend the night at the tobacco barn by the old house. They used a brick furnace and hardwood logs to cure tobacco then, and someone had to watch the fire closely until it was through curing. Lattice, Sam, and I decided to stay with them. Frank and Lenton put us off at the barn and took off. It was quite a while before they returned with the car roaring around the curve on two wheels. When it stopped, Lenton hopped out dancing and shaking his finger so I knew they had the music going.

"Where've you all been?" Lattice and I asked.

Frank just grinned foolishly and said "Off."

Lenton said they'd been to a store to get kerosene oil for Cousin Helen Boney. Lattice started giving Frank a lecture that he didn't want to hear. The car cranked up again and took off before Lenton could finish climbing back inside. When it returned, we got them out and bedded down outside the barn, but near the furnace. I found a wide board, laid it in another corner near the furnace and lay there watching the stars and the logs burning in the fire until I finally fell asleep, rolled up snug in a quilt to ward off the mosquitoes and the night chill.

During this summer Lena Mae and I had become great friends. She was older and I felt flattered that she would notice me. She was always happy and light-hearted. She'd say, "Hello, Mary." Then a little later, "Where's Willie?" It didn't take me long to figure out that she liked my brother.

My deafness never bothered Lena Mae. I could read her lips easily and if I couldn't, she'd just say, "Oh, that's alright, come on Mary." She knew all the dances. The guys were always calling to her, snatching things out of her hands to get her attention. She'd laugh at them. If she walked the street with me in town, she was always very protective toward me, never letting any fast boys or drunks near, looking out for cars and anything else. She had warm brown eyes and was friendly, yet the other Iron Mine girls seemed to keep their distance and avoid her. My own family didn't forbid me to be friends and treated her nice when she'd come to my house, but they didn't encourage me to be friends either. I wondered why. No matter, I remained friends with her for the rest of her days.

Although I had become a part of the school in Raleigh, had formed friendships, and felt a close bond to most of the people I'd come in contact with, I still dreaded the arrival of the letter. It always had the ticket that would put all those miles between me and the people I loved best, not to mention Queen and all of home. It seemed to be late this year and I thought, suppose they forgot about me? I wouldn't have to leave but could be home all winter and sit by the heater at night, eating roasted peanuts and smelling coffee, hot biscuits and sausage, salt pork, or ham frying early in the morning.

I was far from forgotten though. Mama and some others were grading tobacco one day while I washed dishes and tidied the kitchen. All at once Mama rushed in, waving a letter at me, all upset.

"What is it, Mama?" I asked.

"Here, read this and then explain."

She handed me the letter. Looking at the envelope, I saw it was from Raleigh, but saw no ticket or tags. Puzzled, I unfolded the letter and started reading. Shocked, I had to read it twice.

Mr. Lineberry was informing my parents that there'd been some serious violations of school rules in my dormitory the previous year. They were trying to get to the bottom of it and find out who was involved. My name had been given, so my parents were to question me and let him know what I said. If I was one of the guilty ones, I was expelled. If not, and if I'd give the names of the other girls, he'd send my ticket and tags to return to school.

I looked up. Mama was about to cry.

"Mama," I said. "I have not done anything."

"Then how did your name get in it?"

"I don't know."

"Well, who was it breaking rules and what did they do?"

Again, "I don't know."

My thinking machinery seemed to have quit working. Mama meant to get to the truth. She told me to sit down and tell her just what this was all about. She was convinced I knew something. I told her how Percy and I had left our beds to hide and had seen shapes and felt hands touch us.

"Why didn't you go downstairs and tell Mrs. Holbrook?"

"We were afraid to."

"You can tell who all it was now."

"No, I can't tell."

"Why can't you?"

"I didn't see them for one thing and for another, I don't want any of my friends expelled."

"*You're* going to be expelled then."

"That's alright. I don't want to go back to school anyway."

I started crying. I'd tried to stay out of all that had happened, yet someone had put me right smack in the middle of it, and now I was being suspected of everything the others had done. The only person I could think of who'd involve me was Hazel. No one had seen me wherever the girls met their boyfriends and I hadn't seen them. The more I thought of how unfair it was, the madder I got. I quit crying and told Mama all about how Percy and I had run and hid in the closet all night and that the ones involved were talked about but that I'd never seen them, so I had no firsthand proof.

Cora Lee was the only one I knew of, and I wasn't going to tell on her. I thought of how those children felt a kinship for each other because of their deafness. They had a distrust of hearing people, even family. Some even looked forward to school opening so they could be with people who understood them when they talked and didn't giggle and make fun. If they were expelled, who would they have to enjoy life with? The only girls I was fairly sure weren't in it were Percy, Margie, Hill, and Flossie.

Mama dropped the subject for then but it still bothered her; she wanted so badly for me to have an education. Papa said I didn't have to go back if I didn't want to, and I felt grateful to him for taking my side for once. However, I wasn't sure whether he felt sorry for me having to go off from home every year or if he just didn't care whether I learned anything else or not. I could read, write, and count. Frank was also disappointed in me; I don't know how the rest felt. Sometimes I'd see different ones looking at me like they wondered. I tried to put it all out of my mind and just be happy I was home and could do all the things I once had.

I saw the leaves turn color and took Queen and the other dogs out to the pond. It was beautiful, calm, and peaceful, with leaves floating on the water. I could sit up as long as I wanted at night, get up when I wanted, and eat good, home-cooked food. For awhile, I was happy, but then I'd see Mama looking at me and see the sadness. Also, Sam, Willie, and all my friends were in school and had no time to play. I still saw friends at church, but days were short and the weather was cold, so no one went out riding much like in summer. Most of my school clothes were still packed in my trunk. I wore jeans and everyday clothes for the work to be done. Potatoes had to be dug, cotton had to be picked, and cane had to be stripped and made into syrup. I helped with whatever I was told to do.

I found myself thinking more and more of Raleigh, wondering what the kids were doing, if all the leaves had fallen in the woods behind campus, how the fair had been. This was the first time I'd missed the fair in five years. For the first time I really thought about my future, what would become of me if I didn't have Mama and Papa. If I didn't finish school, there'd be no good job for me, only field work. My friends were all still in school. Berthena was planning to enter nurse's training at St. Augustine in Raleigh next fall. Eunice was pretty and lots of boys wanted to marry her. I didn't want to be a wife but I wanted a family, someone to care about me as my parents had done. My brothers would all soon be married; Bennie and Frank already had. I couldn't imagine them wanting me to stay with them. I knew Mama and Queen loved me. I hoped the rest of them at least cared a little, but I'd always been a crying pest; nobody wanted that.

When I went anywhere, I felt everybody looked askance and wondered about me. They did ask if I'd finished school. Mama explained that I'd be a little late going back this year. I'd tell myself I was never going back. I'd build a house out in the woods and fill it with dogs and cats; they'd love me and I'd grow a garden to feed us and we'd be happy.

One of my cats, Nanny, had two cute kittens. I named them Mary Christopher and Willie Columbus for Columbus Day, because they were born in October. They were so cute and fat, chasing dry leaves over the yard. I came home from somewhere with Papa and Eunice one night and couldn't find Nanny any place. Her babies were hungry and I inquired if anyone had seen her. Subud looked at me with his funny smile, not saying anything, so I knew he had seen her. I was ready to pounce on him with questions but Willie stopped me.

"Yes, I've seen her," Willie told me.

"Where?"

"In the field across the ditch."

"What was she doing in there?" I demanded.

"Lying down dead," he informed me.

"No!" I shrieked.

"Well, go see."

I did just that. Finding a flashlight, I stumbled down the road and into the field looking everywhere, but no Nanny. Even the next morning when I returned I found no sign of a cat anywhere in the field.

The boys assured me she had nine lives and had come back to one of them and gone elsewhere to live. I figured that was better than being dead so I tried to be a mother to her kittens. Christopher thrived and grew fat on the milk and scraps I fed them daily, but Columbus must have missed his mother. He grew quiet and wouldn't eat much. I forced the milk in but couldn't make him chew. He developed a cough so I put a tar plaster on his chest. I also crocheted both of them ruffled white collars and put them on their necks.

One day, Frank was working on his car in the yard while the kittens played nearby. Finally he finished, slammed down the hood, got in, and started the motor. I noticed he got out again after backing out of the yard, looked under the hood again, then took off. I messed around awhile longer, then started inside.

Columbus was no longer playing but sitting on the edge of the porch, looking lonely. I wondered where Christopher was and called. She didn't come. Thinking I'd walk down the road a piece, I saw the edge of something crocheted in a patch of dried weeds. Looking closer, I let out a blood-curdling scream. It was Christopher, dead. She had hidden under the hood of Frank's car, and when he started the motor, she had been caught up in it. The little ruffled collar I'd made for her was fluttering in the breeze like the sheet pulled over Pridgen when I had seen her dead. I kept on screaming and my family came running. Mama and Eunice from inside, Subud showed up from some place. Frank was just driving up again.

"What's the matter?" everybody was asking me.

"My kitty's dead."

They all stood there and looked at me, and then looked at each other. Then Mama told me to stop crying, I still had Columbus. But I wanted Christopher too; she was cuter and more playful.

I guess they got tired of my noise. Papa had come in and heard my latest "cut-up" as they called it, so he soon got back in his truck and left. Frank and Subud followed. Mama, Eunice, and Lattice went back inside. I went in search of a casket for Christopher and found a white shoe box with the tissue paper still inside. Wrapping her carefully in the tissue paper, I placed her in the box. Then with a shovel and Queen, I set out for the spot on the ditch bank behind the house which served as a graveyard for my cats. After digging a hole, I looked at my kitty for a last time, laid the box in the hole, and filled it in. I missed Sam being there for this service. He would have to visit the grave when he came in from school.

Towards night, Frank and Subud returned separately; each had a kitten for me. When Papa returned after dark, he had a little, fat, yellow one under his coat that a White neighbor had given him. I named this one Dewey. So I'd lost one kitty and gained three, plus I still had Columbus.

Another thing I gained that year was a brand-new niece. Mable gave birth to her and Bennie's second daughter, Della Mae. The first had died at birth and I never saw her. Naturally, we all had to go see and admire the new addition. Eunice had already been there about a month. Della was a very cute baby and sweet. I was a proud aunt, and it was a joy to see how gentle and loving Bennie was with his little babe. Well, Eunice could come home now; it seemed like she'd been gone for years.

Nobody mentioned my being out of school, but the thought was always there. I was surprised to find I actually missed school, mostly the classes and the library, and yes, a few of the girls. I

My brother Bennie, with his wife Mable and their daughter Della.

thought of school and my future more and more. I guess this was the beginning of growing up. Again, I pondered the question of what would become of me if I lost my parents. I'd picture myself without them, going out to work the farm or work for other farmers. And who would I talk to? Sam spent more time with me than the rest, but he was unpredictable. Sometimes we were close and had fun; then we'd have an argument and he would tell me how bad I was. Eunice wasn't like me, so the only person I never doubted was Mama.

I'd try to picture if something happened to me first, and how it would be if I was found floating in the pond dead, or a car hit me like it did Stephen Allen. Would anybody besides Mama cry? I doubted they would, for I had been a pest before, when I could hear. But at least then I'd felt a part of the family. Now I felt I was being condemned and that I counted as nothing.

At that point, I considered giving in and returning to school. I was almost a senior and once through school, I could get a job doing some of the things I'd learned to do and become independent. That was the word—*independent*. I wouldn't have to ask my family for anything and could send money to Mama and Papa to help make life easier for them. They'd worked hard all their lives and I could see signs of growing older in them both. Papa's hair was graying fast and Mama had a few lines in her face. However, I kept my thoughts to myself and went my usual way, roaming the fields and woods, reading my mystery stories when I had nothing better to do. If my family didn't care that much for me, they just didn't, and I couldn't make them, so I'd enjoy what I could and not worry.

One afternoon Mama was sewing on her machine at the foot of her bed as I lay on the bed reading. I fell asleep and the next thing I knew, it was dark, and hands were touching me. Suddenly, I was back in Raleigh and felt those hands again. Screaming, I scrambled to the foot of the bed, jumped on top of the sewing machine, then to the floor, running for the only light I saw. Papa was sitting by the heater waiting for Mama to fix his supper. I jumped on his lap and hung on. Mama came out of the room behind me looking surprised. So did Papa.

"What the devil ails this girl?" he wanted to know.

Mama said she didn't know, she'd gone in there to wake me up so I could eat supper and that I'd come up screaming and ran from her.

"What's wrong with you?" she asked me.

By now I was crying.

"I thought I was in Raleigh and somebody was touching me in the dark," I told her.

She looked at Papa and said something. I think it was then that they really started believing my account of what had happened at school. Papa patted me until I hushed up. No more was said about it.

Then one day I received a letter from Hill and Flossie. They said they missed me and wanted to know when I was coming back to school. They gave me all the school news and I read the letter over and over. I went out to the pond and thought hard. I didn't want to make a mistake and regret my decision. Returning to the house, I found Mama and, before I could change my mind, told her I was willing to go back to school if they'd let me in.

Her face lit up, she was so glad. Right away, she sat down and wrote Mr. Lineberry, telling him that I had nothing to do with that mess, how Percy and I had run. She also went on to tell him that it was a shame any of them had to be expelled. If they'd done wrong, he ought to punish them if needed, but not put them out for good. It was the only deaf school for Blacks in the state, and if they were expelled there was no other school they could go to and finish as hearing children could. How, then, could they ever learn anything else?

That letter bore fruit. In no time my ticket and tags arrived with a letter telling me what bus to be on. The students were allowed to go home for Christmas now if their parents came or sent for them. I was to be on the bus they were on, returning after the holidays.

That year Christmas was both happy and sad. It was a joy to be home again for the first time in years to help bake cakes, clean up, rake and burn leaves and trash, and shop for Christmas. But I knew I'd be leaving again for Raleigh.

Everyone seemed especially happy. When shopping, nearly all the salespeople smiled and said "Merry Christmas." The streets of Wallace, both Front Street and Back Street, were packed, but if you bumped into someone, Black or White, they'd just laugh and say "Merry Christmas." It was one of the happiest Christmases I was to see for some time. Sam and I found a little holly tree with bright red berries and put it up in our sitting room. Although we had no electricity for lights, our tree was beautiful nonetheless. Our spirits were high, and everything was fun, even cleaning and washing windows and moving furniture. I was on top of a wardrobe doing something and Sam moved the chair I used to climb on so I couldn't get down. We yelled and made so much noise that Mama came with a broom, said we reminded her of two little puppies.

By Christmas Eve, all the cakes and pies were baked, the house was clean and smelling of hidden fruit and Christmas goodies, the ham was baking in the oven, the yard and porch were swept clean, and the wood was stacked high. I sat by the heater, looking through the sparkling window at the woods behind the house with the sun setting clear and golden. I can still see it. I felt so full and happy that I wanted to cry and sing at the same time. It was Christmas, I was with my family and Queen once again, what more could a person want? I refused to even think of Raleigh.

Soon Christmas morning was upon us. Up before daybreak, we gathered, wished each other merry Christmas, opened gifts, and ate a big breakfast of scrambled eggs, sausage, liver pudding, hot biscuits, coffee, cake, and fruit. That night Eunice took me with her to the different nightspots: the Cabin, which belonged to Uncle Foy and his boys; the Savoy farther down the highway; and some more I didn't know the names of. Everywhere young people were doing the jitterbug, the Big Apple, and the Suzy Q.

Our spots knew no age rules in those days. The only drug was white lightning and if it was sold, it was with great secrecy down in the woods or out behind a building. No one saw the transaction, only the results, which were most often a fistfight or hot words. Occasionally, someone got shot or sliced up.

This Christmas night, however, everyone seemed happy. I was asked to dance often, but as usual, only accepted if it was someone I knew well. On the roads, children were out in force, tossing lighted firecrackers in front of oncoming cars and otherwise having a good time; no one appeared to mind the sudden explosions of lights and brilliant colors. After all, it was Christmas—a time to be happy.

I'd had my autumn at home for the first time in five years. An autumn I'd remember always. So now it was time for school again. I didn't have my usual packing to do this time since most of my clothes were still packed. I added Christmas goodies and gifts and was soon on my way. In leaving, I consoled myself with the thought that I'd only have to be gone for four or five months this time instead of the usual nine.

15

Accepted at Last

WHEN I boarded the bus, I saw several kids from school who'd been home for Christmas. They were surprised to see me and I could see them signing to each other.

"Herring's on the bus, going back to school."

Then they started asking me why was I late this year.

"Just because I'm late," I shrugged.

I wasn't in any mood to explain anything to them. Not being put off, they went on to inform me that several other students were also late returning to school this year. I soon would learn that that, to say the least, was an understatement.

Upon arriving at school after dark and going upstairs, what friends I had left fell upon me, hugging me and saying how glad they were to see me back. I hardly had time to set my bag down and remove my coat before I was swamped with news. It had been an even bigger scandal than I'd thought.

Half of my friends had been expelled, both girls and boys: my blue-eyed William, along with James Greene, Raymond, and a whole bunch more. Among the girls who had been expelled were both Cora Lees, Minnie, Rena, and Hazel. Rena had gotten pregnant and her parents raised sand with the school officials. They'd gone to Rena's home to meet with her parents and made Rena give them the names of the other students who were involved.

Not wanting to be the only one, she'd made a list and told all, naming about everybody on the second floor.

I held steadfast to my belief that Hazel had given my name. It turned out that the night she'd made such a to-do over the lights being on, Raymond had been under her bed and when I went closer to see what she wanted, that's when he saw my gown. I started boiling thinking of him lying there and seeing me in my nightclothes. I'd have kicked his teeth out if I'd known they were that close to my feet.

Lots more had been on the list, but after Mama wrote Mr. Lineberry that letter, he'd reconsidered and let them come back. Others could have returned but didn't want to. Percy was late too. Others that were late returning included Buckwheat, Jessie, Madga, Odessa, Beulah, Bonnie, Margie, Flossie, Hill, and Maybur. The boys who came back were Leon, Clifton, Brandon, Robert, Wilbert, and a few more.

Even some of the teachers and matrons got the ax. Miss Hayes, Miss Stewart, Miss Kearney, Mrs. Holbrook, Reverend Williams, and the night watchman, as well as others who just quit. They were blamed for not having caught onto what was happening. I was stunned.

"It's a whole new bunch of teachers and all are young," I was told, "but watch out for the home economics teacher, Miss Watford. She's a real warhorse."

They were truly convinced that she was able to see from the back of her head. The new matron was Mrs. Nelson.

I felt sad that those children had caused so much trouble while just trying to have a good time. I assured everyone that I hadn't given any names. I also told them that Mama hadn't wanted any of them expelled and that she had written Mr. Lineberry and told him that. They said I had a good mama and I saw that at last I had crossed the line and was truly accepted as one of them. They told me to get a bed in the senior room on the north side near them. Mrs. Nelson was new and didn't know where I'd slept before. I was more than glad to move. My old corner on the south side reminded me of too much. I got an empty bed right near Madga and Buckwheat, and I started another year of school.

This year Mrs. Edmondson was again my homeroom teacher. I was a junior and the only classes I had beside hers were home economics and arts and crafts. The old teachers who knew me seemed to look at me with suspicion, but they were nice to me, though I didn't really care. I soon met Miss Watford, the warhorse, only she wasn't one really. Her roommate, Miss Weaver, was the third-grade teacher. They'd also gone to college together. Miss Chisolm was the secretary, Miss Wright, the new nurse, and Miss Freeman taught arts and crafts. Mrs. Whitaker was still there.

We had a new principal, Mr. Mask. Unlike Reverend Williams who lived in Raleigh, Mr. Mask was from Hamlet, so he had to live on campus and his family visited him on the weekends. Mr. Mask was a huge man with a thick black mustache and shiny glasses. What I first noticed about him was his walk, like he had springs on the bottom of this feet, bearing straight down at one, like a train. The first time I saw him coming, I got out of his way when he passed. He gave me no sign that he had seen me, but when I had hopped out of his way, he stopped, looked directly at me and signed, "Who are you?"

Mrs. H. M. Edmondson, my last homeroom teacher.
We stayed with her for most of our major subjects.

"Mary Herring," I said out loud.

"Oh, you talk?"

I nodded.

He stood looking at me a little longer, then walked on.

"That was Mr. Mask," the girls told me.

I said, "Wow."

He was different from Reverend Williams for sure.

Mrs. Edmondson greeted me with a smile and "glad to see you back." I guess she was. She almost didn't have a class: only four seniors and five juniors. The rest had been expelled. Our first class was algebra, and I had a lot of catching up to do.

My next class was on the first floor for home economics, where I met Miss Watford. I'm not sure what I expected. She could have been a schoolgirl herself in looks. She was slim with short, neat hair; glasses; and a quick, direct manner. I saw she also had a sense of humor and I liked that. I told the other girls so.

"Don't let her fool you," they told me.

"You have to have everything just right or you get a big zero. And she can see you from the back of her head. Watch."

Buckwheat made like she was going to open the refrigerator door. Although Miss Watford's back was turned, she immediately told Buckwheat to shut that door.

"See?" they told me.

It didn't keep me from liking her and we hit it off.

Miss Weaver was a different type. She wore expensive clothes and seldom smiled. The girls admired her, but to me she seemed standoffish and cool, never bothering to really learn the signs. She mostly made up her own signs, and her motions were quick and jerky. We had to teach all of the new teachers how to sign.

I took to Miss Chisolm. She was very pretty and always dressed in the latest styles, reminding me of a campus queen. However, Miss Chisolm was warm and friendly and didn't act like a big shot.

There was also a young male teacher, Henry Mitchell. They all seemed to be friends.

Soon after I'd returned, I was called into the office and questioned again about what had happened the year before. Wasn't it ever going to end?

"Did you know what was going on?" I was asked.

"I didn't *know* because I didn't *see* anyone."

"Was there talk among the girls?"

"Yes."

"Why didn't you tell your housemother?"

I shrugged.

"Did you know their names?"

"No."

After a while they let up and gave me a lecture on what was expected of me regarding the rules and regulations. I'd already stopped listening and was imagining that I was home sitting by the pond or doing something I enjoyed doing. Finally I was dismissed. The other girls said they'd been through the same thing when they got back.

Our new infirmary had been completed and Nurse Wright had moved in. Miss Chisolm also had a room over there. It was so clean and new that I started hanging out there when I wasn't in my old place, the library. There were two long wards, one for boys, one for girls, on either side of the main lobby. The infirmary also had a treatment room, an examination room, an operating room, two sun porches, a shiny white kitchen, supply closets, and some smaller bedrooms plus baths. Oh, it was a place to be proud of, all white walls and shiny tile floors. I loved it and wished I could someday be a nurse, but who'd want a deaf nurse?

Mr. Lineberry had taken to visiting the classrooms and the dining room. Sometimes he'd help himself to a biscuit and walk around munching on it, testing our food. He also took to speaking to me and gave the cook orders to serve me rich whole milk at every meal instead of water. I guess I wasn't fat enough already. Miss Watford wasn't afraid to tackle either him or Mr. Mask for anything needed in her department. She made many improvements. We started baking fancy things for the main kitchen in our home economics classes—dried-peach pies, rolls, bread, cornmeal muffins, and doughnuts. They were good, too.

Miss Watford asked for and got permission to take a bunch of us to town to visit a bakery and see how bread was made. It smelled so good in there. We started in the basement and ended our tour in the display room on the street level, where each of us was presented with a large oatmeal raisin cookie, still warm from the oven. Back at school, our assignment for the next day was to write and describe each step for making bread and rolls. For me it was no problem but the other girls complained that they couldn't remember all they'd seen and didn't know the names of the various machines. I let them read my paper to help them remember. They didn't just read, but copied word for word, all except Margie. Miss Watford read them all, gave me a look, and said one word: "Herring." She gave us all *zero*. Well, we'd had a fun trip and a good cookie.

I enjoyed talking with Miss Watford. She was from a farm in eastern North Carolina. She had a large, close family, like mine: two younger sisters, a brother in the Navy, her mom and dad. I told her about my family. I also told her how we felt like prisoners, always watched and shut up, never allowed any freedom. She listened, and things changed; not a whole lot, but they did change. She started borrowing Mr. Mask's car and taking us—Madga, Buckwheat, Jessie, Maybur, Odessa, and myself—for rides into town. Sometimes Percy and Margie went, more often, just us five. We went to the airport and watched planes land and take off. Whites looked at Maybur and wanted to know what that White

My home economics teacher, friend, and mentor, Mrs. Lottie Watford.
This picture was taken on "Going Home Day."

girl was doing with them "niggers." Then Mr. Lineberry and Mr.
Mask started giving us short rides over to the White school where
he'd take us to a supply room with bolts of beautiful print cloth
and let us pick out a couple of pieces to make two or three dresses.
We always put Maybur to sit next to Mr. Lineberry because they
were the same color. We were given permission to walk to the
country store out on the highway in front of the school and buy
snacks if we'd ask first. Other kids could send by us.

One day we had a visitor named Amal Shah, a very handsome
man from India. He'd come to tour our school to see how it was
run so he could help start one in his country. Mr. Lineberry
brought him to our classroom, introduced him, and then asked—
guess who? ME—to escort him all over campus and explain everything to him. I stood up and my knees nearly failed me. I managed
to get started and showed him the third-floor classrooms, then
headed downstairs for my prized home economics classroom

where Miss Watford had a cooking class in session. Outside again, we went across the green to the shoe repair and furniture-making shops.

He could speak and write in English and asked my name. I told him. He said that in his country the rich were very rich, and the poor were very poor with barely enough rice to eat. He must have been one of the rich because his black suit was beautifully fitted, very smooth. He wore one of the whitest shirts I'd ever seen with a black tie. His hair was also jet black, shiny and smooth, his skin a rich brown. We talked and by the time the tour ended and I had him back in the office, we were like old friends. He thanked me and said I was a nice little girl and he'd always remember me. I sure remember him. I had moved up from the scared little girl I'd been over five years before.

All the girls who counted as big wheels had a girl from the junior side to "do" for them—such as scratch their hair and care for their clothes. The girls told me to pick one for myself, but I said I didn't need one. Madga and Jessie assigned one to me anyway: Mildred Ratcliff. Now Mildred was an oddball. She didn't care how she or her clothes looked. She seemed always to wear a sneer and called anybody and everybody a nasty cat, faculty and students alike. I found out she really was a good soul and that her mouth was just made that way. I only let her scratch my head, and I shared my treats with her. For that she was grateful and would scratch as long as I'd let her or until I'd fall asleep.

Along this time, Bonnie got in trouble again. As I've said, she was very strong and a great fighter. One morning she had a run-in with Miss Watford. It was a bad fight and I'm glad I wasn't there for I loved them both. Well Bonnie broke Miss Watford's glasses and she sent for Mr. Slade to help her get Bonnie to the office. He tried. Bonnie got a hold of an iron fire poker and whacked him with it. Mr. Mask was sent for and it took the three of them to get her under control. By that night she was headed for Asheville, expelled. They'd tried to get her to apologize and say she'd do better, but she had refused and talked pretty rough. She said she wanted to go home.

We girls cried when we heard. Then the whole upstairs got angry and showed it after lights out that night. The lights would be turned back on every time Mrs. Nelson came up and cut them off. Finally she turned them off from the switch box. They really went wild then, running up and down the halls screaming, breaking chairs, beating on boxes, the walls, anything to make a noise. Some rolled newspapers in tight rolls, lit them, and ran about whooping. Why they didn't set the place on fire, I don't know. Hill was in bed with her head covered and Margie told them to stop and go to bed, but they kept on. When they ran, I ran too. I don't know whether with them or from them. I was excited and scared. Not one teacher stuck her head out the door, nor did Mrs. Nelson come up again.

We finally wore ourselves out and went to bed. The next morning, Mr. Mask was over early wanting to know what had happened.

We asked *him* what had happened.

He said Mrs. Nelson said there was a big to-do and he wanted to know who it was.

We said the lights were off and we couldn't see in the dark or hear either.

No one was ever punished for that. If he'd expelled one, he'd have to expel all and there'd be no deaf girls, at least not upstairs.

Things went along uneventfully for awhile. I'd become best friends with Miss Watford, also Miss Chisolm and Nurse Wright. When Mr. Mask had to take a carload of deaf children to the clinic or anyplace in town, he'd ask me to ride with him and interpret for them. He called me "Bugger" most of the time. I was also included in all the activities of Madga's crowd. If they wanted to ride or some special privilege, I was the go-between.

One Sunday was especially pretty, though it was still winter. I asked Miss Chisolm if she'd like to go for a walk with us. She agreed, so quite a crowd of us set off for the woods. Once out there, we decided to see if we could hike to the airport, or wherever those planes landed behind our school. Seeing one headed down, we marked the spot and headed that way, but there was a stream or small creek in our way with a makeshift bridge of logs across it. Determined to reach our goal, we held hands and started crossing. We'd nearly all made it when Arwilma from the little girls' room lost her balance, tumbling headfirst into the water. Miss Chisolm was down on her knees in a flash, grabbing for her and almost falling in herself. She had a book she'd been reading, *The Grapes of Wrath*, that did fall.

Some of the larger girls got them back on the ground. Both Arwilma and Miss Chisolm were wet and they had to get back to campus and dry clothes. The dry ones could not go on without a teacher, but then someone noticed we were practically out of the woods and on the edge of a large cemetery. Across from the cemetery stretched the airport. Even as we crowded to the edge and watched, a large silver plane started taxiing for a takeoff. Since we'd seen the airport, we all went on back so the wet ones could dry out. We made it back in time for dinner and no one suffered any ill effects from our adventure.

Our group became known as "Our Gang." Madga was leader as I've said. Buckwheat, Odessa, Jessie, and I made up the rest. We really missed our friends and loved to sit around rehashing the old days. I found I missed William, and even Hazel. Those fights had added spice to our lives I guess.

I still hung out in the library and had started trying to type on those typewriters. Then I had an idea. If the blind girls couldn't see those keys and could learn to type, why couldn't the deaf girls, who could see, learn to do the same thing? I took my idea to Miss Watford. She agreed and said she'd speak to Mr. Mask about it. That's how the senior deaf girls had typing added to their list of things to do. Right away they knew it was me.

"Now, what did you do that for?" Jessie asked me.

"We learn enough now. Who wants to type? That's for the blind kids," Buckwheat put in.

Percy said my eyes would be crossed from reading and typing all the time. Surprisingly Madga stood up for me.

"It's okay. I think I'll like to type."

After that, it was okay for everybody.

I haven't said much about Flossie as she kept out of most of the goings on, but she was really the best friend I had in that school. She was always there for me. She knew my home and the people I knew. When I had spells of homesickness, I could talk it out with her. She kept watch over me if I came down with a cold or flu, fussing until I went to the infirmary, bringing special food from the kitchen. She was glad to be able to learn to type, and said maybe she could get a job someday and get away from her aunt who was so mean to her. "True friends are like diamonds, precious and rare." That was Flossie.

Frances, one of the girls who'd been expelled, lived in Raleigh. One Sunday, she got someone to drop her off at our dorm so she could spend the day with us. How glad we were to see her. We bunched around her getting the latest news. She'd seen someone who'd been to see Rena and said she'd had a baby with one blue eye and one brown eye. Her boyfriend who'd come to see her in the dorm was James Greene, and he had brown eyes. The only blue-eyed guy in the school was William so they said her baby must have belonged to both boys. I'd never heard of such a thing.

My dear friend Flossie Johnson.

Frances caught up on campus news, all about the new teachers and the principal, and went to vespers with us.

Back at the dorm we'd hardly settled down for more scuttle-butt when Mrs. Nelson appeared and said Mr. Mask was downstairs to take Frances home. I said someone was coming back to pick her up later.

"Mr. Mask said now."

We got the hint. All of us went downstairs with her to where Mr. Mask was waiting.

The girls told me to explain to him that Frances was only visiting us for a little while and wasn't planning to stay.

He said that Mr. Lineberry told him to take her home.

"Can we go?" I asked him.

I think he started to refuse, but then he said, "Come on. You can tell me where she stays. And say '*May* we go'. Come on, come on."

He was waving his arms. We scrambled in. Frances, Madga, Jessie, and Buckwheat squeezed in back. I pushed Percy in next to Mr. Mask. When she realized where she was, she reacted like she was sitting beside a snake and started pushing to get back out, but Maybur and I had closed her in.

"Stop wiggling," our principal told us as he took off.

Upon reaching town, he told me to ask Frances where she lived. I passed along the directions, and we soon reached the house she said she lived in. We all told her good-bye and that we'd enjoyed her visit.

Soon this school year was drawing to a close. I guess it seemed so short because I was late arriving and surprisingly, I was having fun. For the first time I seemed to be wholly accepted by the upper girls, and at last we had a little freedom and didn't feel so much like prisoners.

We could, however, see the grim, gray walls of the North Carolina State Prison in the distance on a clear day. Some of the older girls had been there for a visit. One of our own, named Raymond, was locked up in there. I didn't know him because he was in school before my time. Margie and others knew him and talked of him often, how handsome and nice he was. He had graduated or dropped out before I became a student, and he worked in the area doing odd jobs.

One night a White couple he'd worked for heard a noise and got up to investigate. They found an open window and a cap on the ground beneath. The cap was Raymond's and had his name in it. With this evidence they turned him in. At the trial he was found guilty of first-degree burglary and sentenced to the gas chamber. He couldn't talk on the witness stand, but later told some of the deaf girls that it wasn't him in the house that night, that he had lost his cap someplace. No matter, he was sentenced to die.

His mother came to our school one Sunday after visiting him. She looked very old and frail, needing assistance to walk. She said she was doing all she could to get him out and had made an appointment to see the governor. We learned later that she did get to see the governor and had pleaded for her boy's life, telling him how sick it was making her. He took pity on her, and Raymond's death sentence was commuted to life in prison by then-governor, Clyde Hoey. The girls who went to see him came back shocked, saying how he looked like a sick old man, all bent over. They wished they hadn't gone because it depressed them.

The teachers took turns having Sunday school for the students. One Sunday we had a surprise when we entered the junior/senior Sunday school room and saw Miss Weaver writing the lesson outline on the board. We'd never seen her sign that much, so we wondered how she was going to explain the lesson. We hadn't long to wonder. She looked at us, then pointed to the seats.

"Sit down," her looks said.

We sat and stared. What next?

"You," she pointed at one girl. "Pray."

We all signed the Lord's Prayer.

Then with odd jerky little signs she got the lesson across. No one played or talked to each other. All eyes and full attention were on Miss Weaver, trying to figure out what she was saying and what would she say next. It was the most orderly Sunday school class I'd attended. Afterwards when I told Miss Watford about it, she really laughed and asked us how we'd understood her.

We knew Miss Weaver had a boyfriend who brought her back after weekends at home, but had never seen him close up. He started coming more often now, and they'd walk about holding hands, a very nice-looking couple. This turned out to be Lem Graves, a well-known newspaper correspondent. We girls thought that so romantic and thrilling and watched them every chance we got. For ourselves, if anyone had any romantic notions, they were very quiet about it, at least for awhile.

With the coming of spring, young hearts began stirring again, so we looked at what was left of the boys and decided who would go with whom. Madga picked a tall, nice-looking new boy who could talk and hear some: Elbert Wilson. She changed his name to Don, saying she liked that name better. We put Jessie with Clifton, although she still protested that she didn't want him because he was too short and looked like a preacher. Percy got Horace Evans, and Brandy and Leon both started writing me notes. Leon was more interesting, but Brandy was more fun, so I let things stand. It was near time to go home anyway.

At Easter, we'd been practicing songs for a program we were to do in Hamlet at Mr. Mask's church. Mama and Eunice had really done me proud this year. They had sent me a beautiful pale green silk dress, a beige topper (short coat), beige shoes, and even a cute little hat with a flower. We were to leave soon after breakfast, so we hurried to get dressed.

I'd just finished putting on my hat when someone came running through the room signing, "It's snowing! It's snowing!"

I thought it was a joke but looked out anyway. It really was snowing! And in *April!* We were stunned. Soon it was falling heavy and the ground was white, and Mrs. Nelson came up to say the trip was cancelled. By the time night came, the power was out, and we had to use candles. Each of us was given a long white candle. My gang and I put ours together and sat around a warm radiator eating snacks and swapping stories and gossip.

So we didn't get to sign the Easter songs we practiced for so long. By now, I was really into signing them and enjoyed it, fitting the signs to the words, trying to make the motions flow in rhythm with the tune and convey the rise and fall of notes. Two of my favorites for signing were "Ev'ry Time I Feel the Spirit" and "Let Us Break Bread Together." After Easter was past, it seemed no time at all before we were home for another summer's vacation.

THE summer of 1940 was a good summer like the rest. Just being home was happiness. It seemed I belonged to two different worlds—the deaf and the hearing. When I was in school, I was with others like myself and I knew what was being discussed and could just speak up and say what I thought. I fit in and was looked up to by my peers. I took pride in the things I was capable of doing and I had fun with the other kids. I enjoyed the use of bathrooms, running water, and electric lights, but once I was back home, I could shed that life like a snake sheds his skin and was right back with my beginnings: a woodstove to cook on, well-water, oil lamps. I loved it all for it was home.

This summer was not very different from the others except that war clouds were continuing to gather over Europe. More and more boys and young men were being drafted into the armed forces. One of Eunice's admirers, William Glasgow, had gone and one of Gladys's boyfriends, Elroy Wilson, had also been drafted. Now Gladys was dating Elroy's younger brother, C. H., and Thelma had Johnny, another of Elroy's brothers.

In Wallace, N.C., U.S.A., people were dancing to Benny Goodman, Kay Kyser, Fats Waller, The Ink Spots, and Tommy Dorsey. This was also the summer my cousin, Sadie Lee, came down from New York City and spent some time with me. I'd loved and admired Sadie Lee ever since we were babies and Cousin Frank had brought her down to visit. I think I admired the fact that she was a New York girl and nothing ever appeared to faze her. She had been a thin, redheaded little girl who was not one bit bashful. It was always fascinating to watch her speak right up to grown-ups and children alike.

I was so thrilled she was coming to see me now that we were teenagers. When she arrived, she was just as I remembered and we had fun—it was like having a sister my age. Eunice took us with her when she had to work in Little Harlem, and we stayed behind the bar, washing glasses and trying to help out while the guys tried to talk to Sadie. She was taller than me, still redheaded, and still very much outspoken. She wasn't a bit interested in them and would sack them up. Once, one of the guys tried to talk to me. I never knew what he said but Sadie didn't like whatever it was and knocked his glass of beer over. All too soon, Sadie's visit was over and she left to spend time with her aunt in Wilmington before returning to New York. I missed her very much.

However, there were more things to be done. I went to spend a week with Bennie, Mable, and Della. This was a new experience, being able to baby-sit with a cute, tiny baby. Allen was also staying with them to help with farmwork. One day while Mable was helping Bennie in the field, Della got hold of a piece of paper and before I could stop her, she'd popped it in her mouth and started chewing. I couldn't get her to spit it out. I was just about to go into a panic when Allen, who'd come up from the field for a drink of water, saw what was happening and calmly stuck his finger in her mouth and pulled the wad of paper out. I could have fainted from relief.

Another day, they left me a pan of roasted peanuts to eat. I sat on the porch eating them while Della napped. Finishing those, I decided to eat a few apples from a nearby tree. Later that day, Mable's cousin, Lattice, brought over a bucket of beautiful red plums. I proceeded to eat over half of them. That evening, I couldn't eat much supper and we all went to bed early. Waking up late that night, I felt strange—hot and feverish, then icy cold. Next my stomach started feeling like sharp knives were sticking in it all over, then churning. Getting up to go to the night pot, I was too weak to walk so I crawled across the floor. After emptying my miserable stomach, I crawled back to bed, wondering if I was dying and if so, what color coffin they'd put me in and how would my family react. I had to repeat the trip several times before my stomach finally calmed down and I fell into a tired sleep.

By morning I was much better but I was left with a nasty taste in my mouth. Bennie and Mable scolded me for not waking them up. I told them I knew they needed their sleep after working all day. I did ask them to take me home. When I got home, my folks said that it was no wonder I was sick after eating all those plums, peanuts, and apples.

This was also to be the summer that I would finally become a full-fledged member of Peter's Tabernacle Baptist Church. As I mentioned before, I joined the church at age eight but had never been baptized. This summer Mr. Tim told Mama and Papa to bring me down to the creek early one Sunday morning and he'd baptize me before time for church. Eunice got me ready while Mama cooked breakfast. Sam decided he might as well join then too, and true to his word, Subud also joined us. Eunice, Subud, Sam, and I got in the truck and Papa drove us to the creek.

Mr. Tim, Reverend Murphy, and Cousin Archie were already there waiting. No baptism was complete without Cousin Archie. Rolling up his pants legs and taking a long pole, he waded out into the middle of the creek, and tested different spots with the pole until he found just the right one. After Mr. Tim went out into the water, Eunice pushed me to go.

"Oh my goodness," I thought, "here we go."

I wondered if something strange would happen. Would I drown? Suppose my hearing returned? Or would I come up shouting as I'd seen some others do? As it turned out, none of that happened. I just came up wet and gasping to get water out of my eyes and nose. Then it was Sam's and Subud's turns. In the meantime, Eunice wrapped me in a dry sheet until we got back to the house where I bathed, dressed, and ate breakfast. I felt very satisfied with myself at church that Sunday. Now I belonged all the way and could be carried all the way in the church if I should die, and not just halfway as my brothers had told me eight years before.

Even before I joined Peter's Tabernacle, all of us Iron Mine kids used to walk with Mr. Miller to the little church by William Boney's place, where we sang songs, said a Bible verse, and listened to him pray and preach a short sermon. Afterwards, we would escort him back home. We thought he looked nice in his black suit with a bow tie and white shirt. No adults ever joined us, but the kids all sat quietly and listened to him. He never asked for a collection.

The kittens Papa, Frank, and Subud had given me in place of Christopher had all matured into young adults. One I had named Mary Lee, one was Kitty Beau, and the other was Dewey. Columbus had finally wheezed his last before I'd come home, although Eunice had tried her best to save him. Mama said she went about with a bottle of medicine and a spoon in her dress pocket for days, giving him a dose each time he wheezed. I don't know if he had a funeral or not.

Dewey was a beautiful yellow and white cat with green eyes. Each morning he jumped on my bed, found my feet beneath the bedclothes and kneaded them with his paws until I got up. After breakfast when I fed him, he disappeared for the rest of the day. I didn't know where he went until one day I was at Thelma's house and noticed a fat yellow cat lying on the porch along side of Leroy. Both looked so lazy and peaceful. I found out that Leroy had given some fish to Dewey one day. He never forgot the treat and returned each day after that waiting for another meal of seafood. They'd become steadfast friends. You could meet Dewey on the bay road any day on his way to or from Cousin Bert's house, but nights he spent at home on the foot of my bed so he'd be sure to be there to wake me up come morning.

The summer was quickly edging towards autumn and my last year of school. Already, the dust lay thick and ashy white on the grass and bushes beside the roads. Walking the roads barefoot was like walking in soft, warm powder that puffed out at each step. Scores of yellow butterflies fluttered in clusters fighting each other. The leaves looked dull and tired as though they'd be glad when they too wore bright colors and could then drop to the ground and rest.

The war in Europe seemed to be getting worse. Not quite understanding what it was all about, I asked Bennie (my bureau of information) about it. He explained and predicted that America would be involved before long, as France had already fallen. This business about war troubled me.

I wished all our lives could remain peaceful and sweet. But I was soon given a dose of not-so-sweet.

16

Graduation

IT WAS time for school, and I was soon back in Raleigh and my other life. In a few days it was almost like I'd not even been home, that I'd dreamed the summer. Miss Watford and the rest had come back, except Miss Chisolm and Nurse Wright. Our new secretary was Miss Hortense Jones; her sister, Henrietta, had joined the teaching staff. The new nurse was Miss Smith. We had a whole new kitchen staff. Miss King was the head cook, Miss Ray was the second cook, and the two new waitresses were Dorothy and Olivia.

And here I was a senior. Sitting in Mrs. Edmondson's room, I gazed out the window at the same scene I'd looked upon through all that water in my eyes years ago: the two-lane drive up to our administration building, the little white wooden store beside the highway and the few houses around it, and beyond, the woods leading south toward home. Now, as then, the September sun lay on dusty bushes, and treetops were already beginning to turn the same bright colors below fluffy white clouds. I could see myself with my head on the desk in Miss Hayes's room crying to go home. I'd come a long way since then, but I felt sad now also. Miss Hayes and so many more were gone. This would be my last year and then I, too, would be gone, and where? What was I to do after school days? I realized I'd grown to think of this place not as a prison but as a second safe home, and the people in it as sort of another family. They were people I understood and felt comfortable with.

Mrs. Edmondson was rapping on her desk with a ruler to get my attention. When I looked around, she wanted to know where I'd been and told me to copy the assignment from the board.

This year, the senior class of deaf students, besides myself, was Jessie, Buckwheat, Leon, and Clifton. Margie and Madgalene were back as student instructors working under Miss Watford. They still seemed like students since both had their same beds as the year before. Things had loosened up for us quite a bit. We owed that to Miss Watford. I liked her more every day. Her family would come to visit bringing peanuts and other farm goodies like mine did with me. If she had to go to town, she'd borrow Mr. Mask's car, tell a bunch of us to hop in and we'd be only too glad to go.

The food at the school had also improved. Mr. Lineberry decided that the teaching staff should eat at the same time we did and the same food. The teachers were horrified. All these years they had been served special food cooked just for them. They also had their own waitress assisted by two older girls from the deaf department whose duty assignments rotated each week. Although mealtime and the food changed, the teachers kept the waitresses because it was part of our vocational training.

I loved waitressing but had a hard time getting myself assigned to that job. First, I'd been too young, then they said I was too short and clumsy. I guess due to that famous sunbonnet drill. But now being a senior, I'd gained status and at last was given a spotless white apron and cap to go with a blue uniform. The trays were large and round, but I learned to balance them with ease. How I loved passing by the tables where my friends sat, carrying my well-laden tray shoulder-high. I'd balance it on one hand, steady it with the other, and slide it onto the sideboard without spilling a drop of anything. Leon always glared at me every time I passed him. He hated being deaf and hated to see me doing anything he considered deaf-oriented. He wrote notes scolding me for acting like the rest of those "ninnies" as he called them. I just laughed at him.

Life was fun now, even though the war clouds still hung overhead. Mama's letters always had the name of yet another neighborhood boy who'd been drafted. The government had finished Camp Davis and Camp Lejeune for the marines was a little farther south, so marines and soldiers overflowed into Wallace and other nearby towns. We didn't have to worry about any of our boys here on campus being drafted.

Where before, time dragged and seemed endless, now it fairly flew by. There was so much to do: practice with the glee club three afternoons a week, typing class the other two, cooking and sewing classes. I also helped Miss Smith over at the infirmary every chance I got. She let me roll bandages and fill large glass jars with cotton balls, and sit at her desk to copy health reports into a large ledger. There was an electrical panel near the desk. If anyone in the wards squeezed a bulb by their bed, a number would light up on the panel. While sitting at the desk, I'd be watching for a room signal light to come on. How I loved to help in the infirmary.

I still met with my blind friends and they were still hatching up something. I could never stay long enough to really get into things like I once had. We mostly ran on about the latest gossip, clothes, and boyfriends, then I'd have to run. Maybur and I managed a snatch at the swings on the playground now and then, which she loved. She was quite tall now, and her hair reached below her waist. She said she hated it and had Buckwheat to whack it off up to her neck. Mr. Lineberry noticed and didn't like that one bit. He took quite an interest in Maybur, maybe because she looked like his own race, or maybe he knew her family.

He now allowed a few of us to go on shopping trips. My three buddies and I wanted to go after school one evening. Miss Watford said she'd drop us off and pick us up later. At the last minute they decided Margie should go with us since she was older and a graduate. We got out at the post office and agreed to meet Miss Watford on the post office steps at a certain time. We climbed the steps, then told Margie we were going inside to buy stamps and cards and asked her to wait for us. She agreed and told us to behave ourselves and not to talk to any strange men. Once inside, Buckwheat, Jessie, Madga, and I headed for a side door that opened onto another street. We marched along for awhile, happy as larks. I had no idea where we were going. Finally, Madga said we should find the bus station and pretend we were going home. When we couldn't find it, they told me to use my mouth and ask somebody.

"Who?" I demanded. "I don't know these people."

"No problem."

Madga reached out and tapped the first passerby, a short, scraggly-looking man, then gave me the eye to talk.

"Hey, Mister," I stammered. "Can you tell us where the bus station is?"

Not knowing that none of us could hear a word he said, he proceeded to tell us, pointing first in one direction, then another. We all nodded and smiled. When he'd finished I said thanks, and we set off in the direction of the first point. No luck. We tried to remember which way the next point went and headed down another street.

We soon saw a Greyhound bus station sign and headed for it. We marched right up to the ticket window where Madga told me to ask what the fare was to Gastonia, her hometown. The clerk told us, then we asked about the other two: Goldsboro for Buckwheat and Wallace for me. Jessie lived just outside Raleigh so she wouldn't have needed a ticket. I thanked the man, then we marched back out not knowing any more than we did when we went in. Finding our way back to the post office, we went back in by the same side door and on out the front, and there stood poor Margie, still waiting for us. She never knew we didn't buy any stamps but went for a jaunt instead, and that we talked to not one strange man, but two. We finished our shopping and were back on the post office steps waiting when Miss Watford returned to pick us up.

Fair time, Halloween, and Thanksgiving had passed before we realized it. Already the year was about half gone and Christmas was upon us again. Going home for Christmas was taken for granted by most of the kids now. Not for me. I'd forever remember the hurt and loneliness of my first Christmas away from home and my dear family. I'd never take it for granted again, but thanked the dear Lord for opening the way for me to go now. Besides, I had a really special gift awaiting me this year—Frank and Lattice had a new baby girl named Maxine. She'd been born the ninth of December. So now I had two little nieces, and Maxine was right in the same house with me. She was the first baby to live there since Sam. I could hold her to my heart's content, and this I did when I wasn't going someplace with Eunice who still worked in Little Harlem.

Our Christmas break lasted only about a week; our school officials couldn't do without us for long. As much trouble as we seemed to cause them, one would think they'd be overjoyed for us to stay gone as long as possible. Back on campus again, as always, we had to compare notes and discuss everything we'd seen.

Leon had brought back a gift for me. I found the beautifully wrapped gift beneath my pillow the first night back. He'd given it to one of the girls working in the kitchen to give to me. It was

My brother Frank's wife, Lattice, with their three daughters, *left to right*,
Marion, Bennie, and Maxine.

a very pretty raspberry red pullover sweater and matching ski cap.
Another package turned out to be dusting powder and toilet water
from Horace Evans. I got a lot of teasing from the girls but it
wasn't picky like Hazel used to do.

We went through the usual after-Christmas flu and cold season,
then we had to get down to the business of graduating. Miss Watford had us going through all the pattern and fashion books for
ideas on the style of dress we'd like. We'd never had a choice
before. After many sessions of looking and wrangling, we finally
selected a floor-length style with a full flared skirt, puffed sleeves,
and a square-cut neckline, trimmed with eyelet and white satin
ribbons. It took seven yards of white dotted swiss for the dress,
four or five of white taffeta for the slip, and yards and yards of lace
and ribbons. We had to make the dresses ourselves in sewing class.
Fortunately, most of the older deaf girls were first-rate seam-
stresses, especially Margie and Buckwheat.

New things were planned for graduation this year. Mrs. Edmondson and some of the tenured teachers decided that a reunion of all the past graduates should be held each year. Miss Watford proposed having a banquet with dancing afterward in place of a prom, so we'd need formals in addition to our graduation dresses. I was elected president of the class. Brandy would make a farewell speech to my class (he was a junior), and I'd have to respond. We would also have the regular program in the chapel, the baccalaureate sermon, commencement, and a picnic on the green. All in all, there'd be about a week of activities. The planning and excitement reminded me of my Iron Mine school days and naturally, I felt a certain homesickness for the little wooden schoolhouse, the wash-pot of frying fish, and the barrel of lemonade.

After all the meetings and plans worked out, we set to work and time flew. It didn't fly fast enough for us to stay out of mischief. Mrs. Edmondson and her husband had built a nice home in town and moved off campus. They'd had quarters in the blind boys' dorm before and had lived there year-round since Mr. Edmondson worked with the deaf boys in shop. Anyway, she was enjoying her new home and nice roomy kitchen and all the good food she prepared there.

She still informed us what she'd had for breakfast: *hot* biscuits, grits, sausage, eggs, and coffee for her and Mr. Edmondson and milk for Junior, who was also graduating from high school this year at age thirteen. During history class we got a run-down on her dinner menu. On Friday evenings, when she made her weekly shopping list, it was a debate over what to have for dinner: fish or oysters. Some of us nodded through all this rambling or caught and threw notes to the guys across the room. She never noticed with all that food parading in front of her eyes. Unfortunately, it started telling on her by adding extra pounds, which worried her.

She really was a nice-looking lady whenever she got her

makeup on straight and fixed her hair becomingly. One day she brought a bag with her and, just before the last bell, went to the restroom and changed into a black dress. She said she had to go to a funeral or someplace. Being as there wasn't a mirror to show how she looked, she asked us. I said alright but Jessie and Buckwheat said her hair needed fixing and got up to fix it for her, then wrap a turban-style hat about her head. They also added to her makeup, then said how pretty she looked.

Poor Mrs. Edmondson. She smiled and preened and said how people in Atlanta had always said she was pretty and what pretty legs and hips she had.

What she needed right then was a mirror.

The girls had pulled one long curl to dangle out through a crack in her turban, had added too much pink face powder and then bright red lipstick. The rest of us stared, then giggled. It did look funny and they said they'd go back and get her straight before she left. However, someone came for her just as the bell was beginning to ring and there wasn't time. Clifton and Leon said all of us were mean to let her go like that, and I did feel bad, but then decided that the other teachers would notice and fix her up before she got anyplace. I hope so.

No one would ever have gotten away with that with Miss Watford. Our latest project in her department was preparing breakfast for a guest. First we planned the menu, deciding on grapefruit halves, bacon, eggs, toast, and coffee or milk. Then each of us had to cook a certain dish; I was told to scramble the eggs. Everything had to be measured exactly. How many eggs for each person? These were broken into a bowl. Then I had to add salt, pepper, and milk, and beat them for the right length of time. Finally, I had to cook them in a double boiler. The table had to be spread with a white cloth and set correctly—water glass here, coffee cup and saucer there, bread-and-butter plate in its place, all silverware lined up in order, and napkins in place. Now that all was ready, who would be our guest? Who else would have time to leave their rooms this time of day? Mr. Mask, of course.

I scooted upstairs to get him.

"I already had breakfast," he told me.

"But not *our* breakfast. Please come."

He just sat and stared, no smile. I decided I'd better give him the facts so I said this was for our class and if he didn't come we'd get a big fat zero and it would be his fault. That did it.

"Alright."

He rose up like a great bear, heading for the door. I ran before him bearing the good news.

"He's coming! He's coming!"

Then we were ordered to sit and eat with him. It was our turn to stand and stare. The whole meal was a lesson in table manners, but we got through it without spilling, breaking, or getting choked on anything.

Mrs. Edmondson and Miss Mann picked out the songs to be sung and signed for graduation. They were "Let Us Break Bread Together," "I See Glory in the Air," "His Name So Sweet," and "God Bless America." Kate Smith and the war in Europe had made this last song quite popular. How I enjoyed practicing these songs; it seemed like I could hear every one of them.

Even though graduation was the big talk now and everything revolved around it, I still found time to read and visit the library and infirmary. One day Mr. Lineberry came in my classroom grinning and holding a book out for me to take. I looked at it curiously. It was *The Swiss Family Robinson*. I'd seen it on the shelf in the library but hadn't read it yet. He told me to read it.

"Alright and thanks," I said.

Before long I was deep into the adventure of the stranded Robinson family. When I had finished, I found out why he wanted me to read it. The Ambassador Theater in town was running it all week and he wanted me to see the film. He, Miss Watford, and Mr. Mask took three carloads of us to see it that Saturday morning. I'd never been inside a theater like the Ambassador. Thick, soft carpet; dim, rose-tinted lights; a nice smell; and just the right temperature. Percy and I paired off and bought candy and snacks in the lobby. The rest of the gang had scattered about, and we were the first ones to look for a seat.

We found a spot with a good view and settled down to wait for the show to start, nibbling on candy and trying to see each others' signs. An usher came up and tapped us on the shoulder saying something—we didn't know what or even care. We just nodded our heads and grinned. A few more taps and motions and we stopped grinning; this was annoying. Next thing we knew, we were being hauled to our feet and pushed farther over, then set down. Surprise! We were in nice cushioned seats. We'd been sitting on the carpet covering the steps, which were more comfortable than the seats in the balcony at home.

Having read the book I could tell Percy what was being said and done and we both really enjoyed the movie. Technicolor was just coming in and the colors were beautiful. The whole experience was beautiful, new, and exciting. It seemed I was really there with the Robinson family, exploring everything they did.

Back on campus, Percy and I were in for more teasing.

"Boy, you all are dumb," they told us.

Margie said she'd been waving and trying to tell us to get up and sit in seats like the rest of the girls. Jessie said she'd done the same thing.

"We didn't see you all," I told them.

"You must be blind. Go stay with the blind girls." This from Buckwheat.

The discussion then turned to the movie. Some liked it; for

most it was boring. They hadn't really understood that the family had been shipwrecked and had had to make do to survive. They'd rather have seen a romantic picture or dancing. To them that's what movies were all about.

Every day of this spring of 1941 seemed beautiful. Mama wrote that the strawberry plants were full of blooms and that she hoped I'd get home before they ripened and went away. I hoped so too. The very thought of those sweet juicy strawberries was enough to make one's mouth water.

We had so much to do for graduation and the class banquet. Three afternoons a week, three hours were spent working on our graduation dresses and slips—all that white cloth going into one dress. Our hands were scrubbed like a doctor's and we wore a white sheet over our laps. Finally, the dresses shaped up enough for us to try them on to be fitted and to have the hems pinned up. In addition, we had to make dresses for the exhibition. I was working on two: one made from a yellow print and another from a red-white-and-blue stripe. A menu had to be planned for the banquet and other dishes had to be prepared for the home economics exhibit for tasting by the VIPs.

I composed my speech with Mrs. Edmondson's help. Brandy also had his and we practiced together often. Mama and Eunice had sent my formal: pink with a full chiffon skirt, a square-cut neck, and puffed sleeves. Spring was in full swing with warm sun, green grass, and the smell of honeysuckle all over. After lunch those of us not on kitchen duty would gather under a young shade tree near our dorm, gossip, and kid each other until the 1:00 bell when classes started again. Mostly, I'd lie up against the tree and think and dream of days past, days present, and most of all, the days to come. This wouldn't be home to me much longer and war clouds drew nearer. Jukeboxes were playing "I'll Never Smile Again," "Yes Indeed," and other sentimental songs.

The banquet was the first big event. Not too many of the old grads came back, but we could each invite a guest. We all chose our own boys on campus. Of course I picked Leon. He'd started school too late the year he came and wouldn't be able to graduate for another year. The boys arranged two long tables for students and several small ones for faculty in the old dining hall. We girls gathered wild honeysuckle vines from the edge of the woods to twine around the row of columns, and Miss Watford added the finishing touches of flowers and colored lights. It was like a sweet-smelling fairyland when we entered. It was hard to believe it had ever been an old, gloomy, bare-looking place for eating unappetizing food.

Since our dates weren't allowed to call for us at the dorm, we had to meet them at the entrance of the dining hall with all the teachers present. I felt like I imagined Cinderella felt entering the ball. Buckwheat, our beloved hairdresser, had done mine in a pageboy style with bangs, and put a flower on one side. I prayed I wouldn't totter too much in my high-heeled sandals or trip over the dress.

Things were stiff and awkward at first, at least for the students. The guys were splendid in their black or navy suits, white shirts, and bow ties. Someone had set up a phonograph, which seemed natural to me, but the other girls ignored it.

"We can't hear music," Jessie said.

"Yes," Margie agreed. "We'd look crazy trying to dance when we can't hear."

"Well, the blind can hear it and so can the teachers," I pointed out.

"Blind students can't see, and teachers are too old," replied Jessie.

The girls giggled until Madga stepped out, said, "I can dance," and proceeded to do so.

She really could. The deaf students were very apt at learning dance steps just by watching someone else, and they kept up with all the latest moves even though they couldn't hear the music. When some of the blind students who had partial sight started dancing, the rest of us, except Margie, decided to join the fun.

In the meantime, the tables were being readied for our feast. They looked very festive with snowy white cloths, candles, and flowers. When it was time to be seated, I found my place between Leon and Brandy. Mrs. Edmondson made the opening speech as to the purpose of the banquet and welcomed past graduates. Then it was Brandy's turn to bid us farewell and say how we'd worked and learned together. It was a nice speech.

After he sat down and the clapping stopped, I stood up with a thumping heart, sure I was going to make a mistake and disgrace my Class of '41 forever. I looked at all the faces turned my way, waiting expectantly for whatever I had to say. When I glanced down at Leon, he was staring straight at me, looking grim as though to say, "You'd better not mess up. Do it right."

I opened my mouth, and after I'd addressed Mr. Mask and the faculty and fellow students, I felt quite calm and finished my response just right. Leon squeezed my hand and smiled. Mrs. Edmondson told me I'd done fine, but I had to see what Miss Watford thought before I'd really feel right. She was busy directing the waitresses where to set the food, but in passing gave me her special grin, so I knew everything was alright.

Everybody started eating and enjoying all the delicious food— chicken salad, crackers, punch, and other treats. The home ec girls had done themselves proud. Brandy was trying to get Hill to unbend and talk to him. Don and Madga were just gazing at each other. Clifton wanted Jessie to dance with him and she was telling him he was too short.

It seemed like as soon as we'd really started having fun, the

Left to right: Miss Mildred Laws, our principal, George Mask, and Miss Jones on the steps of the administration building (1941).

party was over. The girls who didn't have to clean up were told to go straight to their dorms. The boys too. There was a mix-up in getting sweaters before heading for the stairs, and a few of the guys managed to get in a quick peck before any teachers noticed. Leon was one of them, so that was my first love scene, at age sixteen. Only he wasn't quick enough. I looked and two of the kitchen staff were right beside us and they laughed. I picked up my long dress and fled. I'd never be able to look Miss Ray and Olivia in the face again.

We'd had our graduation invitations printed and mailed early. I just knew my whole family would come, including Papa. He'd never been to see me in all the years I'd been here and this would be my last chance to show off him and Willie. Bennie and Frank had already been seen and admired, and all said Sam was a cute little boy. To me, my papa and brothers were the most handsome males in Iron Mine, and Cousin Bert's boys were next. This was never made known to any of them, but I was thinking how good they'd look, coming into the chapel to see me graduate.

Several days after the class banquet, we had a picnic out on the green that was also fun. We could at least socialize and eat with the boys now, thanks to Miss Watford. Of course we were watched, but no one seemed to care. We enjoyed the thick ham sandwiches, cookies, ice cream, punch, and chips.

Time was speeding by and I was excited, happy, and sad. Our dresses and slips were completed and hung covered with white sheets on hangers, and we had white sandals to go with them. The sermon was scheduled for Sunday evening, commencement would be Wednesday night and we would leave for home Thursday morning. When Sunday arrived, Jessie and I dressed in our graduation dresses. Buckwheat had dressed our hair and the rest gathered around us to admire our finery and tell us how good we looked. Our bouquets were white carnations tied with blue and gold ribbons. The boys, too, looked sharp.

Mrs. Edmondson lined us deaf students up in the hall—all five head—and at the given signal I led the Class of 1941 in to take our seats. Several preachers were there, but Dr. Bullock delivered the sermon. A blind girl was the valedictorian and the blind choir did several songs while we signed. Thelma Freeman sang "Ave Maria," and those who could hear said she was great.

The next few days were spent getting ready for commencement. There'd be an exhibition of crafts and a display of special dishes created by our home ec class. Once again the old dining hall was being spruced up with honeysuckle vines and other flowers. Miss Watford sent me to gather an armful of flowers from a patch growing beside the shoe repair shop on another beautiful, warm May afternoon. The sweet smell of the flowers was enough to make you dizzy. The guys who were in shoe-mending class stuck their heads out the windows wanting to know what I was going to do with those weeds.

"Flowers," I corrected.

I was also told the snakes were going to bite me for stealing their vines.

"It'll be me, so don't worry."

After I'd made several trips with a good armful each time, we had all the columns covered. The dresses, blouses, and skirts we'd made were fastened on dress forms and placed on tables. Miss Leach displayed the crafts and other fancywork down on the other end. A long table covered with a white cloth was placed in the center of the kitchen for food displays. I had made a chocolate cake. Maybur and some other girls made a beautiful salmon salad molded in the shape of a large fish. It lay on a bed of lettuce, garnished with slices of lemon. The exhibit included many other tempting dishes, breads, and rolls.

Now it was Wednesday, the big day, and parents and old grads were arriving. I couldn't be still, running to peep toward the drive to see my folks arrive. It was nearly time to start dressing when one of the girls ran in to tell me that two people had gotten off the bus and one looked like my mama. I was out in front of the office in no time. Mr. Mask was also out there, staring at the two people just coming up the walk, a man and woman. The woman was Mama and I flew to hug her. Turning to see who the other person was, I found him and Mr. Mask pumping each other's hands. It was my uncle, Buddy Vatson.

He was saying to Mr. Mask, "George, you old rascal you. What are you doing here?" and Mr. Mask was asking him the same thing.

I stared.

"I've come to see my niece graduate."

"And I'm here to help her graduate."

Turning to me, Mr. Mask wanted to know why I hadn't told him Buddy Vatson was my uncle.

"I didn't know you knew him," I said.

"Oh yeah. We're old buddies from way back during our college days at Hampton."

Well, this was all news to me, but I wasn't much interested in their college days. That seemed to me a million years ago. I couldn't wait to get Mama off so I could find out where the rest of my family were and what time they'd get here. We left the two college buddies heading for Mr. Mask's office, to catch up on past days I guess. Mama and I headed for the dorm.

"Where's Papa? Why didn't he come with you?" I wanted to know.

"The strawberries are ripening fast and have to be picked, so he's not coming."

I felt like crying.

"What about Eunice and the boys?"

"Eunice stayed to pack and pay off the hands in my place so I could come. Sam is toting them in, and Bennie and Frank are busy too."

I couldn't say anything. I was so disappointed. I'd been so sure that all my folks would be so proud that I'd finally finished school. I'd been sure they'd all come to see me receive my diploma.

Mama knew what I was thinking. She put her arm across my shoulder and told me not to feel bad. They had wanted to come, especially Eunice. But she and Mama couldn't both be gone, and Eunice knew how much it meant to Mama to come see me, so she chose to stay so Mama could come.

"So come on Hon and cheer up. Buddy Vat and I got here and everybody is proud of you."

I then thought, suppose Mama hadn't been able to come? I'd

really be down, then. And after all, Buddy Vat had cared enough to come. Only Margie's sister, Lucy Bell, had come to see her graduate the year before and none came to see Madga, so I was lucky.

Happy and excited again, I took Mama to Mrs. Nelson's rooms so they could talk while I dressed. Again, Jessie and I donned our white dresses. I couldn't wait for Mama to see me. Going downstairs I found Mrs. Nelson had taken her and Buddy Vat to the dining hall for supper. We had to be in chapel early to rehearse some songs one more time. I figured they'd be along. However, after we'd rehearsed, marched in, and taken our seats, I could still see no sign of Mama. I thought maybe she'd slipped in late and was sitting in back someplace instead of in the family section.

When I went up to sign "I See Glory," I looked all over trying to see my Mama. I saw Buddy Vat and an empty chair beside him. I felt sick. Where was my Mama? Had she taken ill? I couldn't keep my mind on what was going on around me for keeping my eyes on the door. Jessie was nudging me to get up. Time for another song, "His Name So Sweet."

We'd hardly started the first verse when at last I spied Mama trying to get into the seat beside Buddy Vat without attracting attention. My heart lightened right up while my hands fairly flew with the signs: "Oh Lord, I've just come from the fountain, I'm just from the fountain, Lord." I know I was grinning. I was so happy, I hardly remember going up to accept my diploma.

The last song was "God Bless America." When we reached the part, "From the mountains, to the prairies, to the oceans white with foam," I could just hear Kate Smith's rich voice singing it as she used to sing "Carolina Moon."

Again, I was happy and sad—happy my Mama who'd wished so much to see me get an education was here to see her wish come true and sad because my school days were over. I'd no longer be

a part of campus life. No more classes. Next year someone else
would be here signing in my place, and I hoped it would be Flossie. After marching out of chapel, the class headed downstairs to
the home ec department where the exhibition was being held.
Mama soon came in, surrounded by the girls who already knew
her and some who didn't.

My first words were, "Mama, where were you? What made you
late?"

She explained that she'd gone back to Mrs. Nelson's room
after eating dinner, and they talked so much they failed to hear
the bell ring for chapel. When they'd finally realized how late it
was, Mrs. Nelson had sent her on to chapel. Mrs. Nelson couldn't
go herself for the little ones' bedtime was close and she couldn't
leave them.

We couldn't get much talking done right then. People kept
coming up, wanting to meet Mama, congratulate me, and say
they'd enjoyed seeing the songs signed. Mr. Lineberry came up
to meet the author of the letter that chastised him for expelling
the children. If either remembered it now, they gave no sign. I
left them deep in conversation. Mr. Mask had Buddy Vat in tow.
I saw them once in the kitchen, sampling the food on display.
Jessie's family had also come—a younger sister and brother along
with her mother.

We girls got together and angled around to where we could
sign to our boys and have a little fun before this wonderful night
was over. Leon was right there. He wasn't smiling much but did
tell me I did great with the signs. He also wanted to meet Mama.

"When I can get close enough I'll introduce you, or you can
push your way through and tell her your name. She'll know," I
told him.

"Would she know me?" Brandy asked.

"Sure, I've told her about all my friends."

That's all Brandy needed. He headed straight for Mama. The rest of us wandered about in a little bunch, pointing out to the boys the different dresses and crafts we had on exhibit, although our names and grades were pinned on each one.

No one ran up and told us to get away from the boys. What a happy night—we could act like normal girls and boys. I still had on my long dress and had to hold it up with one hand to keep from tripping. I was so dizzy with happiness over how well the night had gone. And Mama and Buddy Vat were actually here to share it with me and meet all of my school family. Across the room I could see teachers telling the children it was 11:00 and time to break up and head for our dorms. Leon touched me so that I'd look at him.

"There won't be anyone for me to talk with. The others don't understand things like you do."

"There'll be Flossie and Hill."

"Flossie's okay, like a big sister, but she's still not you."

By then we'd met up with Mama and at last I could introduce them. They both liked each other, but time was up.

Mama and I walked across campus with our arms around each other and it seemed like the campus had never looked more beautiful. Around each lightpost the grass was a tender green, shining with dew; the sky was like velvet, dotted with stars; the windows in the buildings had most of the upstairs windows lighted; and the skyline of Raleigh was just a few miles away. Mrs. Nelson told me to get Mama's bag and my night things and report to the infirmary where we'd been assigned a guest room. Miss Smith was still waiting up for us. Mama and I had a nice room with twin beds near the girls' ward and Buddy Vat had a room on the opposite side of the infirmary.

Once undressed and in bed we couldn't sleep but relived the night and talked and talked about the different people she'd met.

She thought everybody was so nice, especially Miss Watford. Mama loved all the girls, with Margie and Flossie taking first place, but also Catherine, one of my blind friends. And surprise! She liked Mr. Lineberry. They'd had a good talk and one of the boys—she couldn't remember his name—had come up and introduced himself.

"Lorenzo Brandon," I told her.

"He's nice, but funny."

"How about Leon?"

"Oh yes, he seems very intelligent and well-mannered."

Mama was a stickler for those two traits.

She was also impressed with Thelma's and Ira's singing. She'd never heard anyone sing "Ave Maria" in French before.

By now I was getting drowsy. It had been a long, busy day and was after midnight but Mama's excitement hadn't abated. Everybody had been so nice and kind, she loved them all from the cooks and maids on up to Mr. Lineberry. My eyes fell shut. Then she shook me gently and said something that brought my eyes wide open again. It was about Mr. Lineberry.

"What did you say, Mama?"

"I said he told me how smart and intelligent you are and that he hated to see your education end here. He, Miss Watford, and Mr. Mask all said they'd looked into the possibility of you going to Shaw University next year, but you'd need an interpreter for classroom work. They said the state didn't provide for that and it would be too costly."

"Oh, well, I wasn't looking to go to college anyway." I started losing interest, then added, "Thomasina told me there's a college for the deaf in Washington, but it's only for Whites."

"Yes, someone mentioned that too. Mr. Lineberry said he'd like to give you further education by having you come back next year and be a student teacher working under some of the older teachers."

"What?"

I really sat up then. This was something I hadn't even thought about.

"Well, do you want to come back?"

"I don't know, Mama."

Now I was confused. I was sad about being out of school but had already settled in my mind that I'd just go home and help on the farm and run across the fields with my cats and dogs for the rest of my life. At least I wouldn't have to cry and go through leaving home and family again. Now I had to decide what to do.

Again I said, "I don't know. I'll think about it."

But I didn't think long right then because it was so late. The high excitement had run down and I was tired and sleepy.

"Okay," I said. "Let's go to sleep."

Next morning we were up bright and early. Miss Smith came in to say that Buddy Vat was already up and out. We guessed he'd gone in search of his old buddy; however, he hadn't gone far. We caught up with him halfway to my dorm talking with Miss Mann.

He greeted Mama with, "I'll be doggoned. I've run into somebody else I know."

He then told us that Miss Mann was Ethel's old college friend from Hampton. As I've already mentioned, Ethel was his and Mama's niece that he'd raised when their sister Nancy died. He also had sent her to Hampton. So he'd not only met up with his own Hampton buddy, but Ethel's as well—old home week. At the dorm Mrs. Nelson was waiting for Mama to go to breakfast with her. I headed upstairs for my own buddies, or what was left of them. Jessie had left with her family the night before. So had Flora and several more who lived close enough for their people to come and pick them up.

Soon it was time for the bus riders to gather up the last few pieces of hand luggage and be in front of the administration building where the buses would park. I went to get Mama and make sure she wasn't late for the bus. Mrs. Nelson was searching the rooms, making sure none of her charges got left either. The buses were arriving and lining up. Teachers were scurrying around with lists of which students were supposed to board which bus, and separating them into groups.

I had already spotted my bus and headed for it with Mama in tow. Buddy Vat was again in conversation with Mr. Mask and Mr. Lineberry.

"Come here, Bugger," Mr. Mask signed when he saw me.

Oh, mercy, what now? I thought.

However, Mr. Lineberry was grinning and Buddy Vat looked pleased, so it couldn't be too bad. They all looked at me.

"Herring," Mr. Lineberry started signing as best he could.

He wasn't much at it and your eyes and mind had to work hard to understand what he said.

"You come back in September."

I had forgotten what Mama had told me and hadn't thought about it, let alone made my mind up. I tried to think now but couldn't. Did I really want to come back? Would any of my buddies be here?

"You come back," he said again.

"What for?" I asked stupidly.

"Work, help teach deaf children."

"Me? Teach?"

I wanted to giggle and tell some of the other girls what he'd said.

"Will Jessie, Madga, and Margie come back too?"

"Yes," he nodded.

I looked at Mama. She was beaming.

"Well, alright, I'll come back. And thank you."

I waved a hasty good-bye and ran over to where Buckwheat, Madga, and Percy stood with some other girls and boys, taking pictures.

"Hey, I'm coming back in September to teach," I told them. They thought it was a joke and laughed.

"You're a short teacher."

"Well, Jessie will be a tall teacher. She's coming back too."

That was even funnier. They rolled their eyes and almost fell out at the idea of Jessie teaching. Madga and Margie said they'd also come back if Jessie and I were going to be there, and Buckwheat and Flossie were overjoyed. They had thought they were losing all their cronies at one time.

A teacher hurried up to tell all the kids going toward Gastonia to get on their bus. That was Madga's. We hugged her, cried a little, and laughed a lot to hide the crying. Other groups boarded their buses and pulled out. Soon it was our turn, so I found Mama and we boarded and found seats near Flossie, Margie, and Buckwheat. Looking out the window, I saw Buddy Vat still with his old college buddy. I asked Mama if he was going with us or spending the summer there with Mr. Mask. The bus driver settled the question. When the driver got in his seat, Buddy Vat wrung Mr. Mask's hand and slapped his back a final time and boarded also.

Except for me having to get up and help the bus driver unload the right kids in the right town, the trip home was uneventful. Buddy Vat got off in Warsaw.

Eunice was packing strawberries when we got home. As usual, I ran all over the house inspecting every nook and cranny, getting my fill of just being home. Sam refused to let me hug him anymore. He stood by, eyeing me until I'd hugged and kissed everyone else and finished touring the house, then told me to come on. This was my annual tour of the outside fields, garden, and barnyard to see the new baby calf and Mama's pretty, fluffy baby chicks. They looked like little yellow and white balls with tiny legs, running after the mother hen. The pigs were fat and sleek. Queen was shut up for being in heat. The two mules, Ruth and Rhodie, were out being used in the fields someplace so their stable doors stood open with chickens inside scratching among the hay for stray grains of corn. The old red horse drowsed in the sun. Then we went to the strawberry field where they had finished for the day. Aunt Mary had helped Eunice pack, and Mama sat talking while the crates of berries were being loaded on the truck.

Aunt Mary's granddaughter, Edna, was also there waiting to go home. I mentioned before that she was like another sister. She and I traded licks as a greeting and grinned at each other. Frank had brought a jar of white lightning to share with anyone who wanted to share it. Aunt Mary certainly did. By the time she was ready to go home, she was quite joyful, bright-eyed, and flushed but had the presence of mind to ask Mama if she could stop by her garden on the way home for a head of cabbage.

"Help yourself," Mama said.

Papa left with the last load of strawberries for the day, and Eunice headed for the house to bathe and change clothes. Mama, Sam, and I decided to walk a piece with Aunt Mary and Edna.

Upon reaching the garden, Aunt Mary turned off on the cabbage row and stooping, reached out to cut a head of cabbage. I guess her head was dizzy from the sips of white lightning. Once she stooped over, she couldn't stop but stumbled and then went sailing down the row, still stooping and grabbing wildly at the cabbages as she passed them. Edna took off after her. By now Aunt Mary was halfway down and going full speed like a sailboat in the wind while Edna hollered for her to stop. Finally catching up with her sailing grandma, she got a firm grip on her and brought her back. Mama took the knife and cut the cabbage herself.

After we'd returned to the house and had dinner, Sam and I were once again outside. For the first time I realized something had been nagging at the edge of my mind since dinner.

"Sam," I said, "Where's Willie?"

I'd thought he was off in a field with one of the mules until he didn't come in for dinner. Sam pretended he hadn't heard the question. By now suspicious, I asked again.

"Washington," he said.

"What Washington?" I asked, since Washington, North Carolina wasn't far away.

"Washington, D.C."

Willie gone? I couldn't believe it.

"What for?"

He shrugged.

"I'm going to ask Mama."

And off I ran in search of her.

"Mama! Is Willie really in Washington, D.C.?" I shrieked.

She nodded.

"To stay?"

She nodded again.

I was crying by now. I couldn't stand the thought of even one member of my family not being where I could see them. I'd cried for days when Bennie went to Norfolk for a summer a few years before. Now Willie, who had taught me about the woods and about rabbit boxes and tried to teach me to milk the cow, had left. Each of my family had a special place in my life that no other could fill. Now Willie's place was empty.

There's no telling how long I would have cried if Sam hadn't come to tell me that Edna was back. I wasn't surprised because our house was a second home to Edna.

"Where's Aunt Mary?" I asked her.

"Home. She laid down on the first bed she got to and went to sleep," she informed us. Then added in a matter-of-fact way, "I got her money so no one can steal it from her."

We laughed, knowing Aunt Mary kept her money fastened inside the elastic leg of her knee-length bloomers. Playing and talking with Edna for the rest of the evening took my mind off

Willie until that night, when I cried again. He had wanted to go to college at A&T in Greensboro the coming fall, but there wouldn't be enough money from the farm so he'd gone in search of a job in hopes of earning enough to go the next year. And so my first summer as a graduate started off quite sad. However, we were soon busy with farmwork and time passed.

I was surprised by a visit from Margie and Buckwheat one day. Buckwheat had managed to get to Wallace to see Margie, and the two of them had found someone who knew where I lived and hired him to bring them out. It was so good to see them. We sat on the porch catching up on school news. We did feel sort of self-conscious when we'd get carried away by something and sign so fast and excitedly that the others on the porch would stop talking and stare at us and ask me what was being said. I'd tell them and also said that that was the way deaf people felt while hearing people talked and laughed and we couldn't understand.

My nieces, Della and Maxine, were the cutest little things. Della was going on two and Max would be one. I had fun being an aunt, and they were what made being home this summer different from the others. Once I had settled down to being the cook and dishwasher again, it hardly seemed like I'd been away. This year I had Lattice to share my old chores, as she had to be home with the baby. After the crowd went back to the fields, we'd wash and put away the dinner dishes and clean the kitchen. Then we would sit on the end of the porch and have a ball talking and playing with Max like she was a doll.

I also started spending more time with Gladys this summer. She, Thelma, and I had become a threesome, but since Gladys was the oldest girl in the family, she had many duties helping both in the fields and in the house with the cooking, cleaning, and the care of the younger children. To spend time with her, I had to follow her around talking and lending a hand now and then as she worked. Thelma soon would become bored and go home. I also still went to Wallace most Saturdays and spent the day with Eunice in Little Harlem. I enjoyed running errands on Front Street for her, especially to Rexall and Miller's.

This was another lovely summer. I had finished high school and at times I felt quite grown up and ready to date, but had no idea who with. At school, I could run on and kid with any of the boys, but here at home, a lot of them seemed to like me but were self-conscious about trying to talk to me. Most would treat me to something—soda, ice cream, or candy—and just sit and stare unless Eunice or one of my girlfriends happened to be with me. Needless to say, I felt uncomfortable with them.

Turkey was the exception; he could always get me to understand him and make me laugh at his craziness. Leroy and Harding would talk to me, but they were like brothers. The older boys were being drafted fast. The rest of us stuck together and walked the roads on Sunday evenings while Mama sat on Cousin Bert's front porch with her and Cousin Mary Eliza.

We'd disband and go home when the sun started going down. We'd walk home on the bay road with Mama, slapping at the mosquitoes and lightning bugs flitting about. Sometimes the moon would just be coming up, making shadows across the road. I used to love this walk when it was a bunch of us, but now it was only Mama, Sam, and me, unless Eunice happened to be home. I missed Willie so much, also Allen and Subud, who had moved to Philadelphia.

This summer Della was given a baby sister, Shirley. I decided this one was going to look like me. She was another pretty baby and favored her daddy instead, but I resembled him too, so maybe she did favor me a teeny bit.

Willie wrote that he was coming home for a visit. He lived with Papa's cousin, Mary, a large, nice-looking woman whom I'd met only once. Her son Lloyd was Willie's age and he came too. He was a nice, friendly boy. They could only stay a week, but it was just as well; I hardly got to say a dozen words to them. They were always on their way out to see girls or go someplace. Nevertheless, I cried just as hard when the week was up and they had to leave. The rest of the summer passed much as the ones before with Sunday school and church on Sundays, barning tobacco, chopping, and helping Mama can the various vegetables and fruits she put up each year.

This was the summer of '41 and the peacefulness of our country was fast coming to a close. It didn't affect our part of the world so much just yet. Only the best of the young men, Black and White, were being drafted, and of course, some enlisted. Black women were being accepted as Wacs and nurses.

17

From Student to Teacher

IN AUGUST, the letter from Raleigh came with the opening date for school and what bus for me to be on. And although I knew I'd cry and feel sad at leaving my family and home, I did feel more than a little excitement to be going back as a teacher. What would it be like? Would we be given teachers' quarters like Thomasina, Lillie Bell, and Emma had?

Eunice had picked out some really cute clothes for me on our shopping trip—flared or pleated plaid skirts; sloppy joe sweaters; loose, boxy jackets; saddle oxfords; and knee or bobby socks. I had all of them plus some nifty dressy clothes, a beanie, and a pork pie hat that was round with a creased crown and a small brim. I guess I was about the proudest young lady to walk onto the old school campus that year. Buckwheat, Margie, and Flossie rode on the bus with me; Madga, Jessie, and Odessa were already there. It was great, all of us being together again. How our hands flew, all trying to say something at the same time and laughing. All of us chose to sleep in the same beds that we'd had before. Jessie and I were paired to work together one week in home ec while

Margie and Madga did classroom work under Mrs. Whitaker. We'd switch back and forth each week. I loved it.

Leon, Clifton, Buckwheat, and Odessa were seniors this year. It was strange not having to go to class or carry an armload of books around. I missed Mrs. Edmondson's room and the fun we had there. Sometimes I felt a little sad for my bygone school days, for I'd really loved school.

Mrs. Whitaker had the beginners and all the new children who couldn't sign. The ones who were born deaf had to be taught the meaning of sound and what talking meant. This we did by taking a child's hand and placing it on our throats, then making a noise so she could feel the vibrations. Then we made them make noises with their mouths. It took a little while for most of them to catch on. Our next step was to show them a picture of an apple, cat, or dog while we put their hands on our throats and pronounced the word over and over. We'd make motions for them to move their lips the same way and make a sound, or have them try to repeat the word with their mouths and hands at the same time. Whether or not any of them ever correctly pronounced a word orally I don't know—I was deaf too. They did learn sign language quickly. We taught them games, along with reading simple sentences, writing, and arithmetic. Mr. Lineberry would often stop in the door and stand watching and beaming. He seemed glad to see us old grads back.

I was even gladder of my first pay envelope—every thirteen dollars and fifty cents of it. We had free room and board and medical care, so our money could be spent on whatever we wanted. Actually it went a good ways since all we mostly wanted to buy were snacks, toiletries, and funny books for recreation. Most candy and potato chips cost five cents; sodas, five cents; and funny books (like *Archie*, *Batman*, and *Spiderman*), ten cents. Scented soap, toothpaste, and talcum powder seldom cost more than twenty-five cents. I sent some of my pay home to Mama. How good I felt being able to send my folks a little money after years of being on the receiving end.

As student teachers, I'd thought we'd be free to come and go and do as much as we pleased. Not a bit of it—most rules and regulations still applied to us. However, this was beginning to be the most enjoyable year at school.

I was still the lead in signing the spirituals and other songs in chapel. Churches in town and other places invited our group to sign for their programs, and Mr. Mask took the group to his church in Hamlet one Sunday. Afterward, we had a very good dinner at his house. Mrs. Mask had baked cornbread that was a beautiful golden color, like pound cake, and cut in neat little squares. When the plate was passed to Jessie, she shook her head. Later when all had finished with meat and vegetables, Jessie reached out and selected a nice square of bread. She looked surprised when she bit into it but kept on and finished by the time Mrs. Mask came in with dessert. Afterward, back in the dorm, we asked Jessie why she'd turned down the cornbread the first time around, then ate it all alone.

"Stop asking," she fumed at us. "I thought it was cake because it was so pretty and yellow, and saved it for last."

"Well, it was good enough to eat alone," I told her.

The others were laughing too hard to say anything.

"I love cornbread," I added, trying to bolster her ego.

All she said was, "Who cares? I don't like it."

The year was passing quickly. I didn't mind having a boyfriend this year. It was Leon and no surprise to anyone. We both were able to speak clearly and had a lot in common, such as a love of reading, and we understood each other. He kept me supplied with candy bars, chips, sodas, and comics. Jessie finally agreed to acknowledge Clifton as a boyfriend, although she still told him he looked like a preacher. He sure didn't act like one, always blowing a kiss her way when whatever officials were nearby had turned their backs. Madga still had her "Don." Buckwheat settled for Robert Rainy. Margie didn't want one because they were all kids to her, Odessa played the field, and Flossie was a dear sis to all of us, girls and boys alike.

I still had my friends in the blind department and visited them often. They really had a thing going this year to get the school "cleaned up" as they called it. They said they were tired of eating off tin plates, and that the food wasn't good. Most of all, they hated the rules and lack of privacy in the dorms. The long rooms had two rows of beds and no curtains, only shades at the windows. We still had no clothes closets. One of them whose home was right there in Raleigh was secretly reporting to a newspaper when her mother came to see her each Sunday afternoon.

"You help us, you hear?"

"Sure," I said.

One little blind girl had come in late, a couple of months after school started, and I took an interest in her. Every sunny day found her outside with her face upturned toward the sun, one finger pressing on the outer corner of one eye. Then she'd start turning round and round, clapping her hands, only to stop and face the sun again. The blind girls said she was dumb and couldn't learn anything. I found out why. One day she was moved to Mrs. Whitaker's beginners' classroom although she was somewhere between ten and twelve. It had been discovered that she was deaf as well as blind. She must have lost her sight and hearing at some point after learning to talk, but no one at school knew why. She could talk if anyone could get through to her.

We did. After feeling an object, we got her to say what it was with her mouth, then to form signs with her hands. It took a good many repeats, but we started making progress, so she could communicate a little. I was the proudest ever when, upon teaching her one day and letting her feel my hair, she smiled and signed, "Herring." I hugged her.

One morning she was missing from class. Checking to see where she was, I was shocked to be told she had been sent home! Why? Because someone, I never knew who, said it was impossible to teach her anything and it wasted the teachers' time to even try. I felt like crying, and I wasn't the only one. Miss Watford was also upset, for she'd tried to keep her in school. The little girl had realized she was going home or someplace when she and her suitcase were put into a car; she hadn't wanted to go. Miss Watford said it was pitiful because she'd started clapping her hands together and trying to sing, "Lord, Lord, he's been good to me." We never heard from her again and even now I wonder how she fared in life, if she was ever able to do anything, and how she was treated.

Tonsil operations were held at the new school infirmary now. I still loved to hang out over there and help Miss Smith make bandages, fill jars with cotton balls, check the shelves for supplies, and record information in the large books for medical histories. I'd also help prepare food in the spotless little kitchen and feed the patients. When there was nothing to be done, we'd sit in the sun porch or solarium, talk, read magazines, and eat homemade ice cream.

Now the state fair in October, and Thanksgiving in November, were behind us. Christmas was just ahead. We could look forward to going home for Christmas and what a joy! Best of all, I'd have my own money to shop with and get gifts for all those dear to me. Thelma Freeman and I were invited to sing and sign in a Christmas program at a White church in town, along with Miss Mann, our directress. It was the largest church I'd ever been in. We were ushered into a dining room first, where a light supper was being served. I felt a little self-conscious being among so many Whites at one time and us the only Blacks. However, they seemed nice and friendly and I soon felt at ease with them. A waiter brought us bowls of soup and hot tea. Snowy white triangles with two pretty, green holly leaves and bright red berries were also on the table, but I couldn't decide whether they were food or Christmas decorations. I secretly watched Miss Mann to see what she'd do with hers. She picked it up and bit it so it was edible. I found it to be very good—bread with crusts trimmed off, spread with cream cheese. The holly leaves were cut from a leaf vegetable or green peppers, and the berries from pimentos. Dessert was little squares of cake (I thought about Jessie) and ice cream. Each of us also received a small Christmas gift—a lace-trimmed hanky, and a sweet-smelling sachet.

Supper over, we got on with the program. Thelma sang, I signed. They wanted mostly to hear the old spirituals, like "Swing Low, Sweet Chariot," "It's Me O Lord," and "Steal Away." We did those and one or two Christmas carols. When it was over, the young people couldn't wait for us to come off the stage but leaped right up, shaking hands, patting, smiling and saying how much they enjoyed it. They also wanted to know how to sign such things as "Eight to the Bar," "Boogie Beat'll Getcha," and other crazy things. Miss Mann finally got us out and into the car. Back in the dorm, I had to relate the latest experience and they laughed about the bread, saying I was as bad as Jessie.

In recounting this period of my life, let me not forget the most horrifying occurrence for the whole nation. That which we'd feared finally came upon us: the horrors of war. The teachers who subscribed to the *News and Observer* received their newspapers at breakfast. I saw some teachers grouped around a paper and noticed the big black headlines in passing—the United States had declared war on Japan after they'd bombed Pearl Harbor on the seventh of December—Frank's birthday.

I grabbed the first paper I could find and read the awful news. My first thought was to go home. If I had to get bombed, I wanted to be with those I loved best. When I told Miss Watford and Mr. Mask that I wanted to quit and go home and why, they both assured me I wasn't about to be bombed, and that the president was sending planes and men over there to fight them in their own country. I couldn't rest until I wrote Mama about my fears, but she told me the same thing and that we should pray.

We were given our usual Christmas bag from the school, then those whose parents sent for them were put on buses to go home. Not too many were sent for this year because it was a tight time for Blacks where money was concerned. Not many had well-paying jobs because wartime plants had not opened up yet. They soon did and Blacks started making more money than ever before.

However, I was able to enjoy another Christmas at home that wasn't much different from previous Christmases. No one we knew was involved yet. The draft board was calling up all men eighteen years and older to register and start training. Nearby Camp Davis and Camp Lejeune were training soldiers and marines who were coming to Wallace for recreation. It was getting to be an everyday thing to see soldiers and marines on our streets.

There seemed to be a new excitement in the air, but unease and worry too, about what might happen to our boys. Some said not to worry because the Black boys weren't allowed to fly planes and fight up front, only to clean and cook, so they'd be safe. It was still a worry for me. I again thought about Willie, Leroy, Harding, Allen, and Subud.

Back on campus, school life settled into its usual after-Christmas dullness. The cold rainy weather kept us in most of the time.

We had nothing new to talk about, so we just sat around getting our hair scratched and brushed, reading comics, and nodding. Finally, one weekend toward the last of January, the weather was clear and cold, but not too cold. We'd had dinner at noon and sat talking of old days and friends and Madga said she'd love to see Frances. I looked out the window at the skyline of Raleigh showing up clearly in the winter sunshine.

"Well, she isn't far away," I said.

"How far?" she asked.

"A sign out on the highway says five miles."

They all looked at me, then at each other.

Madga said, "Let's go."

"Huh? Go where?" I asked.

"To see Frances."

The rest of us just stared.

"How're we going?" from Buckwheat.

"Walk," was the reply.

Again we stared.

"Too far to walk." This from Jessie.

"No it's not," Madga told her. "It's five miles by highway; if we follow the railroad tracks it will be closer. It's right nearby. Right, Herring?"

"Uh, I don't know. Well, maybe."

I'd shut my mouth and found my wits.

"You're all crazy," Margie told us. "Mr. Mask is going to catch you."

"So what? We're through school now, just working."

"I'm not, I'll get expelled," Buckwheat put in.

"I don't care. I'm going." For the first time Odessa had let her thoughts be known.

Before I knew it my adventurous spirit had control of me. I jumped up waving my arms.

"Let's go. Come on Jessie."

"Crazy girls," Margie said again. "I'm gone. I don't know any-thing. If they ask me, I've not seen you."

"Fine."

The rest of us were too busy deciding what to wear. Since we had to walk, we decided on skirts, sweaters, knee socks, and loaf-ers or saddle shoes. I added my loose red jacket and beanie cap.

"Don't forget your camera, Herring. We'll take pictures."

Madga loved pictures, especially of herself. The five of us walked past Mrs. Nelson's room without a glance, out the back door, and on toward the maids' quarters. Rounding the corner of the woodworking shop, we met Mr. Whitney, the school engineer and plumber, a short, chubby type with lots of thick curly hair, and a sour expression. He loved to fuss at us, but we'd learned long ago it was all a put-on. He was really kind-hearted. Now he glared at us.

"Where do you think you're going?"

Madgalene Williams during our last year at school (1941).

"Off," Madga told him airily.

I know he thought we were just going to the maids' quarters, but we passed right on by them. We had a farther destination.

Upon reaching the railroad tracks we turned north. The tracks soon ran between two high embankments, and we lost sight of our school. The landscape began to look very pretty with large rocks, small hills, and cedar trees. We took turns posing and snapping pictures. We laughed and played, happy as larks. Even the sun seemed to be smiling and happy. The war and all bad things were forgotten.

This mood lasted until we reached a place where the rails crossed a creek and the creek was a good way below us. We stopped in dismay. Go back now when the city lay just before us? We looked right and left for another place to cross—a bridge, road, or anything except a railroad track. Nothing else was to be seen; it was this or go back.

"Come on you guys, let's go," and Madga marched, not back but forward, stepping from one cross tie to the other just as easily as stepping up stairs. Odessa followed, then Jessie inched her way across fearfully, but across she did go. Buckwheat and I stood looking at each other.

"You go first," I said.

"Go yourself."

"Let's hold hands."

So holding hands, we set foot on the rails.

Buckwheat teetered. "Yikes!"

I jumped back and Buckwheat went down on her knees and started crawling. That seemed the safest way if only a train didn't come along, so I followed suit.

We made it! Walking a little farther, we found ourselves in what appeared to be a lumberyard with shacks and outbuildings scattered about. Now we had another problem—how to get past a large dog that was snapping and snarling at us. I told the girls not to run but stand perfectly still.

"So he can eat us better with those big teeth?" Jessie asked.

I noticed a woman in the doorway of a shack watching us. I asked if she'd please call that dog if it was hers. She must have said something to him for he left us alone and we passed her doorway unbitten. I tried to smile to show we were friendly and harmless, but she only stood in her doorway, arms folded, and stared at us suspiciously.

We went about the business of trying to find a street we could recognize, and sure enough, across another street was a white house we'd passed coming into town by car and Highway 70 itself.

"Now I know where we are," I told the girls.

"Good, now find Frances," said Jessie, giving me a little push.

I was trying to remember which street we'd turned into the night we had carried Frances home. Up ahead was a cluster of gray concrete buildings surrounded by a high wire fence. We'd passed there, I was sure. Farther on was a white bungalow that looked like the one where we'd dropped off Frances. I pointed it out to the girls.

"Wrong street," Madga said. "This is Cabarrus. Frances's address is on Martin."

Onward we marched and finally we saw Martin Street. Our spirits lifted. We were getting close.

Just as we reached the neat white house with the number we wanted, a taxi pulled up, discharging a bunch of people. They were headed for the same house. We trailed in behind them and into the living room. The people who lived there seemed overjoyed to see their guests, for everybody was hugging and kissing. They started for us and then asked their guests who we were.

The guests didn't know and everybody stared. I felt another little push.

"Ask where Frances is," one of the girls told me.

"Is Frances Mitchell home?" I asked.

Some shook their heads and all stood and stared. A small, balding man in a black suit stepped out and pointed to the door. We knew what that meant, so we turned and filed out, like a bunch of rejected puppies. All this long walk for nothing.

The little man had followed us out. Now he asked me who we were.

"Frances's friends. Do you know her?"

He bobbed his head yes, then got me to understand that Frances only got her mail at his address—she lived elsewhere.

"Come on, I'll show you."

Oh, goody, we'd see our friend after all. Since I could talk to him, he walked beside me. He couldn't sign but gestured and I could read his speech. He said he'd seen Frances at church that morning. I passed on this information. Then he wanted to know where we stayed.

"School," I told him.

"On Garner Road?"

"Yes."

"How'd you come in town?"

When I passed this question, Jessie said, "Not his business."

Madga said to tell him in a car.

"How will you get back?"

Nosy man.

"In a cab," I told him.

My buddies were giggling about my new boyfriend and how short both of us were. I ignored them.

"There's Frances's house," he pointed.

I looked. It was the same house we'd passed coming into town that I'd believed was the one. Now I looked at them and laughed, but they ignored me.

Frances was surprised and glad to see us. After meeting her aunt and cousins, we sat in her room. When we told her how we'd come to town, the girl laughed until she cried, saying, "You crazy girls." She set out cookies and peanut brittle for us to eat while we swapped news and how the time flew. We saw through the window it would soon be night and we had more than five miles to walk.

Frances wrapped candy for us to take back while we scrambled into our coats and headed for the door. She walked with us as far as the gray buildings with the fence.

"What's that place?" Madga asked Frances.

"The women's prison."

"That's where we're going to be if we get caught out here," I told them.

We found the shack in the lumberyard, but no dog or woman was in sight this time. The winter dark was closing down fast. Luckily, we could still see to cross the creek on the railroad track, but by the time we'd reached the embankments, it was dark and very cold, so we had no time for talk or play. We started trotting even though it was black down between the high banks.

I wondered, *What's that small bright light way up ahead? A train!*

We were in a bunch and close enough to see signs. So I pushed and signed, "Get off the tracks!"

I never knew how I did it, but I was halfway up the bank by the time train reached us, holding on to a bush for dear life as the train rumbled past. Feeling my way back down, I found Buckwheat just below me. We collected into a little bunch and ran as best we could.

When we finally saw the school lights, what a welcome sight they were! That was the only time we were happy to see that place. Passing the maids' quarters, we saw Mr. Whitney again. This time he had a flashlight and shone it on us.

"Where've you been?"

"Off," Madga said.

"You're gonna get it," he assured us.

At our dorm, all the outside lights were on and Mr. Mask was coming down the back steps. Well, Madga, Jessie, and I were through school anyway, so what was there to worry about? Heads up, we marched to meet our fate. However, Mr. Mask only glanced at us, saying hi as he passed. Upstairs, we found everything as usual: girls reading, gossiping, and getting ready for bed. No one knew we'd been out except Margie and she was neither excited nor worried.

"So you crazy girls are back. Did you see Frances?"

When we told her the highlights of our adventure, she laughed, then shook her head.

"Crazy."

Unsure about how our escapade would be taken by the higher-ups, we waited for our summons to either the office or Mrs. Nelson's room. None came. Even when Mrs. Nelson came up to turn out the lights at bedtime, she acted as usual and bid us all goodnight. Nor did Mr. Mask or Miss Watford say anything or act differently the next morning. Life went on as usual.

Hadn't we even been missed? Now we felt indignant. We could leave the grounds, spend a whole day in town, and even come in after dark and no one even cared or missed us. That is, no one except Leon. He and Flossie fussed about the train and the railroad tracks. We could have been killed they said. Well, we weren't.

This was the last part of February and spring was on the way. Maple buds began to swell and redden; the days lasted a little longer; then it was March. The war was getting worse. We had boys in Europe fighting Hitler, boys in the Pacific fighting Japan.

Everywhere were signs of Uncle Sam pointing a finger and saying, "I want you." He meant all able-bodied men and boys over eighteen. Women were wanted to work in aircraft plants and to take over men's jobs to free them to fight.

About this time I received a letter from Mama telling me that my brother Willie had enlisted and was at Fort Dix, New Jersey.

"Oh no, not my brother!"

I started crying so hard that I could hardly finish the letter. The girls came running.

"What's wrong? What's wrong? Is somebody dead?"

"Not yet, but my brother joined the army and will have to fight those mean people."

Flossie sat patting me and saying he'd be alright, that the Lord was with him. I calmed down, but the next day, there was another letter from Mama saying my one and only sister had gone off and married someone they didn't even know and was living in Stony Creek, Virginia. A second letter that day was from Willie with a picture of himself all spic and span and splendid in his new army dress uniform, standing straight and solemn. I broke out crying again, feeling like I'd lost my only sister and Willie.

I wanted to go home where I could talk to Mama, lay my head in her lap, and cry. Then she'd talk to me and make things sound right again. I even went to the office and asked Mr. Mask for permission to go home for Easter, which wasn't far away, but he wouldn't hear of it. I slept with both letters and the picture under my pillow that night and cried myself to sleep.

Flossie and the other girls told me I should be happy for my sister and pointed out that I had a new brother. I hadn't thought of it in that light, so I started wondering about him and how it would be having a new male addition to our family. It might be fun. So I felt better about Eunice, but the worry about Willie and the war stayed with me. I had started to grow up and think about my life and the course it was taking. I discovered I wasn't the only one having serious thoughts.

Sometime after Easter when our thoughts turned homeward, a bunch of us were sitting around gossiping and kidding each other, when someone mentioned "next year." Madga said she didn't think she'd be back next year.

"Are you kidding?"

"No, I'm not kidding. Don wants me to marry him and move to Brooklyn, New York."

We sat stunned. School without Madga was unthinkable; she was our leader, the fun girl, the life of everything.

"I might or I might not. Maybe I'll say yes, maybe no."

We hoped she'd say no, but then Jessie said she didn't know if she'd be back either. Her family was considering moving to Springfield, Massachusetts, as soon as school was out and she couldn't stay down here alone. Another one gone or going. Someone asked what was I going to do.

I didn't know. The only thing I did know was that I didn't want to come back if my buddies didn't. The whole thing was depressing. Here, I'd thought my life lay in a neat plan before me—home in the summer with my folks and Queen, and here on campus through the winter with my friends. I had thought I'd keep working and yet still be sort of a schoolgirl, doing silly things, carefree. Now everything seemed to be falling apart. My family wouldn't all be there, so home would be different. If I returned, my friends wouldn't all be here either, so school would be different. I thought of a song that I used to hear Miss Staten sing: "I'm just between the devil and the deep blue sea."

We became bolder about going across the highway to the store. No longer did we ask permission, but just set out, bought what we wanted, and marched back and no one said anything. We talked openly to the guys when we wanted to and no one said anything about that either. The blind students were still making their plans to blow the whistle on everybody involved in running the school. Miss Watford was quiet and Mr. Mask didn't smile much these days. I don't know if they'd heard rumors or what.

We had another fun day with Mr. Mask when Madga, Jessie, and I asked him to drop us off in town to do a little shopping. He obliged and told us to be on the post office steps at 5:00. Up and down Fayetteville Street we went in and out of every store. I found a beautiful green suit, bought it, and had it packed in a large cardboard box. Jessie found a dress, and Madga a good-sized trunk and some shoes. We had photos made and bought ice cream sodas. Finally broke, we waited on the steps for Mr. Mask. When he did come, he loaded our boxes and bags into the care and then Madga asked him to pick up her trunk at Belk's department store. He just stared.

"A trunk?"

"Sure."

"Where'll we put it? This is a *car.*"

That was his problem, we told him.

It was decided we'd just go on with what we did have and send Mr. Council back with the truck to get the trunk.

Poor Mr. Mask grumbled all the way back to campus while we giggled.

18

Good-bye, School Days! Hello, World!

THERE were only a few more weeks of school and none of us had decided definitely what we'd do the next year. I think we were afraid to talk about our plans for fear of what the others would say. We weren't quite ready to face up to really cutting loose from everything familiar and dear, and this place was a second home now. Some nights I couldn't sleep after lights-out and would raise the shade and stand looking out at the quiet campus. What to do? Come back? Stay home? Get a job? If so, what job? Who wanted to hire a deaf person? I thought of the poster, "Uncle Sam Wants You," but did he mean *me*—someone who couldn't hear?

My deafness hadn't bothered me in the past but now I thought of so many things—the way I was politely passed over when someone in the church wanted something done, the quick snicker when I misunderstood something said to me, and other little things. If it was like that among people who knew me, what would it be like without Mama or someone here at school to make me feel like I was a person too? Then I thought of what Mama always told me: I was just as intelligent as anyone else and could do anything the rest could do; I should hold my head up and be proud; I shouldn't get angry or feel hurt because of a few laughs at my mistakes. She always said it was for the lack of sense on their part, that they didn't know any better. And Jesus was always there beside me.

So encouraged, I considered the possibilities of what I could do. I wanted to help with the war somehow. I could cook, sew, type, help out in nursing—anything else, I was willing to learn. I wanted to work with Uncle Sam, but did Uncle Sam want me?

Should I marry? What sort of marriage could I have? Two deaf people in a house unable to hear what was outside? But did a hearing person want to marry a deaf one? Children? Wouldn't they be ashamed of having a mother who couldn't hear them talk? So I decided marriage and children were out. I'd get tired going in circles and go to bed.

One day, someone came and said the four of us—Madga, Margie, Jessie, and I—were wanted in the office. Oh, wow. We looked at each other. What had we done?

No one was in there except Miss Watford and Mr. Mask. He told us to go into the library and be seated. This sounded grim. Mr. Mask and Miss Watford joined us, looking sort of sad and very serious. Mr. Mask opened things up, with Miss Watford serving as interpreter.

"Butler, you're the oldest and assistant to Mrs. Nelson," he began. "So what have you all been doing breaking rules?"

"Me?" Margie was indignant. "I didn't break the rules. I've done nothing."

"Somebody did." He fixed his eyes on the rest of us. "And you didn't report it."

Silence from everybody. He started again.

"You all used to ask permission to go to the store, now you just walk."

More silence.

"Herring, what do you say?"

"The store is only a little way, just across the road. We didn't think anybody cared."

"And where else did you go? I met you all coming in one night."

So he'd known all along. I looked at my friends.

Madga spoke up: "It's no matter. I'm not coming back next year anyway, so you can expel or fire me now."

My heart went straight down. I wanted to cry and tell her, "Not yet, let's have another year. Just one more."

"Oh, pshaw," Mr. Mask said. "We're not talking about expelling anyone. All of you'll be back. We just want you girls to be more responsible and help Mrs. Nelson with the children. You all are teachers now. We want you to act like it, be more mature."

Then Jessie had her say.

"Don't count on me. My family is moving to Springfield, Massachusetts and I'm going too."

My world was falling apart fast.

"Well, what about you two?" Mr. Mask asked, looking at Margie and me.

Margie said she didn't know, she might come back or go to Philadelphia or stay home where a White lady wanted her to work full-time as a housekeeper.

I was the only one without a corner.

"I'll let you know," I mumbled.

Miss Watford was looking at me and she knew what I was going through, but our principal still tried to bluster it out.

"Oh, you girls go on now and behave and forget about leaving. Come on back. Be here when school opens, alright?"

We filed out and I asked the girls if they'd been kidding about not coming back.

"No way."

Madga and Don were engaged and he had his plans mapped out. Jessie had her plans too. Buckwheat and Odessa said definitely they wouldn't be back if Madga wasn't.

Time was flying by. Suddenly there were only a few days until time for school to close. Everything seemed to take on new meaning for me as my mind hopped back and forth. I'd look at the little kids and see myself as I was seven years ago, scared and lonely. I'd look at the downstairs bedroom and think, *Here's where I slept first.* I remembered the old dining hall, the playground, and walks in the woods. If I didn't come back next year, would I ever see these places again?

One day while packing and going through old letters, I found one that someone had written to Mama. I'd probably brought it back with me after Christmas. I'd made a remark at one time about my desire to be a Red Cross nurse or worker. The letter was asking Mama if she thought they'd have me. After all, I couldn't hear so how could I do anything? Reading that letter was like waving red in front of a bull. My mind was finally made up: I was leaving and would prove to the world that I could be independent and do things just as well as they could, deaf or not. I'd show them.

I told Flossie of my decision.

"Oh no, please come back. I'll be lost without you and your mama."

"Sorry, sis. This is something I have to do. Mama will still write you and keep in touch."

Next to be told was Hill.

"I don't like that," she told me.

I grinned at her.

"Don't like what?"

"You leaving us. This will be a dry and lonesome place with no one to talk with."

"Oh, nonsense. You, Flossie, and Maybur are next in line to be the campus big wheels," I told her.

I'd really miss those three. They were the only ones who still talked like hearing people and we'd had a lot of good talks about home, books, and people—things the others weren't interested in. They, too, seemed to belong to a different world than one of silence. They had never really fit in with the other deaf girls. This was especially true of Hill because of her family being professionals and she herself being more prim and proper.

When I told the others that I, like them, wouldn't be back, they grabbed my hand all at once so that it was a pile of hands all on top of each other while we made a vow to always keep in touch and visit each other. Then they wanted to know why and if I was going to marry Leon and move to Brooklyn with Madga and Don.

"Not me," I told them. "I don't want a husband. I'm going to get a job and build a big house way up in the mountains."

"Herring's crazy," was the comment.

Then before we knew it, we were in the chapel for graduation, and I was leading my group through the songs for the last time. Flossie was training now to take my place. They always wanted a girl who had been able to hear long enough to learn songs and tunes to make the signs more in harmony with the words. Signing the songs made me feel I was actually hearing it all. When we got into the first song, "Let us break bread together on our knees. . . . When I fall on my knees with my face to the rising sun. . . ." I pictured myself in the song and I could just feel the warm sun on my face as I knelt with a bunch of people out among large rocks in the desert.

Later, Thelma sang her specialty, "Ave Maria." Everyone said she had a very sweet voice and that when she and Ira sang together it was something to hear. By the time we'd gone through "Up above My Head" and "His Name So Sweet," and then "God Bless America," my heart was full and so were my eyes.

> God bless America, land that I love.
> Stand beside her and guide her
> Through the night with the light from above.

I wanted Him to bless my school too.

I could see the campus, quiet and serene after lights-out with the airport searchlight passing over. This place that I'd hated mightily and tried to get away from, I now loved as a second home. A part of it would be with me for the rest of my life, or some of me would remain there. I didn't know which.

I wanted God to watch over it and keep it the same. I wanted to know that it was there for me to return to. At the same time, I knew it wouldn't stay the same, and that there'd be changes in the years ahead just as there'd been during the years I'd been there. New children and teachers would come in, old ones would go out just as I was planning to do now. The song ended and we sat down.

I looked at Flossie and said, "Next year, your job."

She didn't reply. Her eyes were full too.

That night, in the dorm once again, we sat around a window where we could see by one of the outside lights on campus. We remembered past years and old friends who'd already gone, like Frances, Percy, and even Hazel. We recalled fun times and sad times. Then Madga brought us back to the present by telling how she planned to furnish her apartment after she and Don were married and living in Brooklyn. She'd have glass-topped tables and crochet pretty doilies and have glass dishes full of candy. She'd name her babies Don Wilson II and Myrna.

Margie said, "Yes, and they'll have pretty pink toes like little kittens."

Jessie said, "Yuck! I don't want any babies. I'm going home to eat my mama's good food."

Buckwheat planned to work in a tobacco factory, make lots of money, and buy pretty clothes, a gold tooth, and gold eyeglasses.

"I already told you what I want to do," I said, "but I want to do war work first."

"War?! You're crazy for sure."

The talk went on 'til the wee hours. We knew this was really our last night this time and couldn't bring ourselves to break it up.

However, morning finally came and again we gathered in front of the administration building to wait for our buses. Mr. Mask was out there to oversee the departures and as usual Miss Watford was busy going from group to group, making sure every child was headed in the right direction. We all sort of clung together as long as possible. At least Margie, Buckwheat, and Flossie would be on the same bus I was. Finally, the bus arrived and we started loading.

Mr. Mask came up to pat my head and say, "Bugger, be sure and be back in September."

I couldn't open my mouth. I looked at Miss Watford. She looked at me, eyes bright behind her glasses. She gave me a quick, tight hug then a little push toward the steps.

"Be a good girl and remember."

I nodded, too full to speak.

Soon the bus was headed down the drive to Highway 70, turning south around the curve that I'd watched so many times from my classrooms. I looked back as we went over the hill and everything looked lonely and deserted in the spring sunshine. Even though I was crying, I'd made my choice: Good-bye, school days! Hello, world!

Epilogue

THE campus changed over the years. A new chapel was built, as well as a gym, a campus store run by students, and a special home ec building that was named in honor of Miss Watford. Best of all, the dorms for the deaf and blind students were connected and the addition was converted into recreation rooms with a stove and a fridge so the kids could fix snacks while watching TV or playing games. Girls and boys could be together, but supervised, of course. Students later were not only allowed to go home for holidays but for weekends as well!

Madga and Don did marry and move to Brooklyn, New York. Leon also married (a hearing girl) and moved to Brooklyn. Jessie moved to Springfield, Massachusetts, Margie to Philadelphia. I lost touch with Buckwheat.

I never did do any work for the Red Cross. About five months after I left school, I moved to Washington, D.C., and lived with my father's cousin, Mary, for a time. In 1942, I landed a job with the Department of the Navy, where I worked as a junior clerk. I communicated with my boss and co-workers through speechreading. They also wrote notes to me. Although everyone in the office was hearing and none of them signed or fingerspelled, I didn't experience any problems communicating with them. I resigned in the mid-1940s to return home and care for my mother. She died in 1954 and my father died in 1971.

I met and married James Wright, a hearing man, after returning to North Carolina. We were married in 1950 and remained married until his death in 1982. I have four daughters, Linda, Mary, Carolyn, and Judy. They are much like me, thinking for themselves and going their own ways. I raised them to value education as my family had raised me. One worked at Gallaudet University (the university for deaf students), one is a law professor, one is an artist, and the fourth is a housewife. I never did pursue teaching, instead I concentrated on raising my own children. I still attend Peter's Tabernacle Baptist Church. My children interpret the services for me because I'm the only deaf member.

My sister Eunice is also widowed. Once I met her husband, Jimmy, I liked him fine. He died in 1987. My oldest brother, Bennie, is now deceased. Frank and Lattice live next door to me. Sam and his wife, Sylvia, live in Goldsboro, North Carolina. Willie and his wife, Lucille, make their home in Depew, New York, near Buffalo.